BODYLOVE

ALSO BY RITA FREEDMAN

Beauty Bound

BODYLOVE

Learning to Like Our Looks—And Ourselves

RITA FREEDMAN, Ph.D.

HARPER & ROW, PUBLISHERS, New York

Cambridge, Grand Rapids, Philadelphia, St. Louis,
San Francisco, London, Singapore, Sydney, Tokyo

1817

Except where public figures are identified by first and last name, all names and identifying details of individuals mentioned in *Bodylove* have been changed to protect their privacy. In some instances composite accounts have been created based on the author's professional expertise.

FIRST EDITION

Designed by Alma Orenstein

Library of Congress Cataloging-in-Publication Data

Freedman, Rita Jackaway.
  Bodylove: learning to like our looks and ourselves.

  Bibliography: p.
  Includes index.
  1. Women—Psychology. 2. Body image. 3. Beauty, Personal. I. Title.
HQ1206.F699   1989   155.6'33   88-45511
ISBN 0-06-016025-X

89 90 91 92 93 CC/RRD 10 9 8 7 6 5 4 3 2 1

To my mother and father

CONTENTS

ACKNOWLEDGMENTS

Writing a book is an isolating process. Yet books aren't born in isolation. In the labor and delivery of this one, three women in particular were working partners and midwives. I've enjoyed their friendship while admiring their talents. Anne Edelstein, my literary agent, brought energy and enthusiasm to the initial ideas for this book. She believed in its value, nurtured its sale, and eventually helped polish the final draft. Her contributions are evident on every page. Irene Kleinsinger, my research assistant, administered the Bodylove Survey. Her creative interviewing skills yielded a wealth of information that enriched the text. Janet Goldstein was the superb editor that every author wants, and I was lucky enough to have. Always available and supportive, she gave the kind of constructive criticism that kept me motivated through countless revisions. Her advice on what to include, what to discard, and how to arrange material was invaluable.

I'm humbly indebted to the patients who have worked with me over the years. In their pursuit of a healthier self-image, they've asked vital questions that lead me down new paths, and they taught me a great deal about the techniques that are presented here. I'm also grateful to the many women who completed the Bodylove Survey and to those who shared their feelings during the interviews.

Personal friends and colleagues read early drafts, patiently listened to my problems, and offered their support. Special thanks to Evelyn Beilenson, Nick Beilenson, Allan Duane, Marie Duane, Gloria Goldstein, Sharon Golub, Harry Green, Terri Heyduk, Jessica Lighter, Jacqueline Plumez, and Vicki Stern. While numerous scholars have shaped my understanding of body image and human behavior, some whose writings are particularly important to this book include Aaron Beck, Thomas Cash, Seymour Fisher, Elaine Hatfield,

Susan Sprecher, and Marcia Hutchinson. I've also been inspired by those, working in the women's movement, who have forged a new perspective on gender roles. I hope that my efforts as a psychologist and as a writer will contribute to this movement for social change.

Finally, I'm deeply grateful to family members who celebrate the milestones with me, especially my son, Adam Jackaway, for his good-natured friendship and my daughter, Gwenyth Jackaway, for her encouragement and concern. This book is dedicated to my parents, Martin and Adele Freedman, in appreciation of their commitment to family, their generous support and active interest in my work. They taught me to respect both mind and body.

BODYLOVE

FROM BODY LOATHING TO BODYLOVE

YES, I DO THINK I'm attractive," she says confidently into the microphone. "Other people might not agree but this is me, and I like how I look." There's a round of applause as Phil Donahue moves on through the audience.

From the stage I look carefully at the woman who has just spoken. She's quite plain—some might even say homely. Her large jaw and broad hips stand out as she faces the camera. She isn't young or tall, like the professional models seated near me. She doesn't have the kind of face that smiles from magazine covers. Yet she's just told millions of viewers that she considers herself attractive.

I silently applaud her healthy self-image, while my thoughts turn to a client I saw the day before, Susan—a young teacher who examines her face with a magnifying mirror, frets over every flaw, and thinks she'll never marry because she isn't pretty enough. Susan has a recurring dream that on her wedding day the groom will lift the veil from her face and turn away in disgust. Her nightmare is like a fairy tale in reverse.

A plain-looking woman declares herself attractive on national television because she views her body with loving eyes, while Susan suffers shame and doubt over imperfections that are only imagined. "I always try hard to do my best," she explains. "Then, when I look in the mirror, I feel like I've failed because I don't look as good as I should." It isn't the reflection in the mirror that's her problem; it's the image she sees in her mind's eye. Although her looks are lovely, her thoughts about her body are not.

Perhaps you know someone like Susan. Or maybe you identify with her yourself. Does the state of your face often dictate the state of your mood? Do you feel too heavy to really enjoy a meal? Does your body seem like an obstacle to be overcome? If so, you owe it to yourself to explore a new relationship with your body. After all, you opened this book for a reason. What you'll find here is a group

2

of simple exercises to help you gain confidence in your appearance and in yourself.

As a psychologist I've worked with many women like Susan who are unhappy with their lives and especially with their looks. I feel their pain as I hear their problems—with weight, age, or sexuality. I watch as these conflicts drain their energy and spill over into their relationships at home and at work. Their struggles are personal and difficult, but not really so unusual. These same problems were expressed again and again by the women I interviewed for this book. I'm sure you experience them, too. We all do in one form or another. In fact, when Eleanor Roosevelt was asked if she had any regrets about her life, she replied, "Just one. I wish I'd been prettier." That is certainly Susan's wish, and it may be yours as well.

This book grew out of my deep concern about women—about how we are seen and especially how we see ourselves. Our preoccupation with appearance goes much deeper than the outer image. It's a basic part of who we are, and it affects the choices we make and the goals we pursue. For beauty is not only a personal and psychological issue, but a social one as well. In this new era of female liberation, are we any freer to accept the naturally feminine bodies we inherited at birth? Are we any happier with our chronic diets than the women who laced themselves into an hourglass figure a century ago? More than ever, it seems we are constricted by beauty standards that are not very liberating.

I don't think we were born wanting to suffer and sacrifice in order to look attractive. Yet we continue to remodel our flesh, much as our grandmothers did, to fit the popular beauty ideal—tweezing, squeezing, dieting, coloring, covering, and uncovering our flesh in order to feel lovely and lovable. Maybe these efforts would be worth it, if we also felt better about ourselves in the end. But often that just isn't the case. "No matter how hard I work at it, I can't seem to get the right look," Susan complains.

One woman in two is dieting most of her life; two out of three has mixed feelings or is depressed when she sees her nude body in the mirror. The majority of ten-year-old girls are already afraid of becoming too fat. A friend is considering a face-lift, while another owns over $1,000 worth of cosmetics. Along with Susan, these women share a similar problem: *body loathing.* Body loathing is a feeling of preoccupation and dissatisfaction with appearance. It creates anxiety about body parts. It causes guilt and shame over flaws that are real or imagined. It arouses self-consciousness and envy.

Body loathing surfaces in many familiar ways. For example, Lynn feels tense each morning just trying to decide what to wear. And Martha views every new wrinkle as a frightening enemy. These women suffer from body loathing, while they long for *bodylove.*

WHAT IS BODYLOVE?

Bodylove is a mixture of emotions, attitudes, and actions that allow you to enjoy the way your body looks and the way it feels. Bodylove enhances self-confidence and heightens physical pleasure. Like other loving relationships, bodylove involves caring and concern. There is joy in personal contact as well as tolerance of flaws. There is a unity that overcomes the separateness between mind and body. We all have the potential to love our bodies. Like any loving relationship, it takes work to realize that potential.

You can work on bodylove in many ways, as we'll see in the chapters ahead. Three steps are essential, however. The first is paying *attention* to physical needs. If you listen with respect instead of mistrust—to pain, pleasure, hunger, fatigue—your body will tell you how to nurture it. The second step is *appreciation* of the pleasures your body can inherently provide—aesthetic, athletic, sensory, and sexual. Finally, there is *acceptance.* By accepting your flaws and limitations you'll be freer to enjoy the lovely parts of yourself; to experience what is and to stop longing for what isn't. Bodylove doesn't mean creating a perfect body; rather, it means living happily in an imperfect one. After all, an imperfect body is the only one you'll ever have.

Although Susan is quite attractive, bodylove eludes her. When she first described her problems to me she sounded very much like a character in a novel by Judith Rossner. "The only time I ever think I'm beautiful," observes Sascha, "is when some man is staring into my face in broad daylight and telling me I'm beautiful. And then as soon as he turns away for a minute I think he's changed his mind. And if he doesn't turn away or change his mind, I start thinking he's one of those idiots with no taste."[1] In the same way, Susan's self-esteem could be built up or broken down by a single glance. Looking good doesn't solve the problem of feeling bad about your looks; it doesn't give you bodylove.

Experts and advertisements are forever telling you to firm up your thighs, restyle your hair, revamp your nose, remodel your clothes—in order to look better. Maybe it's time to reconsider their messages. Time to rediscover the sense of joy that you felt about your body as a child. Consider all the time, effort, and money you've spent over the years to make over your looks. Why not balance these efforts with a different kind of beauty routine—one that nurtures your ego and pampers your pride?

This is not an anti-beauty book. It doesn't criticize you for wanting and trying to look your best. I'm not advising you to throw away your makeup or forget about your appearance. After all, we do live in a world where beauty counts. Good looks are basic to femininity and a real source of women's social power: the power to attract attention, to influence others, and to get things accomplished. While beauty may be only skin deep, it often makes the first impression.

There's a difference, however, between pursuing beauty joyfully and pursuing it desperately. Looking attractive *is* part of the game of living. But playing with your image should feel like fun, not like a contest in which you always wind up on the losing side. For some women like Susan the body has become a battleground. They speak of fighting fat, defeating age, or feeling trapped and frightened. They sound like victims under siege, and they are. Body loathing wounds both mind and body. You can end the costly battle with your body by investing in a new vision of yourself. Bodylove is a powerful tool that can help you get on with other parts of your life.

USING THIS BOOK TO CARE FOR YOUR LOOKS AND YOURSELF

I wish I could become your fairy godmother, wave my wand, and make you "lovely ever after." Unfortunately, there is no quick fix. It took many years of experience to shape your body image. You can't remake it instantly. Change may not be easy, but it *is* possible. The chapters ahead affirm your basic right to love your body and show you how to do it.

I've translated new research on physical attractiveness into exercises that help you move from body loathing to bodylove. These exercises aren't hard. They're based on methods of cognitive and behavioral therapy that work with everyday problems. First you explore what you're thinking and doing in a certain situation. Then you learn to substitute new thoughts and behaviors that can serve you better. If it sounds simple, it is. The techniques are grounded in common sense. They've proven useful with women like Susan, and I'm sure they can help you, too.

Some of the exercises are designed to explore and clarify your attitudes about your body. Others train you to behave less destructively and more compassionately toward it. We'll be using relaxation to overcome resistance, visualization to explore the values you developed as a child, movement to express emotions, and mirrors to rehearse praise. Let your mind and body work together as you progress through the book. And don't be afraid to share your efforts toward change with the people who care about you. Loved ones can help you clarify your problems and work on them.

The exercises will teach you to turn away from the mirror and step off the scale when you're evaluating yourself. You'll start to make better sense of our social nonsense, as we explore the role of society in misshaping your body image. By tuning in to body messages, you'll develop the self-awareness and the self-control to treat your body with respect. Working toward bodylove will free you from chronic self-consciousness and help you more fully enjoy both your body and your life.

You may gain insight and even feel better about yourself simply by reading through the chapters. To benefit most, however, you have to act—that is, *act*ively engage in the exercises. You wouldn't expect to be in great shape after skimming through a fitness book or thinner after reading a diet book. Only by "doing" will you discover which exercises are most valuable for you. Keep a pencil handy to jot down thoughts and responses to questions. Clip a photo of yourself to the inside cover of this book or on your bathroom mirror as a reminder of the body you're trying to befriend.

Bodylove is directed mainly toward women, in part because physical attractiveness is so central to the feminine role. It's not that men aren't troubled by their looks. They are. Balding heads and bulging bellies cause them plenty of anxiety. Men can certainly benefit from reading this book, too. It will sensitize them to their own body-image problems and help them understand the women in their lives. Yet men's problems are somewhat different because they relate to their bodies from a masculine perspective. As Phil Donahue quipped, "Men may do some silly things, but you won't catch them walking in a snowstorm with a cute little hole at the end of their shoe."

HOW OTHERS THINK AND FEEL

At the beginning of each chapter you'll find some questions taken from a body-image survey I developed for this book. For example:

Are you self-conscious about your appearance?
>CONSTANTLY
>OFTEN
>SOMETIMES
>RARELY
>NEVER

How do your current feelings about your body compare with your feelings five years ago?
>MUCH BETTER
>SOMEWHAT BETTER
>THE SAME
>SOMEWHAT WORSE
>MUCH WORSE

Just try to answer these questions thoughtfully. Gathering information about yourself can help you recognize problems and measure your progress.

I used this Bodylove Survey with 200 women to find out how they felt about their bodies. Although my sample wasn't scientifically selected and therefore isn't fully representative of the general population, it did include women of all ages, from all walks of life. As you can see from the following summary, they were single, married, mothers, students, homemakers, and working women from all parts of the country and from various racial, economic, and religious backgrounds. Their responses provide a useful scale against which to compare your own feelings. (The Appendix includes the complete Bodylove Survey and results.)

Along with the survey results, each chapter presents case studies to illustrate common problems. You'll meet Lynn, who struggled with chronic self-consciousness; Ellen, who has been obsessed with her weight all her life; and Kim, who used dance to discover her sexuality. I'm sure you'll recognize your own body-image conflicts through their experiences. You'll also find that the basic problem, which recurs over and over, is one of poor body image.

LOOKING AT BODY IMAGE

Each of us carries around with us an inner view of our outer self. This is your *body image:* "a picture of the body seen through the mind's eye." While this image is built on physical characteristics, it's also separate and distinct from them. It goes beyond the simple fact of being blond or thin, for it's a product of your imagination. Although it's imaginary, body image can feel as real as the body itself. It can be a constant source of strength or a chronic cause of pain.

Body image has many aspects. It's *visual*—what you see when you look at yourself. It's *mental*—how you think about your appearance. It's *emotional*—how you feel about your weight or height. It's *kinesthetic*—how you sense and control your body parts. It's also *historical*—shaped by a lifetime of experience that includes pleasure and pain, praise and criticism.

Your body image is always changing, as the body itself changes with age or illness, with hunger or fatigue. When you're puffed up with pride, it inflates. When you're beaten down by failure, it shrinks. Of course, it's also reshaped by the whims of fashion.

Above all, body image is a social affair. It may be housed in your head, but it's grounded in the everyday experiences that surround you. How you see yourself depends on how you think you're seen by others. Your body image can be jolted by the judgment of a loved one or the whistle of a stranger. Susan is surprised at how quickly a wave of self-consciousness can wash over her when someone new

CHARACTERISTICS OF SUBJECTS IN THE BODYLOVE SAMPLE*

1. Age Range	18–74	WORKING FULL		
UNDER 30	32%	OR PART TIME	54%	
BETWEEN 30–45	35%	OTHER	15%	
OVER 45	33%			

6. Ethnic or Racial Background

2. Residence			
EAST COAST	35%	CAUCASIAN	87%
SOUTH	30%	BLACK	5%
WEST	20%	ASIAN	4%
MIDWEST	15%	HISPANIC AND OTHER	4%

7. Religious Background

3. Marital Status		CATHOLIC	25%
NEVER MARRIED	37%	JEWISH	19%
FIRST MARRIAGE	34%	PROTESTANT	37%
DIVORCED	12%	NONE OR OTHER	19%
REMARRIED	11%		
WIDOWED	4%	8. Economic Level	
OTHER	2%	GETTING BY	11%
		SOMEWHAT SECURE	43%
4. Number of children		FAIRLY PROSPEROUS	35%
NONE	41%	AFFLUENT	11%
ONE	9%		
TWO	20%	9. Educational Background	
THREE OR MORE	23%	LESS THAN HIGH SCHOOL	1%
		HIGH SCHOOL GRADUATE	9%
5. Occupation		SOME COLLEGE	28%
HOMEMAKER AND/OR		COLLEGE GRADUATE	26%
MOTHER	15%	SOME GRADUATE SCHOOL	11%
STUDENT	19%	GRADUATE DEGREE	25%

*Note: In some cases totals do not equal 100 percent because of incomplete or multiple responses.

enters the room. "It's as if I suddenly see myself through their eyes," she says. We all know how a casual comment about our appearance can transform our feelings, for either better or worse.

As you can see, body image is a complex combination of attitudes, feelings, and values. In some ways, it's a bit like intelligence, a trait we know exists but can't easily define or measure. Psychologists use all kinds of techniques to measure body image, including analysis of figure drawings, inkblot tests, and multiple-choice surveys in which body parts are rated in terms of satisfaction. But of all the body-image tests, the one shown below is my favorite.

How accurate is your body image? Probably not very. Like the figure in the cartoon, most of us are rather poor judges of our own appearance. When self-ratings of attractiveness are compared to ratings made by outside observers, little correlation is found. We simply don't see ourselves as others see us.[2]

The mind's eye distorts the body's image, sometimes in a positive direction, sometimes in a negative one. While the outer world may rate you a terrific 10, your inner eye sees only a terrible 2. Or the reverse can be equally true. The direction of distortion is as important as the extent of it. Seeing yourself as more attractive than you really are may boost self-esteem, whereas seeing yourself as less attractive than you are may undermine it, as in Susan's case.

If you're like other women, you probably distort your body image in two particular ways: either by seeing a certain body part as abnormal or by seeing yourself as having the wrong size or shape.

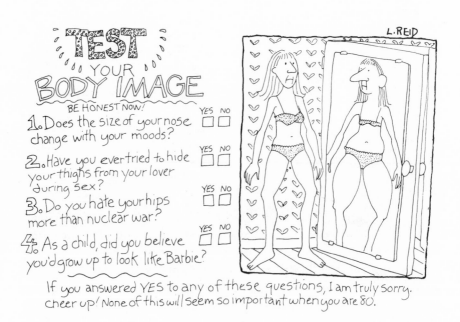

From *Do You Hate Your Hips More Than Nuclear War* by Libby Reid. Copyright © 1987 Libby Reid. All rights reserved. Reprinted by permission of Viking Penguin Inc.

Perhaps you're preoccupied with your "thunder thighs" or "saddle-bag hips." You then generalize from this single feature to your whole appearance, ignoring the parts that *are* attractive, to both yourself and others. These distortions transform body image into a kind of caricature.

EXPLORING FEELINGS AND GOALS

To understand body image more fully, try examining your own feelings by answering a few simple questions:

- Are you frequently self-conscious about your appearance?
- Do certain body parts tend to dominate your thoughts? If so, which ones?
- Do you often compare your looks to those of other women, or to media models?
- Do some body parts seem dramatically different from one day to the next?
- Do people say you look better than you think you do?

A *yes* answer to these questions suggests that your body image may be distorted in a negative direction, and you could benefit from reevaluating your image and learning to care for it in a new way.

In working with Susan, my first step was to help her clarify her goals. You'll also want to give some thought to setting goals for yourself. Jot down a few thoughts about how you would like to feel about your body. Don't focus on how you want to look, but on how you want to feel about your looks. The following list gives you an idea of the goals that other women have chosen and that are covered in the chapters ahead:

Feel less self-conscious around others.

End the constant battle with my weight.

Feel less critical of my appearance.

Become less preoccupied with mirrors, scales, dress size.

Free myself from my family values of how I "should" look.

Have more fun decorating and displaying myself.

Enjoy my sexuality more fully.

Stop demanding perfection.

Enjoy exercise and become more physically fit.

Stop abusing my body with compulsive exercise.

Spend less time and effort on making over.

Spend more time and effort on making over.

Accept my age and worry less about looking older.

Make healthy decisions about changing my looks.

Treat my body with respect.

Reduce shame and guilt about how I've used my body.

Define my looks in my own terms.

Stop using my looks as an excuse for other problems.

These are just some of the many goals that might be important to you. In choosing goals for yourself, try to keep your list short and manageable. Set priorities by deciding what is most important to you *right now,* and work on just a few things at a time. Susan decided to concentrate on her perfectionism and on becoming less critical of her image. She discovered that these were the same problems that got in her way at work.

RESISTING CHANGE AND CHANGING RESISTANCE

To succeed at bodylove you must first admit that you need to change your relationship with your body. Then you have to learn techniques to help you change and muster the courage to use them. In addition, you also need to deal with resistance. If change is the ultimate goal, resistance is the ultimate stumbling block. Since resistance is such a big problem for everyone, I want to warn you about it from the start.

Why do we resist the very changes we say we want to make? First, old habits are like old slippers—hard to throw out because they're so comfortable. You go round and round in the same old groove because it brings you back to a familiar spot. It's easier just to keep doing what you've always done. Second, you're likely to resist change because it creates conflicts and confusion. Known problems seem less threatening than unknown ones. So you stay put on the safe ground of the familiar and cling to your old body-image conflicts.

In order to progress toward bodylove, you'll have to recognize resistance and work to overcome it. You can spot resistance if you start looking for it more honestly. Check yourself against these common resistance tactics. Which ones are your favorite hiding places?

- *Delay.* Do you procrastinate or forget things you really wanted to do?
  "I don't have time to exercise. I'll start next week, next fall, someday."

- *Denial.* Do you see problems in others but not in yourself?
  "My sister really hates her body. She needs this book more than I do."

- *Blame.* Do you reject the possibility of change by blaming either yourself or others for keeping you stuck?
  "I'll always be obsessed with dieting because my mother pushed food on me."

- *Rationalizing.* Do you manufacture "good" reasons instead of admitting the real reasons?
  "I need to have cosmetic surgery because looks are crucial in my business."

- *Fear.* Do you scare yourself into a state of inactivity?
  "I'd become enormous if I ever stopped taking diet pills."

- *Avoidance.* Do you arrive late, get sick, lose things . . . in order to dodge confrontations that feel threatening?
  "Too bad I left that body-image book on the train and never got to the chapter on sexuality."

Think about whether you're a blamer, a rationalizer, an avoider. Once you figure out your usual resistance tactics, it will be easier to catch yourself in the act of resisting. The first step in overcoming resistance is to admit that you're doing it. We all do. Then try to:

- *Break the problem down into small parts.* If you work on them one by one, change will seem less threatening and your resistance will diminish.
- *Set modest goals.* Then you'll be likely to achieve them. Expect success and concentrate more on progress than on setbacks.
- *Begin to act.* Start by doing something tangible. You might avoid mirrors for one day or register for an exercise class. Resistance keeps you stuck, but action serves as a catalyst for further change. Action makes you feel less helpless about your body-image problems.

I'll explain these steps in greater detail as we go along. These techniques for overcoming resistance are part of the behavioral approach that we'll be using in the exercises that follow.

Susan resisted by avoiding situations that made her feel anxious. Thus her progress was slow as she tried to reduce her critical demands for a perfect image. We worked with her dream of being rejected when the groom lifted the bridal veil. While remaining deeply relaxed, Susan visualized her wedding day and saw herself walking down the aisle on her father's arm. She learned to stay calm while revising the end of the dream. Through imagery and relaxation Susan gained confidence that she could be attractive and lovable even when she didn't look perfect.

With time and effort, I saw her slowly grow from a self-*rejecting* to a self-*respecting* young woman. Her body did not change very much during this time, but her vision of it was altered. As she developed greater self-acceptance, Susan began to feel more attractive and to view herself from an inner-directed perspective.

Like Susan, you'll be moving at your own pace as you go through these chapters. People vary in their response to self-help exercises. Some experience rapid relief when they break free of a destructive habit. Others slowly gain a general sense of well-being. Start with those exercises that feel most useful to you, and keep practicing. Don't be discouraged if you fall back into old habits. Go back and review earlier sections when you need to. Remember, there are no foolproof formulas for learning to love your body. Problems tend to persist even as they start to diminish.

It's true that beauty resides as much in the eyes of the beholder as in the face of the beheld. Therefore you can create a lovelier body by teaching your mind's eye to look more lovingly at the mirror's image. In large part you are what you *think* you are. You are what you see in the looking-glass self.

This book challenges you to make over your mind about the nature of your body. Here's an invitation to start a new romance with yourself. Your body can be a loyal friend and a strong ally. Trust it enough to pay attention to its messages. Trust yourself enough to accept the challenge of change so that you can say to yourself—and perhaps even proclaim on some talk show—"Yes I do think I'm an attractive woman. This is me and I like the way I look."

MINDING YOUR BODY

Are you self-conscious about your appearance?
> CONSTANTLY
> OFTEN
> SOMETIMES
> RARELY
> NEVER

Is physical attractiveness important in the daily lives of most people?
> VERY IMPORTANT
> SOMEWHAT IMPORTANT
> NOT SURE
> UNIMPORTANT
> VERY UNIMPORTANT

Do you agree that "good-looking people are usually happier and more successful than less attractive people?"
> STRONGLY AGREE
> AGREE
> NOT SURE
> DISAGREE
> STRONGLY DISAGREE

During the course of the day, how often do you check yourself in a mirror?
> CONSTANTLY
> OFTEN
> SOMETIMES
> RARELY
> NEVER

If you could change one thing about your body, what would it be?

Here's my morning ritual. I open a sleepy eye, take one horrified look at my reflection in the mirror and then repeat with conviction: "I'm me and I'm wonderful. Because God doesn't make junk."

—ERMA BOMBECK

CLARA turns toward the mirror, then steps closer. Something is wrong. Her hand sweeps across her forehead as if to smooth away a wrinkle. Those watching her are fascinated, for Clara has just revealed a remarkable fact. This clever chimpanzee clearly recognizes the hairy face in the mirror as her own. "That's me, and I look strange," her actions proclaim as she tries to rub off the red mark they've put on her forehead. By placing a mirror in Clara's cage, researchers produce a self-conscious chimpanzee with a complexion problem. Remove the mirror and she is happy once again.[1]

At two, my little niece looks in the mirror and is surprised by the dab of lipstick I've secretly put on her nose. Sally reaches up to touch it, just like Clara the chimp. Clowning around a year later, we paint our cheeks with Revlon's latest shade, Scarlet Fantasy. Then, with serious concentration, the smart toddler tries to color her lips alone. Our game is over for this is no joke. The mirror has lured Sally into a makeover routine that will last a lifetime.

My client Lynn also has a special relationship with mirrors. During her first appointment she describes how self-conscious she feels about her appearance. "The worst part is being so concerned with what other people are thinking when they see me," she says. "What do you think when you see yourself?" I ask. Lynn's silence tells me how hard this question is for her. We go over to a mirrored wall and I offer to tell her what I see as we face her reflection together.

"You're a woman of medium height," I begin. "Your body seems strong and solid. You have warm brown eyes that match your hair. Your mouth . . . your skin. . . ." As I describe her features one by one, she studies them. Suddenly Lynn turns away from the mirror, her eyes filled with tears. "I wish I could see that woman, too," she whispers, "but I can't." And so begins our work together.

Lynn finds it hard to accept her appearance: "Sometimes I change clothes five times in the morning, because I'm so unsure about what looks right on me. I keep getting more anxious and then wind up wearing what I had on in the first place. I also seem to be checking myself in the mirror all the time, just to make sure I still look okay."

Some of Lynn's problems may sound familiar. Are there days when you can't find anything to wear? Are you drawn to your mirror for reassurance only to discover some new flaw? In this chapter we'll examine the social and personal stereotypes that influence your perception of your body and yourself. The exercises at the end will teach you how to make peace with your mirror and how to build self-confidence by handling negative thoughts that undermine body image.

Seeing yourself as an attractive woman doesn't always depend on becoming more attractive. For Lynn, for my niece Sally, and for you also, it's not the image in the looking glass that matters most, but how that image reflects back into the mind's eye. To behold your image literally means to "be held" by your own thoughts. You can hold your image roughly or tenderly, with body loathing or with bodylove. In the end you'll discover that the most important person minding your body is you.

When Lynn first came to see me she had experienced a recent shift in self-image caused by several major life changes: a move that separated her from family and friends, a new job where she was highly visible to the public, and a gain in weight resulting from birth-control pills. The pressure of these events caused a surge of body loathing that distorted her body image.

Despite a great many assets and talents, Lynn frequently feels insecure: "Ever since we moved last year, I worry a lot about whether I can handle this new job. When I have to face a special client, I have even more trouble getting ready for work. My body feels huge and out of control, which is how my life feels, also."

During one therapy session, I had Lynn visualize various body parts, letting her mind's eye travel from head to toe. When I asked if she had trouble seeing any parts clearly, she responded, "My nose. I see it differently all the time. It doesn't seem to fit my face, or the face I'd like to have. When I get preoccupied with it, nothing else looks attractive." I asked Lynn to estimate the length and width of her nose and then to draw it life size. Comparing her estimates to the actual size of that feature, we found that she overestimated. In fact, most of us overestimate the size of our body parts. Our body image is truly larger than life.[2]

Lynn seems to have what so many of my patients want: a solid marriage to a man she loves, a well-paying job with a bank, good health, and good looks. Despite all this, she remains anxious and depressed, longing for beauty she already has but can't see. Like many women, Lynn clings to the notion that if only she were prettier she'd also be happier and more confident. In fact, she's using her appearance as a scapegoat for other fears and frustrations that seem harder to face. So she ends up running back to the mirror when things go wrong. By blaming her appearance she tries to gain a sense of potential control over her problems.

She isn't unusual. One of my clients canceled a cruise after three frustrating days of looking for a bathing suit. Another can't enjoy a new friend because, "That woman looks so great I'm wiped out when I stand next to her." A colleague turned down a chance to appear in an important documentary because she felt too old to be seen on camera.

Perhaps you've been using your looks as an excuse for not taking greater responsibility for your life. Doris goes to a singles party but leaves after half an hour of standing on the sidelines. "It's hopeless unless you're gorgeous," she tells me. And Samantha blames her lack of friends on the fact that she's middle-aged and overweight. These women feel sorry for themselves and get stuck in self-pity. Appearance is a handy excuse for maintaining a victim's mentality. It protects them from taking risks, changing jobs, or finding new friends.

Poor body image can have many consequences, both in your head and in your body. It contributes to depression and eating disorders. It undermines self-confidence and inhibits sexual expression. People who feel unattractive have been found to be more fearful of negative evaluations from others. Shame over weight, for example, can cause a general "disowning of the body" and a disrespect for its needs, which then leads to chronic dieting or compulsive exercising.

What are the effects of poor body image in your life? Are you intimidated by more attractive people? Do you hesitate to pursue new goals because you don't want to be looked over too closely? These consequences are all too real. That's why it's important to acknowledge and explore the problem.

UNDERSTANDING THE PROBLEM

Like many women, you may find that you often wind up looking good but not feeling very good about your looks. That's because poor body image has very little to do with how you actually look. Think of the most beautiful woman you know—a celebrity, friend, or relative. What features make her so lovely? Now imagine how that woman must feel about her own body. Here's an interesting fact. Beautiful women have the same insecurities as anyone else.

It's surprising but true that there's hardly any connection between a woman's actual physical attractiveness (as rated by others) and her satisfaction with body image. Studies show that pretty women are as likely as plain ones to be unhappy with their looks. Furthermore, there's very little connection between physical attractiveness and feelings of self-worth. When both attractive and unattractive people filled out a self-esteem survey, their scores turned out to be very similar.[3] There *is* a strong relationship, however, between body image and self-esteem. Regardless of appearance, people who view their bodies favorably also tend to have higher self-esteem. In contrast, those who view their bodies unfavorably tend to have lower self-esteem. In other words, the better your body image, the greater your feelings of self-worth. The diagram below shows the relationships among physical attractiveness, body image, and self-esteem.

What does this diagram tell us? First, that body image is quite independent of physical characteristics. You can feel plain or even homely when really you're lovely. You can feel beautiful when others think you're not. Even when body image is quite inaccurate, it does serve as "subjective reality." If Lynn sees her nose as huge,

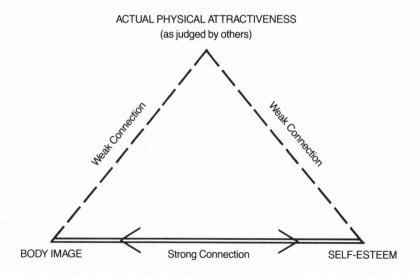

this becomes truth to her. Mind dominates matter when it comes to body image.

Second, the weak connection between physical attractiveness and self-esteem means that changing your looks may or may not improve your self-confidence. Looking better doesn't necessarily make you feel better about your looks or yourself. On the other hand, improving your body image is quite likely to improve your self-esteem—so, working on self-esteem will usually improve your body image, also. Body loathing leads to self-loathing, while body-love leads to self-love. Which is why your feelings about your looks have so much impact on other aspects of your life!

Finally, the diagram shows that body image and self-esteem are highly interdependent. Distortion of one affects the other, and it's hard to determine the direction of influence between them. Lack of self-esteem may stem from an underlying body loathing, while body loathing may be a product of low self-esteem. In other words, when you're down on yourself, you probably are down on your body as well. Lynn's self-esteem was shaken by a move and a new job. As her insecurities grew, she became more self-conscious about her looks. Then, because she felt less attractive, her self-confidence diminished even further. In fact, self-consciousness is a common symptom of poor body image.

THE SELF-CONSCIOUS SELF

One important goal of this book is to help you become less self-conscious about your looks. Self-consciousness is an underlying factor in such problems as age anxiety, weight obsession, and compulsive exercising.

When you're self-conscious you're preoccupied with yourself as a social object. The eyes and thoughts of others seem to invade your personal space, making you ill at ease. If you think about it, "ill at ease" translates to "dis-ease." Self-consciousness is therefore a kind of disease that disrupts your psychological well-being. Lynn describes feeling "a wave of anxiety when I'm with people—at a meeting or in a restaurant. It's as if all eyes are focused on me, judging how I look." She mistakenly assumes that others are minding her body as closely as she is minding it herself.

How often do you feel self-conscious about your appearance? In a 1984 *Glamour* magazine poll, 46 percent of the sample said they felt self-conscious "around almost everyone."[4] Of the women in the

Bodylove Survey (as shown below), only 16 percent said they rarely or never felt it. Think for a moment about when and where you feel most self-conscious. How does it affect your relationships with others?

Are you self-conscious about your appearance?

21%	CONSTANTLY
23%	OFTEN
40%	SOMETIMES
14%	RARELY
2%	NEVER

Those who feel highly self-conscious as well as unattractive may suffer an acute sense of vulnerability. At those times, Lynn says she wants to hide or fix herself up. The restroom serves as her safe retreat. Feelings of self-consciousness keep driving her back to the mirror to confirm that she looks okay, or to "repair" her image as best she can.

Women who are highly self-conscious tend to exaggerate the importance of physical attractiveness. They assume that others are as obsessed with everyone's appearance as they are themselves, which isn't always true. When you're preoccupied with your looks you can't give very much of yourself to others. You may become so shy or awkward that you try to avoid social contacts. Self-consciousness thus becomes a constricting corset that keeps you from moving freely in your social life.

Lynn feels as if she's always competing with a critical inner voice that compares her to other women. When the voice tells her she doesn't measure up, her self-consciousness increases. One woman described this sense of competition:[5]

> Here I am at a table of women . . . and the first thing I do to assess my coworkers . . . is look around to see who is prettier than I. I can always count on being the second prettiest woman in any situation . . . in class, on buses, anywhere. But I always want to be *the* prettiest.

Other women admit their envy, even hatred, of loved ones and strangers who "make" them feel so uncomfortable. "My sister comes to visit twice a year and always wants me to go shopping with her in Manhattan," explains Gretchen. "But she's thin and pretty. Every time I have to go into a dressing room with her, I'm filled with jealousy."

PLAYING THE BEAUTY GAME

Most of us get caught up in the beauty game because beauty *is* a major source of female power. Beauty counts. It buys attention, affection, promotions. But what is this thing called beauty that we all want so badly? How would you define it? Webster says that "beauty gives pleasure to the senses" and that a pretty woman is "pleasing to the eye." Lynn describes beauty as "the cover-girl look." The women I interviewed all had their own thoughts about it:

> "Beauty is a quality that attracts attention. You have to look twice at someone who's beautiful."

> "I used to think that being beautiful meant being thin. But now I realize my thin friends don't feel that much prettier than I do."

> "It's just an illusion. You can't put your finger on it because it's really created in your head."

> "Who knows what beauty is? But I sure spend a lot of time chasing after it."

Beauty isn't easy to define. We're as likely to see it in an innocent girl as in a sexy siren. We proclaim it a natural quality even while we promote it as a packaged illusion. One day we dismiss good looks as trivial, the next day we crown and worship a new Miss America. We hide the fact of our face-lifts, yet flaunt our remade faces. Precise definitions of beauty dissolve in such contradictions.

Although we have trouble defining beauty, we seem to know it when we see it. People tend to agree on who is attractive. In a given culture at a given time, ratings of appearance show great consistency, regardless of the age, sex, or background of the judge.[6] And people also seem to agree that appearance counts. When asked whether physical attractiveness is significant in everyday life, a full 95 percent of the Bodylove Survey said it was somewhat or very important.

Is physical attractiveness important in the daily lives of most people?

39%	VERY IMPORTANT
56%	SOMEWHAT IMPORTANT
3%	NOT SURE
1%	UNIMPORTANT
1%	VERY UNIMPORTANT

Beauty standards are often confusing. They vary from place to place and from day to day. Yet an inherent tension is constantly built into the notion of feminine beauty. Erotic sophistication is sometimes paired with naïve innocence. Other times a delicate grace is required alongside muscular athleticism. These conflicting demands pull us in opposite directions, making the beauty game highly stressful. Lynn complains, "It's harder to dress now that I have this executive job. If I put on something pretty and feminine, I feel self-conscious about not looking businesslike. I just can't seem to win."

These contradictions make it especially difficult for women to love their bodies. Compared to men, women are judged more critically for their appearance. And they judge themselves with the same critical eye. Poor body image has been described as a universal fact of female experience. We may be called "the fair sex," but we tend to see ourselves unfairly. Just consider the following facts:[7]

- The majority of ten-year-old girls in one study rated themselves as *least* attractive in the whole class.
- Half the teenagers in one survey reported that they frequently feel ugly. By college age, only 45 percent of college women felt good about their overall looks, as compared to 75 percent of college men.
- Appearance has become more and more important over the past two decades, yet women feel less and less satisfied with their bodies.
- Most adult women see themselves as heavier than they really are, and heavier than the ideal they think men prefer. The majority describe their bodies as too fat. Women also check their mirrors more often than do men.
- Less than half the females in a national sample agreed with the statement, "I like my looks the way they are." Nearly half said they would consider cosmetic surgery to look better.

No matter how long and how hard we work at it, some parts never seem quite good enough.

LOOKING GOOD CAN DRIVE YOU CRAZY

Whether you're seven or seventy, putting on the feminine role can be hazardous to your mental health. In a well-known study, therapists were asked to rate personality traits they thought were healthy for a normal male, for a normal female, and for a normal adult. While males and adults were judged to be alike, females were rated differently. Normal women were considered more emotional, more submissive, and more dependent than healthy adults. In addition, "preoccupation with appearance" was judged as normal for a healthy woman but not normal for a healthy person![8]

Sometimes it's hard to feel like a normal woman and a normal person at the same time. The demands of both roles often are incompatible, especially when it comes to physical attractiveness. I know, for instance, that high heels are uncomfortable. Yet sometimes I think I should wear them to look right. The healthy person within me says, "Take them off, they feel awful." But the healthy woman within me says, "Leave them on, they look terrific." So I'm caught in a bind. Do I reject the feminine role and put on sensible shoes? Or do I opt for the pretty pumps that are painful but sometimes make me look and feel more attractive?

This is the kind of no-win situation that leads each of us to our own body-image problems. These are the conflicts that create body loathing and that drive us all a bit crazy. Lynn's clothes never seem right. A dress that looks fine at home in the morning doesn't feel "professional" enough when she gets to the bank. We all face such dilemmas again and again because they're a natural by-product of the feminine role. Of course, we weren't born believing that high heels or long hair look pretty. We were taught these "truths" through the process of socialization (discussed further in Chapter 3).

OBJECTIFICATION

As a woman, you're expected to be pretty and to flaunt it. Throughout history, females have been denied many roles in society, but the role of beauty object has been actively promoted. Most girls are encouraged to dress up and show off—to please parents, boyfriends, and especially themselves. After all, girl watching is a national pastime. Women get so used to watching and being watched that it feels like a natural part of daily life. Few of us are consciously aware of this *objectification* . . . or very concerned about it. After all, it's nicer to be looked at than overlooked.

The game of girl watching leads to a kind of self-objectification that further distorts body image and erodes self-esteem. Piece by piece, we start to pick our own bodies apart and then remodel them. One flaw, real or imagined, can dominate the whole image—as with Lynn's nose.

Objectification encourages you to see yourself in terms of parts, and to transform those parts to gain attention. Making over body parts is central to the feminine role—which explains why coloring your lips or cutting your hair can take on so much meaning. You've learned that what's on your head may be considered as important as what's in it. This, too, is another aspect of the normal-woman versus normal-person conflict.

The Bodylove Survey asked: *If you could change one thing about your body, what would it be?* Not a single woman in 200 said she would leave her body alone and change nothing! Each one wanted to change something. And every inch of the body was targeted for overhaul by someone. What did they long for? Wider eyes, fewer freckles, longer legs, smaller feet, better posture, firmer thighs, thinner ankles, thicker hair, longer nails, bigger breasts. . . . (Psychoanalysts should note that genitals were never mentioned.)

Above all else, they wanted to lose weight. Fully two-thirds of the women in the sample were longing for less of themselves, especially in the region between their waist and their knees. "Remove the saddle bags . . . get rid of my hips . . . have a smaller rear . . . melt away this potbelly . . . less cellulite . . . lose the flab," they wrote. Weight obsession is the norm among females today, and it's a major cause of body loathing.

Confused about being a healthy person or a healthy woman and objectified by ourselves and others, it's no wonder we're so self-conscious about our bodies. When society sets impossible standards for feminine beauty, disappointment and failure become inevitable. What can one say about a culture that requires an ideal weight that is dangerously thin? Or that demands an ideal face that looks forever young? Or that worships a foot as small as a doll's or one that's propped up on a three-inch heel? Once a certain look becomes sacred, it redefines normal appearance, even when the demands of society are quite abnormal. These "neurotic" social norms distort body image and erode self-esteem.

THE PROBLEM OF LOOKSISM

To achieve bodylove you have to take a hard look at how society molds body image. You might think that caring for your image is a purely personal matter. In reality, you must cope not only with the face in your own mirror but with the mirror of society as well. And that mirror is distorted with stereotypes.

A stereotype is a widely held belief that members of a certain group are all alike. (Blonds are sexy; southerners are friendly). First, someone is labeled according to a particular trait (blond); then she is judged to have other qualities because of that trait (sex appeal). Stereotypes are dangerous because they make assumptions and ignore individual differences. They're also powerful precisely because so many people believe them to be true.

Looksism is a stereotype that links certain qualities to attractive people and other qualities to unattractive people. Like racism and ageism, looksism influences how we see ourselves and how we're seen by others. Equally important, looksism affects behavior. It leads to discrimination either toward or against those who have a certain look. For example, studies show that:[9]

- Cute babies are held and cuddled more than other babies.
- Good-looking children get more attention from their teachers.
- Pretty women date more often and tend to marry earlier than their plainer sisters.
- Attractive women are more readily hired for jobs that are "appropriate" for females (pink-collar jobs).

There's a tendency to associate good looks with good deeds, and this is where the power of beauty comes in. Attractive people are seen as more sensitive, interesting, sincere, poised, and leading more successful lives than less attractive people. If the package is wrapped well, we assume the contents are also wonderful. Beauty stereotypes aren't all positive, however. Attractive people are also prejudged to be conceited, selfish, vain, snobbish, arrogant, fickle, and sexually demanding.[10] Beauty is nice, but it's not always better.

For instance, good looks can be an obstacle for a woman seeking an executive job, where a highly feminine look may be stereotyped as unprofessional. (Which is one reason Lynn has so much trouble finding the right outfit for work.)

Can you think of times in your own life when looksism worked either for or against you? Were you given special attention as a child because you were so cute? Were you passed over for the cheerleading squad because you weren't cute enough? Sometimes we're unaware of the subtle effects of looksism on us. For example, males were asked to call unknown females who had been described to them as either attractive or unattractive. The women didn't know this information had been given to the callers. Somehow the men unconsciously encouraged the "pretty" women to respond in a friendlier way, whereas the "unattractive" women became less effective on the phone.[11]

It's hard for us to admit or accept that something as "superficial" as looks can push one person ahead and hold another back. So we give lip service to "higher" moral values. We preach that beauty is only skin deep, yet deep down we know how much we value it and how much we fear its loss. We know full well that we do judge books by their covers. We do take others at "face value." Most of us get caught up playing the beauty game, even though the odds are fixed so that only a few can win.

While the women in the Bodylove Survey were sure that physical attractiveness was quite important in daily life, they weren't so sure about its effects on success and happiness. Just as many of them agreed as disagreed with the statement, "Good-looking people are usually happier and more successful than less attractive people."

Do you agree that "good-looking people are usually happier and more successful than less attractive people?"

11%	STRONGLY AGREE
37%	AGREE
16%	NOT SURE
33%	DISAGREE
4%	STRONGLY DISAGREE

You can hear their mixed reactions in these comments:

Myrna. "Basically I think a person's success depends on motivation and how much they're in control of their life. But appearance does play a part, because society's attitudes center on it. Those who fit the norm can initially get what they want, but looks can't carry through entirely. What's underneath also carries a lot of weight."

Isabelle. "If you're beautiful to begin with, people give you the benefit of the doubt. They want to include you. If you're not so attractive, then you have to come across with other things."

Looksism is not a figment of the imagination but a reality that affects your life. How you look influences whether you're looked at. And this in turn changes your body image. While beauty counts, many factors determine whether blond curls or big breasts are an advantage or not in a certain situation. Because appearance communicates, we study the social code and try to send the "right" kinds of body messages. As the cartoon on page 31 shows, looksism prompts us to send false messages, knowing full well that a different person lives behind the façade.

TAKING A LOOK AT LOOKSISM

Stereotypes don't disappear overnight just because we name or expose them. Even so, by looking closely at looksism you can become more aware of how this stereotype influences your own body image. Greater awareness will help you reduce its harmful effects.

EXERCISE • Challenging Looksism in Yourself

All of us carry around our own personal brand of looksism. Try to explore yours by completing the following sentences on paper. Respond rapidly so that your true feelings show.

Because of my looks . . .

Pretty women . . .

I think my body . . .

I wish my body . . .

When I look good . . .

Unattractive women . . .

Bülbül © 1973.

Now check your responses. Do you find any recurring themes? For instance, Charlene wrote that, "Pretty women are lucky women," and "Because of my looks I've had a hard time." Both statements imply that beauty makes life easy. But does it really? Or is that belief a product of looksism?

You'll probably find that at least some of your sentence completions are based on stereotypical attitudes about appearance. Try to challenge each of the responses you made by giving a *counterargument* that makes good sense. Counterarguments are rational statements that refute some belief you automatically assume is true. They are an important technique that we'll be using later on. In this case, counterarguments can help you understand the hidden influence of looksism on your body image.

The best counterarguments are realistic and persuasive. They offer a fresh perspective that can move you beyond the constrictions of a stereotype. Let's take Charlene's responses as an example. She wrote "Pretty women are lucky women."

Counterargument: Pretty women don't always feel lucky. They complain that people won't take them seriously. They worry that they are liked for their looks but not for who they are. They may get hassled and exploited as sex objects, and they feel anxious about losing their beauty as they age.

Charlene also wrote: "Because of my looks I've had a hard time."

Counterargument: In fact, I've been successful sometimes and un-successful other times, even though my looks haven't changed. As I've gotten older, I'm not any better looking. Yet my looks seem to have less influence on my life.

As you try to challenge your responses to the sentences you completed above, remember that stereotypes are powerful because we cling to them as truth.

EXERCISE • Discussing and Recognizing Looksism

Another valuable exercise is to explore the meaning of looksism with family or friends. You can start an interesting discussion by comparing looksism to racism, ageism, or sexism. Ask people if they agree with any of the following statements, and examine your own attitudes during the process.

- You are what you look like.
- Attractive people are happier and more successful than less attractive people.
- Women have to suffer in order to look good.
- Beauty is in the eye of the beholder.

As a final activity, take time to consider how looksism is hidden in media messages that connect good looks with the good life. Open any woman's magazine. Notice how much space is given to depict-ing, defining, and displaying the female body. Notice how much advertising space is devoted to beauty products.

Flip through the pages and count the number of cosmetic ads that promise to produce a lovelier you. It's interesting to jot down a list of the powerful terms used in these ads to connect beauty with success and happiness. In the ads of just one issue of one magazine I found all of these terms: *pure, gentle, sensational, unforgettable, refreshing, clean, healthy, renewed, pumped-up, fresh, bold, outrageous, firm, advanced, glow-ing, incredible, genuine, natural, alive, unique, creative, sensual, upbeat, luscious.* Notice the wide range of characteristics that are connected with being attractive. This is how looksism gets perpetuated. Who wouldn't want luscious lips if they guaranteed a luscious life?

When you use media models as your personal role models, you may be headed for trouble. One study found that exposure to photos of pretty models has a depressing effect. Women tend to rate their own appearance as less attractive after viewing pictures of beautiful models. And men judged women as less attractive after watching just one episode of a TV show featuring a bevy of gorgeous lady cops.[12]

Ads foster looksism by compressing beauty into a few variations of "the right look." Consequently, minority members try to buy straighter hair or rounder eyes, searching for the equality that democracy promises but rarely delivers. The media serve as a kind of magic mirror that reflects an idealized world. In a way, they present today's version of classical myths. Let's look at one ancient myth for insight into the power of reflected beauty.

MIRROR BONDAGE

Imagine a deep forest with a limpid pool. Enter Narcissus, a Greek hunter who is irresistibly handsome. Narcissus has never beheld his own face, so he can't understand what all the fuss is about. While kneeling for a drink, he becomes intoxicated by an image on the surface of the water. Again and again he tries to embrace this vision of beauty, only to see it dissolve in his arms. As he reaches for a kiss, Narcissus falls into the pool, swallowed up by his hungry longing for a lovely face.

The myth of Narcissus depicts an ancient Greek superstition that seeing your own reflection is bad luck. Freud used the term *narcissism* to describe a morbid preoccupation with oneself or one's body. Indeed, reflections can throw you off balance. Like Narcissus, you may be drowning in the vain pursuit of a perfect image.

It's not surprising that mirrors play such an important role in shaping body image. One author explains that mirrors are to image what scales are to weight—a measure of our acceptability or even of our reality. We often turn to them for reassurance, asking the mirror to tell us that we're "still fair enough." But as the anxious queen in *Snow White* discovered, mirrors may only confirm our worst fears.

Katherine tells me that she lives in a house that's heavily mirrored. "Some days are good. When I look I can see good things. Other days I think 'it's just not fair.' I'm not sure what makes a bad day. But I'm very objective and I call it the way I see it. On bad days

I try to avoid being seen by anyone who's important."

"Some mirrors are friendlier than others," Charlene observes. "Some are really hateful and show you everything you don't want to see. I can't stand the ones with the fluorescent lights that make every wrinkle scream out." Who hasn't felt the "triple threat" of the three-way mirrors in fitting rooms, where from every angle you're forced to admit that your body just doesn't fit the ideal.

What really happens when you turn toward your mirror? Studies show that mirrors have three important effects.[13] First, they make you more *self-conscious.* Mirrors are intrusive and hard to ignore. Reflections demand attention and they heighten awareness of "me." Put a chimp like Clara or a toddler like Sally in front of a mirror, and they become absorbed with themselves.

Second, mirrors make you more *critical.* Self-reflection is a setup for self-rejection. Anxiety increases when personal awareness is heightened in some way, whether by mirrors, tape recordings, or the presence of observers. Mirrors can trigger negative thoughts about the body and arouse guilt or shame over inadequacies. "I start my day in front of the mirror, frustrated by all the things I can't change," says Lynn.

Third, mirrors make you more *conforming.* They sensitize you to looksism and motivate compliance with popular beauty standards. From the mirror comes a voice telling you to adopt the "right" image and adapt to society.

Today we have more image feedback than ever before—more mirrors, photos, and media models against which to compare ourselves. Narcissus grew up unaware of his good looks. Today, by the time a youngster like Sally starts school, she's already spent hours inspecting herself in the mirror or watching herself on video tape. Already she wonders, "Do I look okay," "Am I pretty like Mommy?" Primping before her reflection, she too becomes more self-conscious, critical, and conforming.

The Danger Zone of Mirrors

If mirrors threaten self-esteem, why do we enter that danger zone so often? Because mirrors are quite seductive and sometimes helpful. We turn to them for the narcissistic pleasure of seeing a bright smile. We look out of curiosity, to watch a familiar face gradually change. We look with fear or shame, to see what we want no one else to see. We look with a deep need to inspect and control our bodies.

Lynn was increasingly drawn to her mirror for a "fix" of self-reflection. The process of checking up and making over had become automatic. It briefly reassured her she could "do something" about her looks (and perhaps her life). For her, the mirror was a fickle friend, sometimes kind and sometimes cruel.

Mirrors are a bit like slot machines. We're drawn to them and take the gamble because there's an occasional big payoff, even though we often come away unrewarded. In fact, mirrors can be addictive, just like gambling. Some women become obsessed with the smallest details of their appearance and compulsively turn to the mirror for a dose of self-reflection. As with other addictions, the result is both satisfying and destructive. One of these mirror-junkies remarked, "I enjoy the game, but feel like an observer watching a stranger move through the day." Research shows that attractive women spend more time at their mirrors than less attractive women, probably because they get a bigger payoff.

Mind Over Mirror

Mirrors have the power to turn a healthy woman into a cosmetic hypochondriac by making her a "beauty object" in her own eyes. It's part of the objectification we saw earlier. Self-scrutiny leads to preoccupation with trivia—with hairs, spots, wrinkles. Mirrors can turn moles into mountains and scars into craters. Normal changes get magnified into abnormalities. That's why it's better to tone down the mirror's message. Better to keep your distance, literally and figuratively. Adopting a distanced attitude serves as a defense against self-consciousness.

A frequent need to check your appearance puts you in bondage to your mirror. How can you loosen that bond and move beyond the looking glass? Here are some exercises to help you relate more sensibly to the mirrors in your life. The techniques we'll be using derive from cognitive and behavior therapy. They're based on the assumption that thinking, feeling, and doing are interconnected. Changing one alters the other two, as well. What you *do* with your mirror therefore affects how you *think* and *feel* about your looks.

EXERCISE • Assessing Mirror Use

You may be more absorbed with your reflection than you realize. Start by finding out how you really use mirrors during the course of the day. This is called *gathering baseline data.* Baseline data can give you an accurate sense of what you're really doing. It's an actual count of some form of behavior. Baseline data serves as a starting point from which to evaluate yourself and to measure progress. (You'll find this technique mentioned in the chapters ahead.)

1. Begin by guessing what the answer to these questions will be:

- How many mirrors are you intimately involved with—at home, at work, in your purse, in your car, for brief encounters?
- How many specialty mirrors do you keep for specific purposes—magnifying mirrors, makeup mirrors, rearview types?
- How many doses of reflection are you hooked on each day?
- How much time do you spend during each mirror-encounter?

2. Now start to observe yourself and keep some notes. Find out how accurate your guesses were by counting your mirror interactions for a few days. Try not to change any behavior at this time; just gather baseline data. After several days, add up the total and figure out your average daily mirror time. Was it higher or lower than you expected? Only you can decide how much time is too much, but consider whether the time was well spent in helping you achieve bodylove.

3. Take a moment to ask yourself some questions about mirror use and answer them as honestly as you can:

- When I face the mirror, what am I looking *at?* (hair, complexion, clothing, size . . . ?)
- What am I looking *for?* (problems, information, evidence that I'm lovely, proof that I'm not . . . ?)
- What am I expecting (hoping) the mirror will tell me?

    Yes, I'm really as pretty as I thought.

    No, I'm not any different from yesterday.

    It's still there. Keep trying.

    I love you, you gorgeous thing.

    How did a nice person like me get stuck in a body like that?

    You're okay, stop worrying.

    You're not okay, start worrying.

If your mirror habits seem excessive or compulsive, think about cutting back slowly. Remove or cover over a mirror you think you can live without. Give yourself a time quota that is slightly less than baseline for several weeks. Make each mirror-encounter a bit shorter. Cutting down even a few minutes a day adds up over the weeks. Equally important, it's an active step toward becoming less self-conscious, less critical, and less preoccupied with your appearance. To motivate yourself, just imagine how liberating a world without mirrors might feel. Imagine all the time you'd gain for living instead of just for looking. Narcissus might have lead a long and happy life if he hadn't glanced once too often at his own image.

Next time you're in a busy ladies room, stop to watch other women as they watch themselves. How close to the mirror do they stand? Which parts do they fuss over? How many women use the bathroom without also using the mirror? Compare your own behavior to theirs. It's funny how the "rest" room becomes the "powder" room where we do so much serious work. On your next trip to the restroom, give yourself a real rest. Try a mirror boycott and break the connection between bathrooming and beautifying.

LOOKING AND FEELING BETTER BY THINKING BETTER

Because we're so preoccupied with our mirrors, we lose sight of our many other virtues. We make the mistake of equating who we are with how we look. But, in the end, an enduring sense of personal attractiveness can't be based on externals alone. It doesn't come directly from good looks or even from good deeds, but from good thoughts—thoughts that are rational, realistic, and self-enhancing.

In this section, I'll show how you can feel better about your body by thinking better about it. If you often feel self-conscious or depressed about your looks, these feelings may stem from faulty thoughts about body image. Your feelings *are* real, but they're not based on absolute truth about your appearance. And they aren't the only way to feel.

A basic premise of cognitive therapy is that *your thoughts influence how you feel.* Feelings don't float in thin air. They're anchored in *cognitive processes* (which is just another term for thoughts). Lynn says she sometimes feels worse when she looks in the mirror. However, it's not really the act of looking but the act of thinking that creates her bad feelings.[14]

Reprinted by permission of UFS, Inc.

Cognitive Errors

As you probably know, two people can interpret a similar event quite differently. And one person's explanations may be more accurate or more useful than another's. Faulty interpretations of experiences are called *cognitive errors.* They are errors because they are illogical, unproven, exaggerated, or just plain wrong. Once a cognitive error becomes a habit, you may cling to it even when faced with contrary evidence.

Cognitive errors can have a big impact on body image. Recall for instance that, in the previous chapter, Susan believed she was unlovable unless she looked perfect. Her faulty conclusions weren't based on fact, yet they frightened and depressed her. Likewise, Lynn's self-consciousness comes from the cognitive error that people are highly focused on her looks when in reality they're not.

We make cognitive errors all the time. Here's a list of the common types of errors that can lead to body-image problems for many women. See if any of these bad mental habits seems familiar to you.

Extreme thinking. Splitting things into all-or-none categories, then judging them as extremely good or bad. If you don't rate yourself in the good category you quickly label yourself as a total failure. Examples:

"Because of this awful nose, I'll never look decent."

"I can't be as pretty as my sister so I might as well give up."

Rejecting positives. Ignoring or dismissing evidence that you're really okay. Therefore you can go on believing that you're not okay and never will be. Examples:

"Yes, he said I looked nice, but he was only being polite."

"I know I wear a size 8, but I'm still too big."

Thinking in "shoulds." Making unreasonable demands on yourself and on others. These "shoulds" only lead to feelings of guilt, anger, and frustration. Examples:

"My waist should be as small as it was before the baby was born."

"People should always look their best."

Personalizing. Taking things personally and feeling responsible for things that are actually beyond your control. Personalizing leads you to constantly compare yourself with others. Examples:

"They're talking about diets because they think I'm too heavy."

"If she can look that good, then why can't I?"

Jumping to conclusions. Using one small fact as absolute proof of a bigger issue. Therefore, you don't have to think things through. Examples:

"I would have gotten the job if only I weren't so heavy."

"He wants a divorce because I'm getting older."

Emotional reasoning. Using your inner feelings to explain what's happening in the outside world. You assume that your emotions are an accurate reflection of what's really going on. Examples:

"I hate the way I look today, so everyone else must think I look awful."

"If I feel this lonely, it means he doesn't really care about me."

Exaggerating. Magnifying the importance of something. This lets you justify a big emotional reaction to a small event. Examples:

"I'm totally depressed because my hair looks so dreadful."

"I could have died when he caught me without my makeup on."

Automatic Irrational Thoughts

The seven types of cognitive errors just described lead to *automatic irrational thoughts*—thoughts that distort body image and produce bad feelings. For example, Lynn sees an unusual short hairstyle on the cover of a fashion magazine and asks her beautician to give her the haircut shown in the photo. She's not pleased with the results, and the following automatic thoughts and feelings are triggered by her cognitive errors.

AUTOMATIC IRRATIONAL THOUGHTS	COGNITIVE ERRORS	FEELINGS
"I look hideous. This is a disaster."	Exaggerating	Anxious, afraid
"I always make a mess of everything."	Personalizing	Angry at self, stupid
"I'm too ashamed to go out tonight. Everyone will laugh."	Emotional reasoning	Self-conscious, intimidated
"I can't possibly go. I'll die if anyone sees me like this."	Jumping to conclusions	Depressed, lonely, rejected

You don't have to greet your image with negative, self-defeating thoughts that make you feel worse. Instead, as so many average-looking women do, you can welcome it with self-enhancing thoughts that make you feel good. Here's how someone with a positive body image and greater self-esteem might respond to exactly the same situation. Because her thoughts are more rational and constructive, her feelings about herself are better.

RATIONAL THOUGHTS	FEELINGS
"This haircut is awful. I'm sorry I chose it."	Regret, disappointment
"It's not at all like the photo."	Angry at hairdresser
"There's nothing I can do I guess it will grow back eventually."	Acceptance, resignation
"How can I look decent for the party tonight?"	Uncertain
"I'll wear my fabulous African jewelry, and say it's the new primitive look."	Relieved, amused

Consider both women's responses. Which one interprets reality more accurately and constructively? Who feels better in the end? Notice how automatic thoughts trap Lynn in a cycle of self-rejection and body loathing. Notice how the other woman's efforts to be realistic and optimistic preserve her self-esteem. It wasn't the bad haircut in itself that caused Lynn's unhappiness. It was her cognitive errors and automatic self-criticism. One such incident isn't important in and of itself. But cognitive errors can lead to negative interpretations over and over again. And this does have a serious effect on self-esteem and on body image.

THE TRIPLE-COLUMN TECHNIQUE

One way to improve your body image is to correct the cognitive errors that keep you thinking negatively about your looks. The goal is to examine your thoughts, find your mistakes, and learn to think differently. To do this you can use the *triple-column technique,* an approach developed by psychiatrist Aaron Beck.[15]

Here's how this technique worked with Lynn. First, we listed all her automatic thoughts about the "hideous haircut" and put these in column 1. Next, we analyzed the type of cognitive errors she was making and placed these in column 2. Finally, we developed rational counterarguments that could refute the automatic thoughts. These went into column 3. The completed exercise looked like this:

AUTOMATIC THOUGHT	TYPE OF COGNITIVE ERROR	RATIONAL COUNTERARGUMENT
"I look hideous. This is a disaster."	Exaggerating	"It's not great, but it's not hideous. Looking scalped isn't really earthshaking."
"I always make such a mess of everything."	Personalizing	"I wanted a new look and this is really different. It didn't turn out as I expected this time. But that doesn't mean I mess up all the time."
"I'm ashamed to go out. Everyone will laugh."	Emotional reasoning	"I'm entitled to make a mistake. Some people may laugh, others will sympathize. Most won't care."
"I can't go. I'll die if anyone sees me."	Jumping to conclusions; exaggeration	"I can decide to go or not to go. Either way I won't die. At home I'll be safe, but lonely. If I go, I'll have more to risk but also more to gain."

Developing good counterarguments is a crucial step. The arguments must be accurate and realistic enough so you can "buy into them." The more persuasive the argument, the more effectively it refutes the automatic thought. Lynn's irrational thoughts are negative and self-defeating. They're put-downs. The rational counterarguments are positive and self-defensive. They're buildups that refute the put-downs. You'll find that if you identify the type of cognitive error that lies beneath the automatic thought, it will help you develop better counterarguments.

In using the triple-column technique, try to read your responses aloud, so you can hear the cognitive errors and make better counterarguments. In Lynn's case I played the part of her automatic thoughts, reading them out to her while she argued back against them. You can do this by yourself or with a friend. You'll find that working with a partner reduces your feelings of isolation and adds an element of fun. This exercise not only helped Lynn feel better about her hair but taught her a valuable skill to use with other body-image problems.

A Triple-Column Attack on Self-Consciousness

Self-consciousness about appearance is often triggered by automatic thoughts that come from cognitive errors. The triple-column technique can help you attack and reduce self-conscious feelings.

1. Begin by gathering some baseline data. For one week, keep track of self-conscious feelings whenever they occur—at work, while socializing, or on the street. Where, when, and how often do you feel self-conscious about your looks? Try to catch hold of the feeling *while it's happening.* Carry a pad and paper to jot down the automatic thoughts that occur just before you experience that uneasy sense of being watched or judged by others. Note that the "others" who are judging you may not actually be there, but may be present only in your imagination.

2. List your automatic thoughts as fully as possible in column 1. Then consider which type of cognitive errors you're making, and write the category in column 2. Finally, spend some time constructing good counterarguments that challenge your faulty thinking. Make the arguments short and persuasive. These serve as your defensive weapons the next time you're feeling self-conscious in a similar situation. Here's how the completed exercise might look.

AUTOMATIC THOUGHT	COGNITIVE ERROR	RATIONAL COUNTERARGUMENT
"Everyone's staring at me, thinking how plain I look."	Extreme thinking	"When one person looks my way it doesn't mean everyone is staring. I don't really know what they're thinking even if they do look."
"I should look better than I do today."	Thinking in "shoulds"	"I'm tired and premenstrual. No one can look their best all the time."
"I'm not dressed right so I'll never get the job. I might as well leave now."	Jumping to conclusions	"I have a great resumé. They're more concerned with what I'm saying than what I'm wearing."
"If I feel so tense it must mean he finds me ugly."	Emotional reasoning	"I'm tense because I'm shy. It has nothing to do with how he views me."
"They're talking about diets because they know I've gained weight."	Personalizing	"They always talk about diets no matter what I weigh. I don't look any heavier than I did last week."

3. It's important to actually work through your responses on paper. The written word has special impact. It forces you to put vague feelings into precise phrases and to decide exactly what you mean. On paper you can see which kinds of cognitive errors you make repeatedly. It's an active step toward overcoming resistance. Do you exaggerate, personalize, or jump to conclusions all the time? Once your counterarguments are on paper, read them out loud, restate them in different ways, rehearse them until they flow easily.

Analyzing and correcting cognitive errors will help you gradually gain control of automatic thoughts and of the self-conscious feelings they evoke. Eventually you'll be able to short-circuit bad feelings by catching your automatic thoughts as soon as they occur and refuting them immediately. With practice, cognitive errors will slowly give way to more rational patterns of thought that then become good habits.

Lynn found that she was most self-conscious in business settings where she had to deal with male executives. One of her constant automatic thoughts was, "I don't look professional enough. He's thinking about how I look, not what I'm saying." She rehearsed counterarguments that stressed her competence in the field and was able to short-circuit self-consciousness before it took hold.

To summarize the triple-column technique for handling cognitive errors about body image:

- Tune in to negative feelings about your body or your looks.
- Write down the thoughts that occurred just before the feelings began.
- Consider which of the seven types of cognitive errors you're making. (Check the list.)
- Develop rational responses to use as counterarguments.
- Write them down and rehearse them out loud.
- Challenge automatic thoughts about your appearance as soon as they occur.

FACING THE CHALLENGE

This chapter sets the stage for understanding body-image conflicts and introduces you to some basic cognitive and behavioral techniques for change. You may want to take time to read it again, and to repeat the exercises during the weeks ahead. Go at a comfortable pace and be assured that you *can* improve your body image.

Here are the major points we've covered so far:

1. *Self-esteem is closely tied to your body image.* Your actual physical appearance has less to do with body image than you might think. If you feel good about your looks, you'll probably feel better about yourself and vice versa, regardless of what you look like.

2. *Our culture sets up difficult standards that objectify women.* These lead to heightened self-consciousness that make body loathing a universal problem for healthy women.

3. *Looksism is a form of stereotyping.* It links certain (favorable or unfavorable) traits with appearance. If you become more sensitive to looksism, you'll realize how it affects and prejudices your view of yourself and others.

4. *Mirrors are a danger zone.* They can make you more critical and more conforming. Reducing your mirror time is a useful step toward bodylove.

5. *You can feel better about your looks and yourself if you think more constructively.* Learn to challenge cognitive errors with good counterarguments and thus short-circuit the automatic thoughts that make you unhappy about your body.

As you see, working on bodylove is a real challenge. You're trying to change patterns that are firmly entrenched. Remember that your body image has grown out of a lifetime of experience. That's why it can't be transformed overnight. People vary in their response to self-help exercises. Some feel rapid relief when they break free of a destructive habit, such as mirror addiction. For others, small steps slowly lead to a general sense of well-being. Small steps *can* be highly significant if they prove to you that change is possible.

In order to achieve bodylove you'll need to work as hard at minding the inside as you do at minding the outside of your body. A beautiful body image isn't found in the mirror; it's reflected in the mind's eye. To get a clearer view of what's going on in your mind, let's look back into childhood, for the seeds of body loathing and bodylove are planted early in life. You'll see how outworn values from the past can be replaced by healthy praise in the present.

CONFRONTING IMAGES: PAST AND PRESENT

What were your mother's attitudes toward your appearance when you were growing up?

> VERY POSITIVE AND ACCEPTING
> GENERALLY POSITIVE
> MIXED
> GENERALLY NEGATIVE AND CRITICAL
> VERY NEGATIVE
> I DON'T KNOW

What were your father's attitudes toward your appearance while you were growing up?

> VERY POSITIVE AND ACCEPTING
> GENERALLY POSITIVE
> MIXED
> GENERALLY NEGATIVE
> VERY NEGATIVE
> I DON'T KNOW

How do you feel when someone compliments you about your appearance?

> VERY DELIGHTED
> SOMEWHAT PLEASED
> MIXED FEELINGS
> SELF-CONSCIOUS
> VERY UNCOMFORTABLE

When you take a long look at your nude body in a full-length mirror, how do you feel?

> PROUD
> CONTENT
> MIXED FEELINGS
> ANXIOUS OR DEPRESSED
> REPULSED

It seemed as impossible for me to know how I looked as it was important. Some people said I looked exactly like my mother, the most beautiful woman in the world: Others said I resembled my father, who though very wise, was not particularly comely.

—ALIX KATES SHULMAN

Y OUR family history is a crucial part of how you see your body today, for body image is conceived and confounded in childhood. It grows out of your earliest experiences, as part of the socialization process. Most little girls are praised for being sweet, neat, and cute. Like them, you probably were encouraged to look critically at your body and to look to others for approval. But do these habits of self-scrutiny help you now? It isn't easy to separate the values that please others from the values that please yourself. To do so you need to question the many "shoulds" that influence body image, including the ultimate: you should please people by looking pretty.

Trying too hard to please can be harmful if you never stop to define who you want to be or what you want to look like. On the road toward bodylove most of us must shed some of the ill-fitting parental and social values we internalized long ago. In addition we must also break free of feminine stereotypes that hold us in the grip of looksism.

This chapter explores your album of childhood memories. Uncovering lost images from the past can show you how your conflicts with your body began. You'll be using visual imagery to help sort out family values, and using mirrors to help create a more compassionate reflection of yourself. In the end, you'll understand why it's so important to become your own loving parent—one who accepts and appreciates you as you are.

I collect antique photo albums. Carefully preserved, these albums display a whole family of strangers. Turning the pages, I try to guess which daughter belongs to which mother, and I wonder how they liked their faces.

In my own family album there's a six-year-old with a missing tooth who sits patiently while her hair is braided. When I ask about that picture my mother smiles. "Even when you were born, you had a head full of thick brown hair," she recalls. "And, oh, how Dad loved your beautiful long braids." And, oh, how I've struggled to untangle my feelings about my hair! Here's a personal body-image problem that I'll share in this chapter—the long and short of how I grew and cut and used my hair to bond with men or to break away from them. It's a problem that I never outgrew and which still makes me self-conscious.

If you have photos from childhood, take them out. If not, try to find some of these pictures. Perhaps they're packed away or still with your parents. Photographs can be an important window onto the past, revealing the history of body-image conflicts. Through photos you may find the lovely child hidden somewhere inside your head. Choose a favorite snapshot of yourself before age ten, one that immediately makes you smile. Place it near the phone, and while you're chatting with others, try to make friends with this little girl. She's still a part of who you are today.

LEARNING SOCIAL VALUES

You began life as an extension of your mother's body and she provided your first lessons in body image. Like a mirror she reflected your sounds and smiles. In her eyes you saw pride or shame. As an infant you learned that your body had its own boundaries apart from hers, and these early lessons in body awareness helped you develop a separate sense of self.

Social interactions also taught you that certain physical features are admired while others are not. Cultural values, including the stereotypes of looksism, are passed down from one generation to the next. Of course, we live in many social systems at once. Family, community, ethnic, racial, and religious groups all pull us in different directions. You got to know your own childish body through these many social filters, and gradually developed strong feelings about dark skin, fat hips, long hair, and so forth.

Think about the values that were important to your family. Did your parents worship neatness or thinness? Did your father hug and hold you when you looked pretty? Did your mother nag and scold you when you got messy? Were you taught to sit straight, eat right, bathe often? Were you ever caught playing doctor, or "playing with yourself"? These are the shadows that may still haunt your body image today, causing self-consciousness and anxiety.

They were the shadows that Jane saw and which she brought to my office. An ambitious college student, Jane was socially withdrawn and rarely dated. Her major complaint was a preoccupation with her complexion. "I know most people don't see these blotches but I think they look awful," she explained. "Sometimes they seem to fade away, and then they come back. It makes me nervous, so I stay home a lot. Then I don't have to worry."

Jane brought in some photo albums and together we turned the pages. An only child, she had been constantly photographed, dressed up like a princess, and shown off like a prize possession. One picture, taken when she was six, showed Jane's handsome father escorting her at an Easter parade while her mother seems hidden in the background. "Dad called me his 'perfect little doll,'" she recalled. "My mother always told me how lucky I was to be blond like him instead of dark like her. She thought I'd have all the dates she never had, because I was pretty." For Jane, it wasn't parental rejection of her appearance that caused problems, but parental overinvestment in it. Being "Daddy's doll" was a burden she could no longer carry easily.

PARENTAL PRAISE

Parental praise is a crucial part of the socialization process. It can build self-esteem, but sometimes it backfires. This happens when praise inflates the value of physical attractiveness or gives excessive meaning to certain features. Jane's baby-doll looks were a source of parental pride and pleasure, as were my own thick braids. However, too much investment in the body as a showpiece taught Jane that love is contingent on looks. Over time she internalized her parents' attitudes. For her, self-love became dependent on looking perfect. For me, long hair became an important feminine tool for pleasing others, especially men.

Perhaps you know from your own experiences that self-consciousness and hypersensitivity about your looks can come from praise as well as criticism. Two out of three women in the Bodylove Survey felt that their parents were generally accepting of their appearance when they were growing up, while one out of four reported parental feelings that were mixed or negative. Think about whether your parents generally were proud or critical of your looks. Which features did they fuss over and which did they want to help you "correct"?

What were your mother's attitudes toward your appearance when you were growing up? What were your father's attitudes?

	MOTHER	FATHER
VERY POSITIVE AND ACCEPTING	33%	26%
GENERALLY POSITIVE	37%	38%
MIXED FEELINGS	13%	13%
GENERALLY NEGATIVE AND CRITICAL	8%	5%
VERY NEGATIVE	3%	3%
DON'T KNOW	6%	15%

Carolann recalls a childhood full of criticism. "My mother always told me to go comb my hair, stand up straight, do something. Those comments stay with you for a lifetime. Even when you think you look good, you're on such a tentative basis. You can never overcome what you feel inside," she explained. "My mother was pretty on the outside, but not on the inside. So I could never use her as a model of attractiveness."

Martha, the mother of a grown daughter, described how hard she had tried to give Trisha good feelings about her body. "I always told her 'Oh, you look so darling.' She really did look beautiful to me from the day she was born and I wanted her to know it. But when she was in college she told me she didn't like those comments because they made her feel self-conscious, as if she had to look special all the time. It never dawned on me that compliments could be a negative thing. Now I see that it's hard to balance out."

During childhood, Ellen's father teased her about her weight. Consequently, she sees herself as much heavier than she really is. This is how parental praise or criticism leads to cognitive errors and to the automatic thoughts that follow from them. Ellen constantly thinks in extremes with respect to weight. Just because she isn't thin, she labels herself as "much too fat."

These examples illustrate the importance of family interaction in setting the foundation for body image. Among other things, socialization teaches you that beauty is a valuable trait for pleasing others, especially if you're a girl.

GROWING INTO THE FAIR SEX

Why are females so much more likely than males to believe that their future is bound up in their looks? Why do so many young women like Jane feel unhappy with their skin or weight, while young men generally feel more satisfied with their bodies? These gender differences are learned in childhood and continue to affect us years later in the form of pride or shame.

While baby boys and girls are similar in most ways, they're seen and expected to turn out differently right from birth. When parents were asked what kind of person they wanted their child to become, "being attractive" was mentioned as an important quality far more often for daughters than for sons. These parents also rated their newborn daughters as delicate and cute, while they saw their sons as hardy and active (despite the fact that there were no measurable differences between the babies).[1]

Girls are quickly wrapped up in a pretty pink world of ruffles and roses. Throughout childhood, they're given more clothing and get more compliments about their appearance than boys. All too often I catch myself telling my niece Sally how pretty she looks. These comments seem to automatically pour out from the same well of compliments that my Dad gave me when I wore my braids like a crown on my head.

In fact fathers sex-type their children even more than mothers do. Husbands urge their wives to keep their daughters' hair long and to dress them up. Sally's father describes her as "coy and sexy" and calls her "a cute little vamp." Most fathers enjoy this kind of flirtation with their daughters, especially during the so-called Oedipal stage, ages three to five. One of my earliest memories is having dessert each night on my father's lap while he played with my hair, both of us enjoying these warm strokes that brought us closer. Jane's father took her to visit his folks every Sunday, and loved to see her "dressed up for Grandma."

Studies show that preschoolers judge appearance in much the same way that adults do and are already guilty of looksism. They can accurately rate the attractiveness of classmates, and they prefer to play with kids who are better looking.[2] When I asked first-graders how girls and boys differed, they told me: "Girls play at being pretty, but boys play cars." "Girls are cute and they don't get as muddy as boys." "Girls have more clothes, but boys are stronger." Slowly but surely, Sally learns to view her body as an object of attraction while her brother learns to view his as an instrument of power.

Learning the rules of gender begins early in life. By age three, Sally confidently declares, "I'm a girl, not a boy!" Polishing her nails, she starts to act out the ornamental feminine role, and enjoys doing it. Her books, clothes, and toys teach her the subtleties of looking feminine. Television becomes her babysitter, transmitting endless hours of cultural values about beauty.

Perhaps you grew up like Sally, playing with Barbie and with your very own makeup sets. These cosmetic "toys" are advertised as "the fun way for a girl to learn beauty secrets." Sally also learns that her pretty face needs improvement, and this message plants a seed of doubt in her head. So she begins to greet her own reflection with new thoughts: "Am I pretty enough? Should I be prettier?" These are the same uncertainties that Jane expressed, and which trace back to her early childhood experiences. Even young children sometimes feel deeply ashamed about their "flaws."

"Of *course* I need to wear a top. How else do you expect me to keep an aura of mystery?"

SHAME ON YOU

Shame is a feeling of inadequacy mixed with the fear that some defect may be exposed to others. Shame can come from having a body that develops too soon or skin that's "off color." As Joyce recalls,

> I was very little when I became terribly self-conscious about my complexion. My relatives from India would visit and say "My God, this girl is getting darker every year—it's such a shame. Look how light her mother is." I got the message that they thought I'd never get married because of my color. I fantasized about an electrical bar of soap that I'd plug into a wall. This magical soap would wash away all the dirty skin and I wouldn't have to be ashamed anymore.

The residue of these early experiences doesn't wash away so easily. Some analysts believe that males are more likely to feel guilty about what they've done, whereas females are more likely to feel ashamed about who they are. Women's shame is rooted deep in ancient myths connecting the female body to evil and contamination. Eve corrupted paradise by opening her mouth to the apple, while Pandora polluted the world by exposing the contents of her 'box.' Historically, women are depicted as beautiful, but also are seen as frightening and shameful because their bodies go out of control.

Aristotle called the female body "a deformity which occurs in the ordinary course of nature." Darwin concluded that males had reached a higher stage of development than females. In our own century, Freud described the "inadequate" genitals of a little girl and her envy and longing for a penis she can never have. Such myths still echo through history and in fairy tales. They fill our children's heads with shame that distorts their body images.

Though worshiped as beauty objects, females are still regarded as inferior. Children learn early that the cosmetic makeovers that transform females into members of the "fair sex" are in part a way to cover the shameful inadequacies of being the "other sex." As a ten-year-old boy explained, "If I'd been born a girl, I would have to be pretty and no one would be interested in my brains."

ADOLESCENT IMAGES

By the time she had reached adolescence, Jane had become more and more anxious about her looks. Perhaps puberty was a painful time for you, also. It is for most girls. One of the striking sex differences that emerges at adolescence is a greater self-consciousness in females. A survey of eight- to fifteen-year-olds showed that at every age level, girls worry more about their appearance than boys. Twice as many high school girls as boys want to change their looks, and they are dissatisfied with a greater number of body parts than boys. Largely as a result of the values they learn during childhood, girls enter puberty with a stronger need to feel attractive than boys do. Therefore they suffer greater insecurity when their developing bodies feel awkward and out of control.[3]

Media images only make matters worse. Advertisers know that talking to a girl in her teens can make her a customer forever. Teenage girls are bombarded with one essential message about their purpose in life: learning the art of body adornment through clothing, cosmetics, jewelry, hair products, perfumes. As a result, the natural adolescent search for a personal identity gets distorted into a search for a packaged image. A growing girl is more or less directed to her mirror to discover who she is.

Can you recall your own self-conscious feelings during puberty? Try looking at some teenage photos to remind yourself of how you looked and felt during that vulnerable stage. Some of your current body-image conflicts probably trace back to it. Do you remember any specific events that made bodylove more difficult during that stage?

Like many women, Jane says she felt worse about her body after puberty than before it. She carries in her wallet a sixth-grade graduation picture that she describes as "the last photo I really like of myself." Joyce recalls, "I truly believed that my dark skin was a punishment for something I'd done wrong. Very early I came to the conclusion that I'd never be pretty, so I'd better be good at other things. I was just beginning to gain some self-confidence when my periods began, and I felt dirty all over again."

Conflicts about body image that begin in childhood tend to surface in more dramatic form during adolescence. For instance, some girls become ambivalent about the role of beauty object even before they reach puberty. Eileen, who is now in her forties, recalls the parental values that led to her strong anti-makeup attitudes:

> When I was very little, my mother often said she'd be ready to go "as soon as she put on her face." I couldn't understand what she meant because she seemed to have a face already. My father and uncles made comments about how women were always shopping for clothes, as if it were female foolishness to be concerned with looks and makeup. Sometime in Junior high school I bought that message from my Dad. I decided, if this is so silly, I won't have any part of it. I didn't want to be just one of those foolish women. My mother encouraged me to look more stylish and wear more makeup, but I wouldn't shop with her and said I had enough to wear.

Many a mother tries to act out her unrealized dreams through her daughter. She may see her child as an extension of herself, and try to control the girl's looks as if she were managing her own body. In reaction, a daughter may rebel against the pressure in one way or another. The mother-daughter tug-of-war over beauty takes many forms. To get psychologically separated, a girl may concentrate on how *not* to look or be like her mother. At the same time, mothers are caught between wanting their girls to grow up into lovely women and hating to grow older themselves.

Mothers send mixed messages. There is pride mixed with envy, encouragement mixed with fear. Jane explains that, "Mom tells me how pretty I am and nags me to go out more. But then she criticizes the guys I date and the clothes and makeup that I wear." Jane has trouble gaining control of how she wants to be seen, while her mother has trouble letting go.

Fathers also send double messages: be a sexy knockout but stay my little girl. One day a man may suddenly see his own child as seductive. Feeling anxious over this sexual attraction he may withdraw or reject her. Other fathers are guilty of sexually abusing their daughters or stepdaughters, which leaves deep scars of shame on the self-image of these girls. (This type of body shame is discussed more fully in Chapter 6.)

Most men feel the loss when a teenage daughter transfers her affection from Father to Prince Charming. Your own father's reactions to the sexuality of your adolescent body may still affect you today. Did you get the message that it was safe to be sexual? Were you taught that sex was dangerous or sinful? The desire to be sexually attractive and the confusion over sexual urges can create body-image distortions that persist over a lifetime.

Perhaps you used conflicts over makeup or clothing as a way to rebel and separate from your parents. A friend of mine refused to permit her daughter to have several holes pierced in her ears. The seventh-grader defiantly took a needle and bravely did it herself, thus asserting the right to display her body as she wished.

My own first adolescent rebellion over appearance took place on a spring day in my eleventh year. My breasts were budding into puberty and my pigtails had been pulled once too often. For weeks I'd been pleading and arguing. "How long do you expect me to wear these stupid braids?" With scissors in hand, I gave my mother an ultimatum: "Either you cut them off right now, or I'll do it myself!" Poor Mom, caught between the passions of father and daughter. As the scissors passed from my hands to hers, we became cosmetic allies (as we would many times in the future). Together we performed the ritual and watched the floor gather up my curls.

That evening I faced my father, felt his shock, and survived his anger. Without the braids that had bound me to him as Daddy's little girl, I was free to grow up and away from him into womanhood. Only recently did I come to realize the full impact of that event on our relationship, as I'll describe later. Yet, by age fifteen I had rediscovered long hair as a seductive lure. Like the other cheerleaders, I tied a white bow in my ponytail and searched the faces of the football players for the adoring look I used to see in my father's eyes.

PICTURE THIS

In this section, you'll travel back in time to explore parental values and your reactions to them. Through a process called *visualization* you can re-experience your childhood body within the safety of your own imagination. Stepping back into the past will help you move beyond it into a healthier body image.

Earlier you saw how cognitive errors can trigger negative feelings. Mental images also arouse feelings. Think of what it's like to awaken from a nightmare, trembling over a picture in the mind's eye. The power of mental imagery is now being used in novel

ways—for instance, to control pain or to improve athletic performance. A skater may first imagine herself doing a perfect spin and
then try to imitate the image.

Visualization is the conscious production of mental imagery.
Thoughts *can* control and change the images you see in your mind.
To understand how visualization works, close your eyes and repeat
the word "apple." An apple image probably appeared. Although
intangible, this apple really exists in your mind. By concentrating
you can change its color or make it spin in the air. Try it. Body image
is also intangible but real. Like the apple, it can be brought to mind
and altered by consciously imagining it differently. Therefore you
can transform your body image by learning to visualize it more
accurately and more attractively.

The next exercise uses *guided imagery* to evoke certain childhood
scenes. The instructions help guide you to visualize specific events
or conflicts you felt long ago. These may be history now, yet they
can cause fresh problems every time you look in the mirror or climb
on the scale. Visualizing scenes from childhood can give you a new
perspective on the past and help you change the way you think
about yourself.

As you recover lost memories through guided imagery, strong
feelings may emerge. Try not to block or retreat from these emotions, but hang on to them if you can. Stay open to the feelings as
long as possible, even if there's pain or sadness. If you become too
anxious, open your eyes to end the scene and try to go back to it
later. It may take some practice, but by reliving childhood scenes
through visualization, you can stir up the ghosts that inhabit your
body image—and perhaps lay some of them to rest.

Of course, it's impossible to read and visualize at the same time,
so I suggest the following procedure. First read through the exercise
to get a sense of it. Then set aside enough time (about ten minutes)
to practice the visualization without interruption from people or
phone calls. Review the guided instructions once more just before
you start. You may find it helpful to record the instructions. Just
read them slowly onto a tape, leaving pauses where appropriate.
You can then visualize along with the tape and repeat the process
until the images are clear. These exercises focus first on your mother
because most likely she taught you your earliest lessons in body
awareness and was your primary social model for a long time. (Use
the person who served as the primary mother figure in your life as
the mother in each of the scenes.)

EXERCISE • Album Update

1. *Practice in visualization.* Begin all visualization exercises by sitting or lying down. Get comfortable, close your eyes, and take time to clear your mind. Then let your imagination begin to search through your memory album. Drift back to adolescence and visualize yourself as a high school senior standing outside the school talking with friends. Notice the details of your hair and clothing, your posture, and your expressions. Concentrate until you see yourself clearly in that setting, looking just as you did then. Can you control the image by making it smile, laugh, or move around?

Now turn back the pages of your album still further. This time visualize yourself in the playground of your elementary school. In this scene you are younger, smaller, more childlike. Bring the details into focus as your eyes travel up and down that young body. What did you look like then? Were you sturdy, healthy, pretty? Feel how real this image is as you focus in on the details. Now try to shift back and forth from the high school to the grade school scene. Use your thoughts to control the images you see. What parts of your body image change in each scene and what parts stay the same? Repeat this exercise a few times, adding new details as you learn to control your visualizations.

2. *The dependent baby.* This time, imagine yourself as a toddler with your mother. Think of how the two of you looked, walking together in the park. You are a very small and helpless child; she is a young woman. Visualize her face as it was then, and your own little body. You start running after a ball, but suddenly trip and fall hard on the pavement. Feel the pain of this accident, see the bruise on your knee and the expression on your face. What is your response? Do you cry loudly or silently? Your mother runs to you. Does she react with fear, sympathy, or anger? Does she say that you "should" be more careful, "should" hug and kiss her to feel better, "should" be brave and not cry, or "shouldn't" run so fast? Notice how small and dependent you are. What do you need from your mother at that moment? What do you want to say to her?

Jane saw her mother as confused and frightened. "When I visualized the park scene, my mother looked upset and didn't know what to do. She was afraid that I'd have a scar on my knee and felt guilty because she didn't hold my hand. Now that I think about it, maybe my mother was always worried about protecting me, keeping me safe and perfect." Slowly Jane began to understand a connection between her current anxiety about her skin and her mother's concerns about protecting her as a child.

3. *The adorable princess.* Visualize yourself growing from a toddler into a child of about six. At this age you've already learned to enjoy and display yourself as a pretty object. Imagine yourself getting ready for a birthday party or some special holiday that you remember well. You're dressing up in your prettiest party outfit, with petticoats, patent-leather shoes, hair ribbons. See the "little girl you" standing before a mirror and looking like a princess. How does she feel about her reflection? Now visualize your mother coming into the room. What does she say, and what do her eyes tell you? That you should brush your hair again, shouldn't spoil the dress, should show Daddy how nice you look? Does she want you to stay little and lovely forever? What do you want to say to her at that moment?

Jane recalls those dress-up times as fun. "I got a lot of attention from my relatives and loved all the compliments. I remember that Mom was very proud and really got a big kick out of showing me off." As we talked about this further, Jane considered whether her strong desire to keep on making her mother proud of how she looked was preventing her from moving into a more adult role.

4. *The active child.* Turn your album to age ten. See how much bigger and stronger you've grown. You can climb trees and jump rope. You're in control of your body and of the environment. Visualize yourself mastering some difficult activity, like diving off a high board or riding a horse. Now you call out, "Hey, Mom, look what I can do." How do you feel about your active body as your mother watches you? How does your mother respond? Does she cheer you on or does she caution or criticize? Do you end up thinking you should do better, or shouldn't be doing this at all?

While visualizing this scene, Jane got in touch with her mother's overprotectedness again. "Mom got worried as she saw me going off for a long bike ride. She would always say 'Don't get hurt' and 'I'll be glad when you're home'." Today Jane uses the same stay-at-home defense against getting hurt when she feels afraid of moving out into the social world.

Here are some follow-up questions:

- Can you find one word to describe how your body looks in each scene?

- What other important values did your mother teach you about how your body "should" be used or displayed?
- Do these "shoulds" serve you well today? Or would you be better off replacing them with values that are tailored to your own personal needs and to the body you live in now?

While you practice visualizing these scenes over the next few days, try some spontaneous imagery. Use your imagination to go beyond the guidelines of the instructions and search for real childhood memories to relive. Become your own guide as the imagery unfolds. You might want to repeat the sequence of images just given, substituting your father, grandmother, or siblings. Be sure to take enough time to explore your reactions and feelings to each of the visualizations.

Who are the special people who influenced your feelings about your body during childhood? Perhaps you had a favorite aunt who took you shopping for a birthday dress. Or a grandmother whose unconditional love boosted your self-esteem. Don't forget the dance teacher, the coach at school, or the counselor at camp. And don't forget the men who have touched your life and your body in important ways over the years—boyfriends, uncles, brothers. Now look over your list. Was there one person in particular whom you associate with body loathing or bodylove? If so, keep that person in mind as you work on the remaining exercises in this chapter.

Chances are that some of your current beauty conflicts probably took shape in adolescence, as mine did. This is the stage when eating disorders are triggered, when complexion problems surface, when makeup is used as a rite of passage into womanhood. There is competition for boyfriends, greater peer pressure, and a strong desire to fit in. Visualizing your teenage body can give you insight into these conflicts and help you resolve them.

EXERCISE • Revisiting Your Teenage Body

1. Relax, close your eyes, and take a few deep breaths to clear your mind. Focus inward and drift back to age fifteen, about the time when you started high school. You're almost fully grown and your body is fairly well developed. See yourself at home in the morning, stepping out of the shower. Notice your wet skin and the contours of your young figure. Try to move inside this image as you stand fresh and clean before the mirror. Now let your eyes travel up and down the imaginary reflection. Notice your hair as you wore it then, your complexion, your expression.

2. Stop for a moment to admire those parts of your body that you liked most. Enjoy seeing them as they looked then. Once you have a clear image, focus on the parts of your body that you disliked. What was wrong with those body parts and how did you feel about them? Did they make you embarrassed, disgusted, ashamed? Were you a late maturer? Was weight a problem for you then? Which parts of you felt too fat or too thin? When you lived in that young body, were you longing to be someone else—someone taller, thinner, fairer?

3. Now visualize yourself getting dressed for school. Do you feel as attractive as your friends? Are you self-conscious about your looks in front of them? Stay in the same time frame and bring your mother (or mother figure) into the scene. Try to recall what she looked like when you were fifteen. Notice the clothes she wore and the look on her face. Was she pretty? In what ways did you resemble her and how were you different?

4. Imagine your mother looking you over before you leave for school. She's checking your outfit, your hair, your makeup. What is she thinking? Do her eyes tell you that you're getting too heavy? That you look more like her every day? That you're becoming a beautiful woman? Let the scene develop. What does she say to you? Hear the sound of her voice and see the look on her face. Is there something you want to say to her in reply?

Here are some follow-up questions:

- Can you find one word that best describes your adolescent body?
- How did your mother influence your feelings about your body then? Does her voice still echo in your mind when you look in the mirror?
- What were your mother's attitudes about her own appearance, and do you feel the same way about your body now as she felt about hers then?

Jane recalls her feelings at fifteen. "The best word to describe how I looked is 'sweet.' Sometimes I felt grown up and sexy, but

I still tried to be a sweet little girl for my father. Mom wanted me to be popular, but she got angry when I started hanging around with older guys. At twenty I don't feel so sweet or naïve anymore. I'm just not sure what I should be instead."

You might want to repeat this exercise several times until you become more at ease with your teenage self. Try to recall and relive several specific events when you remember having real tension with your parents over beauty issues. Some women can identify special points in their history during or after adolescence, when their body image shifted dramatically: "The day my braces came off," "The year I grew taller than my mother," "When I stopped wearing a bikini because of all the stretch marks after pregnancy." For me, there was another rebellious haircut that altered my self-image and pushed me into a new phase of personal growth.

At thirty-three, I wore my hair long and loose, like a flag of femininity. My life was overloaded with a career, two children, an unfinished dissertation, and a floundering marriage. One day I impulsively separated from my long hair and soon afterward from the husband who loved it. As I had many years before, I again used my body to proclaim my right to independence. By first renouncing my role as an attractive object, I felt freer to move on toward a new identity. At the time, I wasn't aware of the meaning behind that haircut. Now, looking through my memory album, I see its connection to the little girl with the long hair that Mommy braided and that Daddy loved.

CONFLICTING VALUES

Parental values continue to influence body image long after adolescence. Eileen, who had rebelled against her mother by wearing no makeup for years, explains her current conflict:

> Here I am at forty-eight, and not only my mother but also my father were putting pressure on me to get rid of the gray streaks in my hair. I would hear from one and then from the other, "You really ought to do something about that gray." For a while I just screened out their remarks, but deep down it bothered me. Then I saw some pictures of myself after a vacation and I realized how gray I'd become. Somehow, my self-image had lagged behind the

real changes. Those photos plus my parents' prodding had an impact. As you can see, the gray is gone—for a while.

As in adolescence, Eileen is still torn between personal feelings, parental values, and the social pressure to conform.

EXERCISE • Confronting Outworn Feelings and Values

By now, I hope you've been able to identify some of the family and social values that shaped your body image during childhood. It's time to confront and challenge the ones that don't serve you well anymore—those that underlie your body loathing and obstruct your bodylove.

1. *Visual confrontation.* Try to return to some of the scenes you've just practiced and carry them through to a new conclusion. What did you want to say as a teenager when you heard your mother's critical remarks or saw her judgmental look? What did you want to say as a child when you were told not to eat so much because you'd get fat?

In the safety of your visual fantasy, bring back those moments and express your frustration, sadness, or anger. Berate your brother for teasing you about your large breasts, or confront the uncle who touched you in ways that made you ashamed. Tell them how they hurt you, how they made you feel awkward and self-conscious. By expressing the negative feelings that you've harbored for so long you can start to gain control of them. Facing these confrontations through visualization will help you resolve the conflicts you still feel. It may also help you deal more effectively with family influences as they continue in your life today.

2. *Cognitive confrontations.* Start by making a list of the family values you've uncovered through the exercises in this chapter. Be sure to put them down on paper so you can clearly identify and express them. Jane's list included such things as:

It's important to show off your looks in front of relatives.

If you're pretty you'll be popular.

Be careful so nothing happens to your body.

Consider the parental values on your own list. Which ones feel alien to your current value system? Which ones get in the way of how you want to see yourself today?

Now construct some counterarguments that refute the "truth" of these attitudes you've collected along the way. Work on your counterarguments until they really make good sense to you. Rehearse them out loud until they feel comfortable and automatic. You might want to have an imaginary dialogue or argument with parents, for example, to persuade them that there are many different ways to view one's body and many different yardsticks against which to measure attractiveness.

As you confront and break free of old values, think about people within or outside your family who have different values about appearance—values that you admire. Why not adopt them as new role models, and examine what makes them attractive in your eyes? You'll probably find that these models radiate self-esteem because they've learned to minimize self-criticism and maximize self-praise. Let's look at how that's done.

From Downers to Uppers

Some people are real pros when it comes to punishing themselves. It's as if they've taken over the role of the critical parent who constantly judges. Socialized by years of experience, they've mastered the art of the powerful put-down. Jane began one of her therapy sessions with an especially vicious attack: "Look at these blotches. They're so disgusting I can't stand myself." When I hear this kind of assault, I instinctively want to cry out, *"Stop!* You're beating up my patient. Would you abuse anyone else this way? Come on, give her a break."

If you, too, are a master at putting down your appearance, isn't it about time to catch yourself and *stop?* Of course, you're the only one who can give yourself a break from the critical attacks that wound your self-esteem. But breaking free of years of habitual body loathing isn't easy.

Before going any further, why not find out how often you're a victim of your own verbal assaults? Gather some baseline data. On a note pad, keep track of the self-critical downers that you fire at yourself over the next few days. Then reverse the process and start to count the times you give self-compliments, or uppers. If you find that the list of downers is even half as long as the list of uppers, you'll certainly benefit from the following exercises.

EXERCISE • Raising Praise Levels

Here are some simple behavioral techniques to reduce self-criticism and increase self-praise. Behavior therapy stresses the use of *reinforcements* to change actions and thoughts. The trick is to catch yourself when you're feeling good about your looks, then reinforce this feeling with praise.

1. Put up some reminder notes around the house. For example, "Have you said something nice about your body today?" Or, "Give yourself a break, think an upper." These will remind you to be more generous in handing out verbal rewards to yourself.

2. Self-praise doesn't come naturally to everyone. Can you spontaneously write down at least twenty meaningful compliments about your body or your general appearance? This may not be easy, so take a few minutes to actually put them on paper. Make sure you include only things you truly believe. Ask yourself what you like about your body. Go over it from head to foot and then as a whole. Check to see if your list is loaded with stereotypes that equate attractiveness with being thin or having perfect features. Perhaps you're still giving yourself the same praise that you heard from parents or from others. With a little creativity you can expand self-praise into less conventional areas. Here are some items from Eileen's list:

I have an air of confidence about me.

My hair is great for sports.

Without makeup I look more natural.

My hips are curvy and feminine.

The praise list you construct will confirm that you *are* worthy of your own admiration. Work on developing your praise list with a loved one or a friend, to get a new perspective on the beautiful parts of your appearance that you tend to overlook.

3. This praise list is a valuable defensive weapon against body loathing. Next time you hear your own internal voice attacking your appearance, shout *"Stop"* (shout out loud if you're alone). Then refute the negative voice by using the items on your praise list. Argue back with conviction until you drown out the downers with a massive dose of uppers. One woman described her use of self-praise this way: "So when I say I'm gorgeous it's partly a ploy and partly I really mean it. I have enough nerve to bring it off, but I certainly have my own insecurities. Yet at some pretty profound level, I really do mean it."

EXERCISE • Say It Nicely

Remember that the way you talk to yourself about your body affects how you feel about it. Lynn slowly learned to catch her critical downers and rephrase them into more neutral or even positive statements (a process called *reframing cognitions*). For example:

DOWNER	REPHRASED TO	NEUTRAL OR UPPER
"My skin looks disgusting."		"I'm disturbed about my skin."
"I've never looked worse."		"I usually look better than this."
"I hate my fat hips."		"My hips are the biggest part of me."

Reframing critical statements helps you correct cognitive errors such as personalizing, exaggerating, and thinking in extremes. Keep track of which characteristics are the target of most of your negative attacks. Is there something in your past history that explains why you're so down on your weight or your skin?

Handling Compliments

There's no doubt that praise from others has a strong impact on body image. Praise is healthy if it enhances self-esteem without dictating what you "should" look like. When my niece visits, I try hard to compliment her in ways that go beyond looking pretty. For instance, I tell Sally that her eyes are shining with excitement, that her legs look strong, that the sound of her voice makes me happy. Most of the women in the Bodylove Survey felt good about being told they looked good. What about you? Are compliments from certain people especially important to you?

How do you feel when someone compliments you about your appearance?

46%   VERY DELIGHTED
44%   SOMEWHAT PLEASED
5%   MIXED FEELINGS
5%   SELF-CONSCIOUS
2%   VERY UNCOMFORTABLE

Handling praise is a fine art. First you must recognize praise. It can be subtle, for instance, when it comes in the form of a quick glance or in the hidden flattery of imitation. Do you automatically dismiss compliments or tune them out? By picking up on compliments and accepting them graciously you can build the self-esteem that leads to bodylove.

A good receiver gets the most out of praise by warmly accepting it with pleasure in her voice and face. This encourages follow-up comments that give an extra boost. A bad receiver reacts with embarrassment or false modesty. She ignores or rejects praise, and thus she gets little benefit from it, even as she discourages the giver from offering future compliments. When Claudia's friend called her for advice on what to wear to an interview "because you always look just right," Claudia automatically rejected the remark by replying "not always." The best response to any compliment is a thank-you, followed by some additional expression of your appreciation.

Instead of waiting for compliments to drift your way, you can learn to actively elicit the attention and admiration you need. Try to:

- *Prompt with questions.* "How do you like my new . . . (jewelry, haircut)?"
- *Express pleasure.* "I feel so great . . . (since I began exercising)."
- *Share good news.* "I've found the perfect . . . (dress for the wedding)."
- *Give out more compliments.* You're likely to get some back in

Reprinted by permission of UFS, Inc.

return. Admiring others will help you to overcome envy and truly enjoy the beauty of another person.

As we saw earlier, praise can have negative as well as positive effects. It causes problems when it invades your privacy, makes you self-conscious, or constantly compares you to others. This is why we sometimes react to it with mixed feelings. In Jane's case, constant compliments about her looks during childhood left her feeling insecure about measuring up to her parents standards. She learned through therapy to stop listening for their compliments and to start using her own self-praise instead. Jane was able to reduce the impact of parental praise by ignoring it or changing the subject. She thereby stopped playing the game of being "Daddy's little doll." Once she got herself out of this old role, her self-praise took on new meaning.

Making Mirrors Work for You

Compliments and self-praise can be good for your self-esteem and therefore good for your body image. They resocialize your attitudes about your appearance and help you bury old, worn-out images from the past. But you'll have to go a step further to actually view your reflection less critically. Surprisingly, you can turn to your mirror for support. Although mirrors do tend to make us more critical and self-conscious, they can be useful tools for transforming body image when constructively combined with the power of visualization.

First, how do you react when seeing your nude body in a full-length mirror? Nearly half the women in our sample had mixed feelings (which shows how two-faced mirrors can be).

When you take a long look at your nude body in a full-length mirror, how do you feel?

8%	PROUD
30%	CONTENT
47%	MIXED FEELINGS
14%	ANXIOUS OR DEPRESSED
2%	REPULSED

EXERCISE • Measuring Mirror Distress

You can assess your anxiety about your own reflection by scaling it. *Scaling* is a behavioral technique for evaluating feelings and monitoring progress against a certain standard. While facing a well-lit mirror, look over your nude body. Don't focus on a particular feature, but scan your body as a whole. Gaze at yourself for about half a minute. Now rate your level of anxiety on a scale from 0 to 100:

$$\left(\begin{array}{c} \text{No} \\ \text{Anxiety} \end{array} \; 0 \ldots 10 \ldots 20 \ldots 30 \ldots 40 \ldots 50 \ldots 60 \ldots 70 \ldots 80 \ldots 90 \ldots 100 \; \begin{array}{c} \text{High} \\ \text{Anxiety} \end{array} \right)$$

This number serves as your baseline *mirror distress level.*[4] Write it down so you can refer to it later. Your distress level will vary somewhat depending on your health, mood, and other daily factors. When the level goes down and stays down with some consistency, it means you're making progress toward bodylove.

EXERCISE • Creating a Compassionate Ideal

You'll need a well-lit full-length mirror and complete privacy for at least ten minutes. It's best to do this exercise while nude, but wear a leotard or underwear if you prefer.

1. Stand comfortably before the mirror and slowly scan your whole body as if you were seeing it for the first time. Slowly let your eyes move from your feet upward, and ask yourself how you feel about what you're seeing.

2. Choose an area of your body that you like because you think it's quite attractive. Focus on it and admire this lovely feature. Try to think of one word that best describes that part of your body (i.e., smooth, solid, muscular, feminine). Then close your eyes and visualize that part, just as it looks in the mirror. Concentrate on the word you chose and slowly transform the image in your mind to make it more like the word (smoother, more graceful). Use your power of visualization to make that feature as lovely as possible.

3. Open your eyes and study that feature again. Try to superimpose the idealized image that you visualized onto the real image that you see in the mirror. Look compassionately at yourself while you bring the real and the ideal images as close together as you can. You're trying to create a compassionate ideal that blends reality with visual fantasy. Let this compassionate ideal sink into your body image so they are fused.

4. Once again, scan your nude reflection as a whole, but this time focus in on a body part that you feel is unattractive, perhaps the one that you would most like to change. Focus your attention on that problem area for a full minute. Now find a word that describes the way you want to change what you see (i.e., firmer, smaller). Close your eyes and, using your power of visualization, get a clear picture of it in your mind. Keep thinking of the word you've chosen to improve this part and try to transform the image in your mind until it's slightly more "attractive." Keep the idealized image in your mind and enjoy viewing it. Now open your eyes and look compassionately at that body part in the mirror. Try to bring the compassionate ideal and the real image closer together. Concentrate until you can see the body part as you just imagined it, in a more positive way.

Repeat this exercise using various body parts and alternating between features you like more and ones you like less. With practice, this mirror exercise can help you experience your nude reflection more positively and less stressfully. Each week or so, go back to the scaling technique and reassess your mirror distress level. Then compare it with your baseline number to see if your anxiety is going down.

Try to look at your reflection through the eyes of an adoring companion or a nurturing parent, one who understands your limitations and compassionately forgives you for them. Remember, the overall goal is to achieve bodylove by accepting and appreciating your body as it is.

EXERCISE • Mirror Affirmations

Another way to use your mirror as a therapeutic ally is by practicing *mirror affirmations.* An affirmation is a declaration about yourself. Often it's a commitment to growth and change. A good example is Erma Bombeck's daily declaration: "I'm me and I'm wonderful. Because God doesn't make junk." By repeating an affirmation over and over with conviction, as you would a ritual prayer, you establish healthier ways of thinking about yourself.

1. Mirror affirmations are practiced by standing quietly before the mirror and gazing into your eyes. Just repeat your affirmation several times out loud. For example:

I, Rita, can look feminine whatever the length of my hair.

I, Jane, don't need perfect skin to be pretty.

I, _____, accept my body with all its womanly fullness.

Let the mirror echo your affirmations back to you while you maintain eye contact with the compassionate person within you. Your affirmations should reflect your own values and desires, not those of your parents, your mate, or the voices from your past.

2. Go a step further with your mirror. Choose an item from your praise list and silently rehearse it each time you approach a mirror. For instance, you might repeat "My eyes are a great color" every time you turn to the mirror to dress or make up this week. Be sure to repeat one statement for several days so it really becomes a habit. Then replace it with another item from the praise list. If you get used to approaching your mirror with active self-praise, the mirror eventually becomes a "positive stimulus cue." It will trigger good thoughts and feelings and thus serve as a reliable source of compliments for you.

PARENTING YOURSELF

The exercises in this chapter are laden with emotion. Therefore you may feel a good deal of resistance to working on them. Jane resisted by rationalizing and avoiding. "I'm trying to make Dean's List this term, so I really don't have time to work with my mirror. Besides, it won't help my social life anyway, because the guys at school are all creeps." For her, as for all of us, it seems easier to avoid than to work on problems.

Giving yourself a break means breaking through resistance, breaking free from cognitive errors, breaking loose from the stereotypes of looksism and objectification. It also means breaking out of the constricting values learned in childhood. Ask yourself if you really want to stay stuck in the status quo of old habits that haven't worked well for you in the past.

Although family and culture have certainly contributed to your body-image conflicts, it's all too easy to get stuck blaming others. Or blaming your body or yourself for things beyond your control. Remember that "blaming" is only another resistance tactic. It's time to move beyond blame; to forgive others for their errors and to forgive your body for its flaws. It's time to take responsibility for reshaping your own body image.

Start by questioning parental "shoulds," re-examining your adolescent rebellions, and reconsidering feminine stereotypes. A young lawyer remarked that, "My mother's bathroom looks like a cosmetic department. She owns at least ten of everything. I'm trying to separate her fear of not looking glamorous enough from the sensuality that I really enjoy. I'd like to combine the good parts of my mother's approach with what I really want for myself."

It may be hard to see yourself outside the framework of family expectations. But you *are* a unique individual. No one has a body or a childhood history that's just like yours. That's why you can't fit comfortably into a mold shaped by others.

Remember that body image is a screen between you and your mirror. It can enhance and protect you as well as torment you. It's a screen made of past dreams and future longings. It echoes with the sound of your mother's voice and the faces of a thousand cover girls who have left a mark on your memory. You must decide which of the values from your past are helpful to you and which are harmful. Decide which of the cultural pressures—for glamour, fitness, thinness, youthfulness, sexiness—prevent you from loving your body. Here are some major points to remember as you work with your images from the past:

1. *Body-image develops in childhood.* Your feelings and attitudes about your body today trace back to early childhood. Through praise and criticism you were socialized to see yourself through the eyes of your family and culture.

2. *Social and familial relationships affect body-image.* As a small child you learned to use your looks to please others and to hide the shame of being "just a girl."

3. *Adolescence aggravates body-image conflicts.* During adolescence appearance is used to rebel from parents, to establish an identity, and to mature into an adult sexual role. Such changes can lead to vulnerability and insecurity, which increase body-image conflicts.

4. *Visualization leads to insight.* Visualization can help you explore childhood experiences and confront feelings and values that inhibit bodylove.

5. *You can reinforce good feelings about your looks with self-praise.* Try to get more praise in your life by giving it to yourself and by eliciting it from others. Mirrors can help you affirm your beauty and find a more compassionate ideal in your own reflection.

As you start to break free of constricting values you'll be able to grow into your own nurturing parent. Eileen, for example, describes a shift in attitudes as she adjusts to middle age: "It's strange, but I'm becoming fashion conscious for the first time in my life. Somehow it makes me feel more secure to dress fashionably and to get rid of the gray streaks in my hair. For me, I think it's a sign of self-acceptance to stop rebelling and to fit in better. I seem to want that now, more than ever before." As Eileen re-socializes her body, she acts like a good parent who is forgiving and generous with healthy praise. The energy that was previously directed against her body becomes available to care for it and to bury the ghosts of a childhood past.

Those ghosts can surface unexpectedly, as I discovered one day while having lunch with my father. He sat across from me, aging but as astute and active as ever. I was past forty, and my hair had a touch of gray. We met to resolve a conflict and wound up sharing a moment of intimacy. As we discussed our problem he said, "You know, everything changed between us when you cut your hair. . . . We never seemed as close after that." I stared back in confusion. What was he talking about? My hair had been short for years.

Then Dad recalled in detail my act of adolescent rebellion. Although I thought I'd forgotten that event, I instantly remembered it as he described, for the first time in thirty years, what happened. I relived the pain, the sorrow, and the anger he felt when he saw me without my braids. Only then did I realize its impact on him and on me. Only then did I start to understand my lifelong love-hate relationship with my hair. Love and hair were braided together in my childhood to form a knot that I'm still trying to untangle. I know that if I face it and break free of it, I'll see myself differently and enjoy a fuller sense of bodylove.

WEIGHTY MATTERS

At the present time, are you dieting in order to lose weight?

Do you believe that your current weight is:
MORE THAN 15 POUNDS UNDERWEIGHT
3–10 POUNDS UNDERWEIGHT
JUST RIGHT
1–5 POUNDS OVERWEIGHT
5–10 POUNDS OVERWEIGHT
10–20 POUNDS OVERWEIGHT
20–50 POUNDS OVERWEIGHT
MORE THAN 50 POUNDS OVERWEIGHT

What do you think your weight will be five years from now?
MUCH LESS (20 OR MORE POUNDS)
SLIGHTLY LESS (5–10 POUNDS)
THE SAME
SLIGHTLY MORE (5–10 POUNDS)
SOMEWHAT MORE (10–20 POUNDS)
MUCH MORE (OVER 30 POUNDS)

How often do you weigh yourself?
RARELY
ONCE A MONTH
ONCE A WEEK
EVERY FEW DAYS
ONCE A DAY
TWICE A DAY OR MORE

Elephants live longer than people—maybe that's because they never worry about trying to lose weight.

OES the following saga sound familiar? You resolve one last time to trim down by starting some new diet scheme from Scarsdale or Beverly Hills. Pounds drop off nicely at first, boosting your morale. You're convinced that "this time it's going to work." Weight loss eventually tapers off and each pound becomes harder to shed. As hunger accumulates, you start to lose control and to cheat, perhaps to binge. Old eating patterns creep back as your weight creeps up to pre-diet levels, or even higher. You're left feeling discouraged with yourself, disgusted with your body, and wondering what went wrong. It's a common tale. Yet rarely do you question your motives for dieting in the first place. The potential rewards seem so obvious. Everyone is doing it, so no one bothers to ask why. Dieting just seems like the thing to do.

As a young woman with two small children I never questioned why I was so concerned with being a few inches too hippy and a few pounds too heavy. Ellen also never questions the "fact" that she "should lose at least ten pounds." Fat seems like her natural foe. "When I'm under 130—even at 129½, I can live with myself," she says. "But when I see 138, like I did last week, I start to panic."

Ellen focuses on the numbers. She's devastated when a slight gain pushes her over some arbitrary point of acceptability. When a slight loss drops her into a new category, she's overjoyed. As in gambling, it's the occasional payoff that keeps so many of us addicted to our dieting mentality.

This chapter is meant for women of every size who must survive in a culture where "you can't be too rich or too thin." It's for those like Maritina, who aren't overweight but still feel fat. It's for those like Ellen, who have always felt too big, too flabby, or too hungry to be content with themselves. It's for those whose weight bounces up and down but never settles for long at the right place.

Weight is now one of the most basic ingredients of how a woman judges her own attractiveness and how she is judged by others. Feeling too heavy may inhibit you from enjoying movement and exercise. It may prevent you from reaching out for social relationships or from expressing yourself sexually. If you're unhappy with your weight, you're likely to be unhappy with your overall appearance as well.

You don't necessarily have to lose weight to reshape your body image to a size you can fit into more comfortably. By understanding your weight conflicts and your natural weight limitations you can reduce the importance of fat as a measure of self-worth. You'll see how looksism causes weight preoccupation. And I hope you'll begin to realize that getting thin isn't really the antidote to feeling fat. After all, many thin women still fear fat. A central theme of *Bodylove* is that you shouldn't have to suffer or torment your body in order to feel better about your looks and yourself.

Ellen had been unhappy for years. After a rapid gain of weight in adolescence, she became obsessed with controlling it. Many girls feel frightened and helpless as they watch their tomboy bodies disappear into the fleshy curves of womanhood. Ellen just wanted to be as thin as her friends and as thin as the models in the teen magazines. But her body had a mind of its own.

> I was fourteen and I seemed to blow up overnight. . . . It felt like my body had been attacked by a bicycle pump. I ate practically nothing all through high school, and secretly took diet pills. But nothing really helped. My mother was on the heavy side and I knew how unhappy she was about it. I swore I'd never look like her, but then I saw it happening to me. I've been hungry and dieting for as long as I can remember. Just once I'd like to eat a regular meal and not feel guilty.

Humans are unique among animals. We alone starve our bodies to feed our hunger to be thin. Each year thousands of women lose their lives in pursuit of a leaner body. They die from anorexia, from bulimia, from intestinal bypass surgery. Remove the *t* from "diet," and you discover the hidden consequence that it conceals. While most of us do survive our fight against fat, we silently suffer the daily disabilities of weight obsession and chronic dieting.

Actually, the word *diet* simply means a food plan. But in this chapter I'll be using the term as it's generally understood—to refer to a plan that restricts calories in order to reduce weight.

THE DIETER'S MENTALITY

Whether you're fat, thin, or average, chances are you've been on a recent diet or have thought about starting one. Few of us escape the slender trap of the dieter's mentality.

"Of course I'm dieting—who isn't?" says Debra, a forty-two-year-old homemaker with three children. "My sister is constantly passing me articles on the latest diet gimmick that she's about to try, and asking me to do it with her. My husband feels free to make comments about my weight, but my friends are the worst. They're always talking about their own fat or someone else's."

Our current cultural climate causes a great many women to reject their perfectly normal bodies as abnormally heavy. A body that feels too big casts a shadow over its own image. Recall that the relationship between actual appearance and self-esteem is rather low, but the relationship between body image and self-esteem is much higher. A person who feels fat can have just as many body conflicts as one who actually is fat. In fact, research shows that a high proportion of women who think they're too heavy really aren't.[1]

Consider whether you may be one of them. Ellen certainly was. Although Ellen's body isn't the ideal size depicted in the fashion ads, her body image had become inflated with years of body loathing. Like most women, she sees herself as bigger than she really is, and she feels ashamed of it.

Shame is part of the dieter's mentality: shame of looking too heavy, shame of not being able to stick to a diet or to keep off the weight that's been lost. In a self-perpetuating cycle, the shame of feeling too fat leads first to dieting, then to binging, and then to more shame at having broken the diet. In his pioneering work on sexuality, Alfred Kinsey discovered that the most embarrassing thing you could ask had nothing to do with intercourse. The question that more women refused to answer than any other on his survey was, "What do you weigh?" When I first asked Ellen, she simply replied "too much."

The dieter's mentality can have serious repercussions. Weight obsession and chronic dieting have been identified as the most prevalent forms of emotional disorders among women today. Yet most of us never connect such symptoms as depression, anxiety, or insomnia with the dieting process. Therefore, we continue to inflict on ourselves the psychological and physical damage caused by calorie restriction. It's painful to try to squeeze yourself into a constricting ideal that's promoted by family, friends, and social pressure.

Of course, eating is a social act that has deep emotional meaning. Early in life food gets mixed up with love and looks, with power and morality. All of us eat sometimes to feed the hungers caused by stress or loneliness. But dieting creates its own emotional hungers. A dieting woman is doubly deprived. She's unhappy because she's undernourished and undernurtured. She envies those who can spontaneously eat when they're sad and she feels guilty when she uses food for solace. After an unsuccessful diet she's left with the added shame of having failed again.

As you well know, there's an endless variety of diets to feed the dieter's mentality. Ellen has tried them all, including fasting, weight-watching groups, liquid protein formulas. Recently she quit smoking and, as a result, gained about five pounds. This triggered all the old feelings of intense anxiety and self-disgust. "I just want to get down to the right size so I can feel good about myself," she explained in therapy. "It's not for my husband, not for my mother anymore, but just for me . . . to prove I can do it." We began our work together by sorting out her motives and eventually agreed on some goals as priorities: first, to normalize her relationship with food; and second, to focus on improving her body image.

Many of you can work on your own to break free of the dieter's mentality and end your obsession with thinness. However, if you have more severe eating problems you may need professional help. To evaluate the seriousness of your own situation, consider these questions:

- Has your weight changed significantly for no apparent reason?
- Are you 20 percent below or 40 percent above the recommended weight for your height?
- Do you frequently lose control and binge excessively?
- Do you vomit or take laxatives, diuretics, or diet pills in order to control your weight?
- Do you have irregular menstrual periods because of low body fat?

If you suffer from any of these symptoms, pay careful attention to this chapter. It will give you a new perspective on your weight problems and may help break down your resistance to getting outside help.

FAT FACTS—SLIM PICKINGS

Consider the following facts about women and their weight:[2]

- On any given day, a high proportion of females are dieting—nearly half the ten-year-olds, two-thirds of the high school girls, and one-third of adult women.
- About 1 percent of college women are anorexic, while another 4 to 13 percent are identified as bulimic.
- Two-thirds of adult women are afraid of getting fat, and 95 percent of them overestimate their body size.
- Women over sixty report that "gaining weight" is their second most serious concern (the first being loss of memory).

The Bodylove Survey confirms these findings. When asked, "If you could change one thing about your body, what would it be?," two out of three women named weight loss or reduction of hips, thighs, and stomach. On the day of the survey almost one-third of our sample was dieting. Nearly half rated themselves as five to twenty pounds overweight and only 17 percent of the group thought their weight was just right.

Do you believe that your current weight is:

6%	3–15 POUNDS UNDERWEIGHT
17%	JUST RIGHT
17%	1–5 POUNDS OVERWEIGHT
23%	5–10 POUNDS OVERWEIGHT
22%	10–20 POUNDS OVERWEIGHT
11%	20–50 POUNDS OVERWEIGHT
5%	MORE THAN 50 POUNDS OVERWEIGHT

Weight conflicts are more common and more serious among women than men. As we saw in the last chapter, boys are socialized during childhood to view their bodies in terms of effectiveness, while girls see theirs in terms of attractiveness. Females tend to rate their figures as heavier than the ideal they desire, and heavier than the ideal they believe men prefer. In contrast, most males view their weight as quite close to ideal. Men's perceptions keep them generally satisfied with their body image, whereas women's misperceptions create a dieter's mentality that undermines their self-esteem. Thus the "healthy" woman becomes preoccupied with trying to control her weight, while the healthy man is less concerned and more accepting of his.[3]

I've seen many clients whose feelings about themselves are dominated by their efforts at weight control. "It was a good week," they announce at the start of a session, "I feel thinner." On "bad" weeks they describe a painful sense of failure at having skipped an exercise class or cheated on a dessert. This is how self-esteem gets mixed up in the dieter's mentality. It's hard for someone to give self-praise when she feels out of control. Most people assume that weight *is* controllable and that it should be controlled. Therefore they blame themselves for not being as thin, or firm, or flat as they "should" be.

Marilyn tells me, "My older sister Anna has always been very careful about what she eats, and she has always been thin. When I was young Mom would remind me that I was getting a little heavy and should be careful like Anna. Now when my weight goes up, I feel out of control and remember how disciplined my sister is."

Ellen lives with a morbid fear of gaining weight. One day she turned to me and protested, "How can you possibly understand how I feel when you're not heavy?" Some therapists write about eating disorders because of their own struggles. Their books reveal years of personal pain and growth. I can't give you a first-hand account of my agonies as an anorexic or my bouts with bulimia. I feel fortunate that my weight has been average and stable most of my life. Yet I do know how frustrated Ellen feels, because I've felt that way too, as have most average-weight women in one way or another.

There was a time when I carefully monitored every meal, compulsively weighed in twice a day, and constantly longed to be just a little thinner. Like Ellen, my self-conscious preoccupation traced back to adolescence—to that sixteenth summer when I fell in love with my new boyfriend and out of love with my new body. I'd been working at a camp, helping myself to extra helpings of everything and filling free time with junk food.

I returned home eight weeks later and eight pounds heavier—heavier than I had ever been. Having finally grown into my maximum adult size, I felt grossly overgrown. I hated my fleshy hips as much as I hated the slim-hipped beauties I seemed to see everywhere. For the next ten years I tried to eat slightly less than I really wanted and always weighed slightly more. A nagging discontent distorted my body image. Those were the years when Twiggy or her equivalent smiled from the cover of every magazine.

THE SHRINKING IDEAL

Being heavy hasn't always been considered unattractive. For centuries, fat was fashionable in western culture, and a full-bodied maternal look was idealized. At the turn of this century, doctors encouraged plumpness as a sign of good health, much as they push thinness today. In those days, a typical chorus girl was 5'4" and weighed 140 pounds. Then came the flapper era, and the slimming of the American woman began in earnest.

As families grew smaller and women took jobs outside the home, our perceptions of feminine beauty reflected these social changes. The beauty ideal shifted from looking like an earth mother to looking like a playgirl. Today we are weighed (and often rejected) by a culture that scales female beauty down to a smaller size than ever before.

Beauty contests became increasingly popular, and the winners grew taller and thinner over the years. So did the *Playboy* centerfolds. Analysis of advertisements shows that the use of plump models has decreased steadily in the past thirty years.[4] Commercial images provide powerful models for social comparison. They become the yardstick against which we weigh and measure ourselves. The significant increase in eating disorders since 1970 is blamed in part on pervasive media images in which a very thin body type predominates, and where positive social qualities are linked with being thin while negative ones are paired with being heavy. A dieter's mentality is thereby reinforced every time you turn on your TV set.

FATISM AS A FACT OF LIFE

The cultural message that fat is offensive is not very thinly disguised. A well-known actress announces emphatically that, "no matter what your age, if you're overweight, you won't look very good." As we've already seen, looksism is a harsh truth. And looksism gives birth to *fatism,* another cruel stereotype that affects us all, no matter what we weigh. Fat people have been called "the last safe minority to pick on." Stereotypes are learned early in life. When asked to choose the photograph of a child they would like as a friend, youngsters pick the fat child last, after they choose photos of handicapped and disfigured children.[5]

Ellen watches her two teenage daughters as their bodies grow more like her own. "If you let yourself get heavy," she warns them, "you're going to have a hard time, too." Her fears are not unfounded in a culture that's so guilty of looksism and so unforgiving of overweight. To check your own fat bias, rapidly complete each of the following sentences on paper:

I think fat women . . .

Thin women are . . .

Fat people should . . .

If I were very fat (or, Because I'm very fat) . . .

If I were very thin (or, Because I'm very thin) . . .

Here are some typical responses given to the above statements:

Fat women "probably hate themselves . . . should get help . . . must be really unhappy about their bodies . . . are a turn-off . . . aren't very appealing."

Thin women are "lucky when it comes to buying clothes . . . used to getting more attention . . . able to eat whatever they want and enjoy their food . . . the kind of people I hate and envy most."

Fat people should "realize how awful they look . . . do something about themselves . . . take more pride in their looks."

As with other stereotypes, looksism starts with false beliefs and ends with overt discrimination. Weight bias is real. It influences job interviews, promotions, college admissions. Heavy people have a harder time finding dates, mates, jobs, and friends. Research confirms that the psychological and social consequences of fatism are real and unjust. Yet most of us contribute to it, partly through our attitudes toward our own bodies.[6]

What traits are commonly associated with weight? Thin people are stereotyped as prettier, healthier, sexier, more disciplined, and better. Fat people are seen as ugly, bad, undisciplined, sloppy, weak, and unclean. As you can see, there are moral connotations to weight. Thin equals good while fat equals bad. In other words, if you're fat you're no good and it's your own fault.

This is how fatism gets justified by perfectly nice people. This is why other nice people feel deeply ashamed of their bodies and of their "inability" to control them. Weight shame spills over into self-image. Ellen explains, "When I feel fat I feel ugly . . . because fat people don't seem to care about their appearance and I know that's the message my body conveys."

DIET MYTHOLOGY

Fatism is partly a product of false assumptions or myths. These myths are kept alive by propaganda from many sources. It prompts the basic belief that dieting improves the quality of life. We're encouraged to live and look rich, but to starve in the midst of plenty. The diet and exercise industry is estimated at $10 billion a year. New and intriguing diet books appear every week with titles like *Eat Yourself Beautiful, God's Answer to Fat Loss, I Love America Diet,* and *The Last Best Diet Book*—all feeding what is described as a "perpetually seducible market."

Here are some of the myths that contribute to fatism and to the dieter's mentality. As you read them I think you'll find at least a few that you firmly believe are true. Carefully review the facts, and consider how these misconceptions have shaped your own body image, as well as your view of others.[7]

MYTH: Fat people eat more food or more calories than thin people.
FACT: *Food intake and obesity are not always related. Some people eat a lot and stay slim; others eat little but still look heavy.*

MYTH: Weight is controllable, so anyone can get thin by working at it.

FACT: *Weight is largely determined by genetic factors. The range of control differs among people, but it remains rather small for many people.*

MYTH: Dieting helps you become thinner.

FACT: *Most pounds that are lost through dieting will be regained within a year.*

MYTH: Dieting is good for you.

FACT: *Highly restrictive diets can cause damaging physical and psychological side effects and lead to eventual weight gain in some cases.*

MYTH: Fat people are lazy and emotionally unstable.

FACT: *Fat and thin people don't score differently on most psychological tests, nor have most forms of psychotherapy proved effective in long-term weight reduction.*

MYTH: If you eat 3,500 fewer calories, you will lose one pound.

FACT: *The relationship between cutting calories and losing weight depends on many factors. The type of food counts as much as the calories it contains.*

MYTH: Thin people are happier than fat ones.

FACT: *There's little evidence that happiness is directly related to weight.*

MYTH: Women have become thinner over the past twenty years.

FACT: *The beauty ideal is thinner, but women are actually a bit heavier than they were several decades ago.*

MYTH: Your "proper" weight can be determined from height-weight charts.

FACT: *Charts based on statistical norms aren't accurate for everyone and are frequently revised as medical and social fads change.*

These are some of the false assumptions that perpetuate fatism and that make us so self-conscious about our weight. Although the cost of these myths is high, still we have a hard time letting go of them. You may find it helpful to copy this list and post it for daily review. Challenging weight myths and replacing them with truths is a major step in improving your body image. Myths are like automatic irrational thoughts that habitually distort your feelings about yourself.

Recall that cognitive errors can be overcome by challenging them with good rational counterarguments. Take enough time to work on this important step by using the triple-column technique outlined in Chapter 2. When you catch yourself thinking irrational thoughts about your weight, jot them down, figure out the cognitive error, and challenge it with facts that are more accurate. By replacing myths with truths, you'll start to think about your weight more realistically and less fearfully.

EVALUATING SYMPTOMS

You probably know how painful and exhausting a diet can be. But you may not realize that there are also serious psychological dangers involved in restricting your food intake. Dieting magnifies the importance of food, causing obsessions and fears, guilt and shame that remain long after the diet is over. Dieting distorts hunger awareness. By inhibiting the natural response to the hunger drive, dieting leads to binge eating and compulsive cravings, especially for sweets. It undermines the body's subsequent ability to regulate weight and appetite. Lethargy, anxiety, irritability, and depression are all common side effects of chronic dieting. The constant stress that the dieter must endure can make dieting much more damaging than the condition it pretends to cure. It can also lead to serious eating disorders.

Eating disorders are defined as "irrational thoughts, feelings, or actions concerning food." The distinction between an eating disorder and an everyday weight problem isn't always clear. Serious symptoms are now so common they seem normal. Do you frequently think about weight and wish you were thinner? (*weight obsession*). Are you afraid you'll get fat unless you constantly control what you eat? (*fat phobia*). Do you feel anxious or depressed when you eat things you "shouldn't" or when you eat more food than you "should"? (*compulsive dieting*).

Following are the symptoms commonly associated with eating disorders, as listed by Susan Kano in her excellent workbook, *Making Peace with Food*.[8] If you recognize these problems in yourself, it's time to reassess your relationship with weight and with food. Your ideas about what's healthy for you may have reached unhealthy proportions. Consider how frequently you experience these symptoms:

OFTEN	SOME- TIMES	NEVER	SYMPTOM
_____	_____	_____	Chronic desire to be thin or thinner
_____	_____	_____	Preoccupation with eating or dieting
_____	_____	_____	Fear of losing control of eating
_____	_____	_____	Preoccupation with body size and body image
_____	_____	_____	Fear of gaining weight
_____	_____	_____	Unstable self-esteem that is affected by weight control
_____	_____	_____	Excessive/obsessive exercising
_____	_____	_____	Frequent binge eating
_____	_____	_____	Purging through laxatives, diuretics, or vomiting
_____	_____	_____	Weight gain or loss of 20 percent or more up and down
_____	_____	_____	Menstrual periods that are irregular or absent
_____	_____	_____	Compulsive weighing

These problems are common by-products of the dieter's mentality. They derive from the basic cognitive error that weight is easily controllable and should be controlled. In fact, what you weigh today may have been "set" before you were even born.

UNDERSTANDING SETPOINT THEORY

It may be your biological fate to be fatter than you wish. In the same way that genes control your hair and eye color, they also influence your weight. You were born with a sensitive weight-regulating system that maintains appetite, metabolism, and body fat. These determine what is called your natural setpoint weight. This setpoint isn't really a point, but a weight range that shifts in response to various factors.

Your body is programmed to keep within its natural weight range. When you start dieting, your setpoint mechanism becomes a fierce opponent fighting to maintain its proper balance. As you eat less, the body has its own devices that defend you from losing weight. Metabolism slows down, appetite increases, and calories are used more efficiently. Physical and psychological stress build as you continue to diet, and nature fights back.

Our weight-regulating systems probably evolved to protect us from starvation during periods of famine. After you've been dieting for a while, your body may gradually push the setpoint up higher, as if it were preparing for another period of starvation. This results in the typical weight-gain rebound that most dieters experience after a diet is abandoned.

Dieting may therefore make it even harder for you to stay at what was a previously comfortable weight level. Despite your heroic efforts to eat less, you may wind up raising your "fat thermostat" which ultimately causes you to weigh more. (See the Resource section on food and weight for further information about setpoint theory.)

People differ. Some have a wide weight range, others a narrow one. Some can gain and lose easily, while others have setpoints that aren't easily reset. For obvious reasons, your body is threatened more by weight loss than by weight gain. So it's probably easier to put weight on than to take it off. And it's also easier to remain at the higher end of your natural weight range than at the lower end of it.

The natural weight that your body is set to maintain often differs from three other weight goals that are probably important to you:

1. The present cultural ideal of physical beauty.
2. The medical ideal advocated for good health.
3. Your personal beauty ideal.

The cultural, medical, and personal ideals do change over time, just as your setpoint range may also change.

Look at Marsha, for example—a 5'6" college student. Her natural setpoint range is 140 to 150 pounds and she can easily maintain that weight. Right now, the cultural ideal for someone of her build is about 120 to 130 pounds. But her personal concept of ideal beauty is a super-thin 115. Clearly she can't satisfy all of these ideals at once. Because her personal ideal is so low, and her natural setpoint is much higher, she constantly feels too fat and is chronically dieting. Consider your own personal-weight ideal—the weight you would like to attain and remain. How does it compare with the cultural ideal that is now admired? Is your personal ideal higher or lower than the medical ideal that's recommended for someone of your height and age? Now let's try to get an idea of your setpoint range so you can see how it compares with these other ideals.

Sizing Up Your Natural Weight Range

What should you weigh? It's hard to say. Assessing your natural weight range may help you see and accept your body as nature designed it. Start off with a "guesstimate."

1. *Guesstimate.* Where do you think your weight would stabilize if you exercised moderately every other day and ate all the "healthy" food you wanted? (Note: healthy food is high in nutrients and low in fat, salt, and refined sugar.)

I guess that my natural weight range is between _____ and _____ pounds.

2. *Weight history.* Take a weight history to improve your guess. Start with an image of yourself at about age fifteen and try to recall your weight at five-year intervals. (Use photos and special events like graduations to jog your memory.) As you recall your weight patterns, consider your activity level and your efforts to diet at each age. Make a chart that includes your age, weight, activity level, dieting efforts, and any other relevant factors. Here's what Ellen's weight history looked like:

AGE	WEIGHT	ACTIVITY LEVEL	DIETING EFFORTS
15	125	Low	Constant dieting, pills
20	133	Low	Moderate, college food
25	122	High	Smoking, went to diet doctor
30	135	Moderate	Moderate, after 2 children
37	138	Moderate	Stopped smoking

3. *Average weight.* Examine your weight change over time and calculate the average. Ellen's weight varied by about sixteen pounds (122–138) and her overall average is 131. What is your average weight _____? What is the total amount of variation _____? Now look at your highest and lowest adult weights. What special factors lead to these extremes? Illness, dorm food, depression, exercise, dieting, smoking?

4. *Dieting effects.* Has your weight gone up and down by 20 percent or more? This may mean that your setpoint has become

somewhat higher as a result of yo-yo dieting, so take this into account. When you stop dieting, does your body generally return to a particular weight? Can you stay at this range without much effort? Make note of that weight range.

5. *Genetic factors.* Is there a tendency to be heavy on either side of your family? You may have those same "fat" genes. Were you heavy as a child? If so, your setpoint may be higher than most people and you must keep this in mind.

6. *Age.* Have you gained a few pounds each decade after reaching age thirty? This is common and may continue unless you keep increasing your activity level or are very careful about the kind of foods you eat.

7. *Activity level.* Are you naturally active or inactive? Can you see how changes in exercise levels have affected your weight at different times in your life?

8. *Other factors.* Additional factors that can influence your setpoint include hormonal changes, stress, alcohol, nicotine, and other drugs and medications. Take these into account when you look at the fluctuations in your weight history.

Using This Information

Now try to estimate your natural weight range once again, using your weight history as a guide. Remember, it's not what you want to weigh, but the weight your body seems to dictate over time. The range might be as narrow as five pounds (115–120) or as broad as thirty or more (140–170). There is no simple test or specific formula for computing your setpoint. But you can get a sense of it by honestly reviewing your weight history. Think carefully and come up with a revised estimate based on fact rather than on fantasy.

Considering my weight history, my setpoint range is probably between _____ *and* _____ *pounds.*

If you're still unsure of your setpoint, try to experiment with it over time by letting your natural weight-regulating system operate freely. See if you can maintain your present weight for three months by eating what you need to satisfy your appetite. If you can't maintain a stable weight level, then consider whether (1) you're trying to live below your setpoint, (2) you're not active enough, or (3) you're eating unhealthy foods.

Setpoint theory doesn't mean that you have no control at all over your weight. It does mean that the amount of control is limited by genetic factors, and that this degree of control varies from person to person. Your natural range can be shifted up or down to some extent. If you're highly active every day, eat very few sweet or fatty foods (but do eat sufficient calories), you might comfortably maintain a lower weight. If you become less active or eat foods with a high sugar and fat content, your weight may drift upward even though your caloric intake remains the same.

As you begin to appreciate the power of setpoint, you'll realize that terms such as "normal weight" and "overweight" take on new meaning when they are reconsidered in light of setpoint theory. What looks overweight or underweight to others might be normal for your body. It's certainly not normal for everyone to want to be a size 6 or 8. It's not normal to constantly starve or dread every meal in order to maintain a "normal" weight. If you think you're too fat, stop and ask, "Too fat for whom or for what?" Think about the cultural pressures that create that label. Consider the factors in your past and the people in your present that make you feel too heavy. Your weight problem may really be a labeling problem in a culture that has only two extreme categories: fat or thin.

Recall that half the women in the Bodylove Survey felt they were between one and twenty pounds overweight. Many of them are probably within their natural weight range and are only overweight in terms of their personal ideal. How about you? Have you been struggling for years to stay at a certain weight or to lose five or ten more pounds? Do the benefits really justify the costs? Living at 5 percent below your natural setpoint may be a much greater strain on your health than being 5 percent above your personal ideal. If, with great effort, you manage to keep yourself somewhat below your natural setpoint, you may be constantly hungry, restless, irritable, craving sweets, and overly concerned with food.

From working with clients, I know that setpoint theory feels very threatening to most women. It's hard for anyone who's been hooked on the dieter's mentality to accept the notion that weight is largely controlled by genetic factors. Most women are afraid that if they stop dieting they'll start gaining endlessly. That if the body is set free of constraints, it will become enormous. Be reassured that this almost never happens. You may also feel a sense of defeat or shame, as if "giving in" to setpoint means you've failed at dieting. But try to remind yourself that working with nature rather than against it isn't a failure.

Why not experiment for a while by accepting setpoint theory and allowing your body to regulate itself? You can always return to the dieter's mentality when and if you choose. Your feelings of fear may be strong, but they aren't based on fact. Fear only adds to your resistance to change.

SELF-SABOTAGE THROUGH RESISTANCE

As you know, resistance can be one of your greatest obstacles in achieving bodylove. Resistance is especially strong when you're faced with accepting a setpoint that's heavier than your personal ideal—and perhaps heavier than the cultural and medical ideals, as well.

At age thirty-eight, Ellen's setpoint was probably somewhere between 130 and 140 pounds. Accepting this as her natural weight range meant giving up the idea that she should lose at least ten pounds. Dieting had been a way of life, and letting go of the dieter's mentality meant changing all kinds of automatic thoughts that were basic to her body image. Not surprisingly, she resisted, insisting that she should and could be thinner. As you read over Ellen's list of resistance theme songs, I'm sure some of them will sound all too familiar to you. Can you refute each of these automatic thoughts with a good rational counterargument?

> If I stop dieting, I'll never stop eating.
>
> I'm good when I'm dieting and bad when I'm not.
>
> My stomach is so big I have to do something about it.
>
> I really should be thinner than I am.
>
> If I lose weight I'll like myself better.
>
> If I lose weight other people will like me better.

Remember that we each have our own resistance styles. Ellen was a rationalizer. She had excellent reasons why the other diets had failed and the next one would work. Procrastinators say they'll stop dieting some day, but not right now. Avoiders don't pay any attention to the facts. Recall your own resistance style and remember that resistance will keep you stuck in your present state of weight conflict unless you work to overcome it.

Resistance is a form of self-sabotage, but you're subjected to a great deal of social sabotage as well. Accepting your natural setpoint is very hard when dieting is constantly being reinforced. Reinforcement comes from the media in a stream of fatism and weight-loss propaganda. It comes from well-meaning loved ones who encourage you to lose weight for your own good. This stream of social sabotage can keep you trapped in the dieter's dilemma. If you're married or in a coupled relationship, it's important to consider your partner's attitudes toward your weight and toward women's weight in general. Is it adding to your weight anxiety? How could your partner help you overcome your own resistance to accepting your natural weight?

For a few months several years ago, Ellen was a slimmer 125. Despite what she had always believed (and continued to believe), being thinner hadn't really changed her life very much. She remembers feeling a sense of achievement, and she enjoyed buying new clothes and feeling trim. But the more she thought about it, the more she had to admit that things weren't really so different then. Her work as a librarian went on as before; her marriage had its usual ups and downs.

Every naturally slender woman knows that being thin doesn't guarantee bliss, or even peace. Paradoxically, this fact may only serve to increase your resistance to accepting setpoint. The dieter's mentality is one way you may be hiding from other sources of your unhappiness. If you give up the struggle with weight, other problems will become more obvious, and this can be a frightening prospect. Ellen observed one day, "I guess it's not just my weight that's weighing me down." This insight was a breakthrough in helping her overcome her resistant attitudes and start seeing her setpoint range as normal and healthy for her.

EXERCISE • Questioning Resistance to Setpoint

If you feel a lot of resistance to your natural weight range, ask yourself the following questions. They can help you clarify why setpoint theory feels so frightening, but also why it may be worth the risk.

- What do you gain from your perpetual struggle with weight? And what do you lose from it?
- What are you afraid you will lose by giving up the dieter's mentality?
- What might you gain by accepting your natural weight range and making peace with your natural body size?

To carry this exercise further, try putting your responses on paper and taking a hard look at them. Some of your expected gains from dieting are probably based on myth rather than fact. Check them against the list of myths presented earlier to see if you can pick up any cognitive errors that should be challenged. Now look at your fears about giving up the dieter's mentality. Are these fears realistic or exaggerated? What would change in your life if you overcame your fear and accepted your natural weight range?

Part of the dieter's mentality is the expectation of getting thinner next month, next year, next life. Hope remains high, even though it's clear that time tends to remodel most people by pulling down certain parts and padding out the rest. Still, we may cling to the belief that getting older doesn't have to mean getting heavier. After all, there's Fonda at fifty—living proof that age can mean fit, not fat.

When asked to estimate their weight five years from now, one-third of our sample expected to slim down and half predicted their weight would stay the same, despite the natural tendency for weight to increase with age. This denial of the reality of weight gain with age stems from a deep fear of fat that can begin quite early in childhood.

What do you think your weight will be five years from now?

11%	MUCH LESS (20 OR MORE POUNDS)
23%	SLIGHTLY LESS (5–10 POUNDS)
52%	REMAIN THE SAME
13%	SLIGHTLY MORE (5–10 POUNDS)
1%	SOMEWHAT MORE (10–20 POUNDS)
1%	MUCH MORE (OVER 30 POUNDS)

RELAXING IMAGES

You saw in the last chapter how visual imagery alters feelings about the body. Visualization can also be combined with relaxation to reduce specific fears and phobias. For instance, if you remain fully relaxed while imagining yourself taking a test or giving a speech, you eventually start to feel less tense about doing those things and can face them more easily.

When relaxation is combined with "fat imagery," it can help reduce tension about "excess" weight. Relaxation inhibits anxiety. The condition of being relaxed counteracts the condition of being afraid, so that a kind of counterconditioning occurs. This therapeutic technique has been called *desensitization* because it gradually reduces your sensitivity to something fearful.

In order to desensitize a particular fear, relaxation plus imagery must be paired over and over again. The goal is to recondition yourself to react calmly rather than tensely. The following imagery exercise will give you an idea of the process. You'll have to practice repeatedly, however, to reduce anxiety about your natural weight range.

EXERCISE • Learning Relaxation

There are dozens of gourmet recipes around for learning to relax. (See the resource section on relaxation.) Some are complex techniques, but I think it's easier to get started if you don't make a big deal of it. Only a few ingredients are really essential.

1. Take time out (about twenty minutes) and label it "For Relaxation and Visualization." Sit or lie comfortably in a quiet place. Close your eyes and dim the lights to block out visual stimuli. Loosen your clothing and shoes. Check over your muscles to see which ones feel tense. Neck, shoulder, and face muscles are especially likely to need release. Just go slowly from head to foot and relax all parts of your body.

2. Breathe slowly and deeply. Fill your lungs as you inhale and concentrate on letting go as you slowly exhale. Try to turn off your mind and focus inward on your breathing. If thoughts intrude, simply repeat a phrase such as, "I'm calm and content." Begin the visualization by seeing yourself as you are now, in this relaxed position. Then go on to the guided imagery that follows.

EXERCISE • Accepting Your Setpoint

1. Start by visualizing yourself in a huge and elegant bathroom with polished mirrors everywhere. There's a skylight filled with bright sunshine and ferns hanging all around. You're relaxing in a fabulous marble tub filled with perfumed water. You feel at ease in your body as it floats in the warmth. Just enjoy the way your body looks and feels in this vision. Stay there as long as you want—luxurious, content, and fully relaxed.

2. When you're ready, watch as you step out of the tub and onto a nearby scale. Looking down you can see that your weight is exactly in the middle of your setpoint range. The scale tells you that you weigh just what your body requires. Remain calm and relaxed as you think about being the right weight for you—the weight nature intended.

3. The sun comes through the skylight and your body gleams with bath oil. Now visualize yourself turning to the mirrors all around you and studying how your body looks at that natural weight. Stay relaxed as you visualize your curves, your muscles, the ripples of your flesh. Remember, female bodies are supposed to have extra padding on their hips, thighs, stomach, breasts. Breathe deeply and remain calm.

4. You're still in that beautiful bathroom feeling at peace with yourself. Watch as you study your female body—its lines and fullness. Visualize yourself from different angles. Notice where your body is especially fat, and how this fat changes your form. When you have explored and accepted yourself from all angles, visualize your imaginary self, repeating a mirror affirmation. Watch as she gazes into the mirror and repeats, "My body is lovely at its proper setpoint weight."

5. Slowly come back to reality by imagining yourself in the present scene. The goal of this exercise is to help you accept your natural weight range and accept a body that may be heavier (or thinner) than you wish. If this visualization makes you anxious, you should try to repeat it a number of times to desensitize your fears. Remember that estrogen pads the female body with fat on certain

places. Fearing fat means fearing the most feminine parts of yourself.

LIFE AT LARGE

It's hard enough to live in an average body when average won't do in a thin society. How can someone adjust to living in a big body? There's no denying that heavy women have a special challenge in their pursuit of bodylove. They generally are more self-conscious than thinner women and more concerned about their looks. For those who were heavy in childhood, the struggle toward a comfortable body image is especially difficult. Some try to psychologically dissociate from their fat, pretending it's not really them. As Kathy described it:

> When I'm fat, I don't live in my body. My head is going "Hey, this isn't me." It's a tape running through my head like static and it interferes. . . . This doesn't count because I am fat. I'm not really here because I'm fat.

Given all the problems caused by fatism, can a heavy woman be a happy woman? The answer is yes, of course she can. Not only happy but successful, productive, and well adjusted. There are many big women who move well beyond their weight and into life. In fact, research shows little connection between weight and psychological well-being. Despite the social stigma that heavy women must face, it doesn't necessarily make them miserable. Here is a contrasting voice to the one above:

> I really am fine as a fat woman. I'm often beautiful. I will never be thin. It's taken me many years to accept this about myself. I will not postpone my life any longer, not for anyone's standard of beauty. There are so many of us it profits none of us to have to battle . . . for the right to exist.

Organizations like the National Association to Aid Fat Americans are working to change cultural attitudes and combat fatism. Such groups help their members to reduce shame and build self-confidence. (See the resources section on food and weight.) If your natural setpoint is clearly high, you might benefit from joining a support group. By sharing with others and hearing their experiences, you can end the isolation and shame that come from feeling that your size is somehow your fault.

If you're heavy, take some time to make a list and collect photos of heavy heroines who can serve as role models for you. There are hundreds of wonderful large women, from Queen Victoria to Nell Carter, who have led admirable lives, brought joy to themselves and others, and made a real impact on the world. You can learn to identify with them and with their full-bodied potential.

It was fat women themselves who started throwing the *F* word around, creating slogans like Fat Liberation, Fat Oppression, and Fat Pride. They exposed the secret that fat was a fact of female life. And they began to ask some important questions: How can we be strong and healthy but also dieting and starving at the same time? Is weight obsession a sign that women are still afraid to grow into the proportions and the positions of a full-grown adult?

Looksism and fatism affect all of us, no matter what we weigh. To challenge these stereotypes we can start opening our mouths: to share our obsessive thoughts about food and our fear of getting fat; to describe the binges, admit the purges, and question the despotism of slenderness. By speaking out we bring weight conflicts out of the pantry closet and relabel them as social problems rather than purely personal ones. At the same time we must learn to close our mouths: not to reject food, but to stop talking incessantly about dieting; to stop complimenting each other for minor weight loss as if it were a major accomplishment. Collectively we can work to scale down the importance of weight.

WEIGHING IN LESS OFTEN

Every spring I have a medical checkup. Most years I check out just a little heavier than I checked in the year before. Now I'm working hard to broaden my ideal image and make room for middle-age. The doctor's scale is a bit on the low side. Usually I come home and find myself comparing it to my own scale, the one I've used all too often over the years.

Scales, like mirrors, can be tormenting and addictive. Fighting them isn't easy, as you probably know. For Ellen, for me, and for countless other women, climbing on the scale is one sure "weigh" to increase anxiety. How often do most women do it? Half of those in the Bodylove Survey said they weigh in only rarely or monthly, but one-third do so more than once a week.

How often do you weigh yourself?

28%	RARELY
21%	ONCE A MONTH
20%	ONCE A WEEK
15%	EVERY FEW DAYS
15%	ONCE A DAY
2%	TWICE A DAY OR MORE

How often should you weigh yourself? If your activity levels and eating patterns are stable, once a month is plenty. If you're working to alter your weight by changing your eating and exercise habits, then weighing about once a week is enough to help monitor progress. Recording your weight at the beginning of each month will show you trends over time. It's these long-term trends rather than weekly fluctuations that are important. Daily weight changes up or down a few pounds are normal and unimportant. By constantly monitoring them you only magnify their meaning.

Debra's addiction to her scale was as compelling as any drug habit. Sometimes she stepped on and off several times in a row to confirm the machine's accuracy. Weighing was a ritual of confirmation for her, as it is for many women. Debra's scale measured more than mere poundage, for pounds had become the measure of her value as a person. The following exercises can help you climb off your scale if you think you're on it too often.

EXERCISE • Scaling Down the Scale

1. *Monitoring.* Begin by gathering baseline data to find out how often you weigh in. Try not to change your weighing behavior while you're counting it. For a month, tape a chart on the scale and record the date and time of each weigh-in along with your weight. At the end, figure out how often you've weighed yourself during the month and compute the weekly (or daily) average.

2. *Withdrawal.* Set a daily or weekly quota that is just slightly lower than your baseline average. Try hard to weigh only on

schedule; for example, once a day before dressing; once a week on Friday; once a month on the first Sunday. Continue to keep track of your scale activity and slowly cut back. Move the scale out of the bathroom or bedroom to a less accessible place (in the basement or on a high shelf). The more effort required, the less likely you'll be tempted to use it. Could you get rid of the scale altogether—like throwing away an addictive substance?

3. *Blind weighing.* You probably know your weight before measuring it. Try recording an estimate before you weigh in, and then write down the actual weight beside the estimate. You may discover that the scale usually feeds information you already have. Now tape over the face of the scale for a while and practice accepting your estimates as fact.

4. *Demolition.* Another exercise that can feel wonderful is to actually sacrifice your scale as a symbolic act of freedom. Vent your anger at all the grief it's caused you by actually breaking it to pieces. Get a hammer, screwdriver, or other weapons, and beat up the scale instead of beating up your body by chronic dieting. Why not invite a friend over and have a demolition party?

CONSUMING PASSIONS

The dieter's mentality often leads to a compulsive attitude toward weight, and in turn to a compulsive relationship with food. If you sometimes lose control of your eating behavior, pay close attention here. Binge eating is a common problem—one that isn't so easy to solve.

Although Monica strongly resists the idea that she should stop dieting, she readily agrees that her eating patterns aren't normal. Years ago a college roommate had introduced her to the art of binging, and she has been doing it once or twice a week ever since. Like other compulsive eaters, she consumes large quantities of sweets or other high-calorie foods during a binge, always very quickly and very privately. When a binge takes over, she can't stop herself: "Nothing else seems to matter once I start. It's as if someone else gets inside my head and I lose all control. After a binge, I feel so bloated and guilty, all I want to do is sleep."

Monica doesn't vomit, but she does experience other symptoms of bulimia such as depression and self-loathing. Whether she is "good" and controls her binges, or "bad" and gives in to them, food dominates her life. Like other compulsive eaters, Monica sees herself as much heavier than she really is. Binge eating can almost always be traced back to a serious and often successful attempt to lose weight. Although the pounds may have been regained long ago, the dieter is left with a long-term eating problem.

It's important for you to remember that a major cause of compulsive overeating is chronic undereating. Dieting creates a powerful hunger drive. Whether or not you want to feed it, your body demands to be fed. The setpoint mechanism interprets weight loss as a major threat to health and life. Often, some emotional stress will break down the self-discipline that has been keeping you on the diet. A trivial upset—something as small as getting a parking ticket—can be the last straw that triggers the binge. In effect, your setpoint works relentlessly to overpower your willpower.[9]

EXERCISE • Binge Control

Here are some techniques to help you gain control of the urge to eat compulsively:

1. Gather baseline data by keeping records of your binges. Jot down when, where, and what you eat. This will help you chart your progress more accurately.

2. Develop delay tactics to postpone the binge a few minutes. For example, decide on a special binge outfit that you must change into before you start every binge. Then call up for a weather report. While you're changing or making the phone call, your urge to binge may subside.

3. Resolve to always begin a binge with a mirror affirmation. For example, stand before your reflection and repeat: "It's healthy to eat when I'm hungry and to stop when I'm full. I give myself permission to have whatever I want." This ritual helps convert the binge from "bad compulsive behavior" into good permitted behavior. It will give you a sense of being in control rather than being taken over by the binge.

4. Try always to binge in front of the mirror so you're not so "alone." Watch yourself eat and notice the difference between eating compulsively and eating consciously.

5. Set a timer to interrupt the binge every five minutes. When it rings, stop eating for a moment, repeat your affirmation, and ask yourself whether you've had enough. You may want to continue binging, but make this a conscious decision. If so, reset the timer for another five minutes. If not, then throw out all remaining binge food.

Monica reported that, "I chose a really tight pair of jeans for my binge outfit so the binge became so uncomfortable I could hardly breathe. My sister is the only one who knows about my eating problem, and she said I could call her as a delay tactic. She doesn't try to talk me out of eating but just chats for a while, and this helps me get over the urge to go crazy with food."

If you're a compulsive eater, set modest goals for yourself, go slowly, and don't expect total success. For some women like Monica, binge eating is an addictive disorder that needs professional help. Consider whether you may be in that category. Have you been binging on a weekly basis over a long period of time? Do you eat so much at a binge that you feel sick? Do you try to hide your binging behavior? Remember that binge eating is generally caused by chronic dieting. In many cases, compulsive eaters have lost the ability to recognize or respond to the natural signals of when to start or stop eating. Ironically, they need to rediscover their hunger.

FROM FAMINE TO FEAST

Would you starve someone you love? Dieting is destructive when it denies you the basic right to nourish and nurture yourself. "To nurture" means to support or sustain with care and concern. Food is an essential part of self-nurturing. Whether you're thin or fat, your body needs nourishment. Loving your body means trusting your natural weight-control system and tuning in to the hunger signals it sends.

Chronic dieting creates a state of mistrust between mind and body. When you don't trust your body to regulate itself, you feel compelled to diet. And when your body, in turn, stops trusting you to feed it properly, it fights back by causing binges or by adding extra pounds. This mind-body tug-of-war traps you in a self-defeating cycle. The mind wants less weight, the body wants more nourishment. Your body cries out, but you pay no attention. There is a breakdown in hunger awareness, a loss of sensitivity to the very hunger signals that keep you healthy, even when they are loud and insistent.

If you're so used to dieting that you've lost track of what it feels like to be hungry or full, it's time to get reconnected to these feelings. It's time to pay better attention to your body's messages and to respect them. You can start by declaring a Hunger Awareness Week. For seven days, listen carefully to body signals. Notice your cravings, your thirst, and your restlessness. Feel the pangs that grow from your stomach, that roll from your mouth, or that float through your head when you're hungry. For one whole week try to respond to these urges. Do you feel like snacking every hour? Do you hate food in the morning but feel famished all evening? Does hunger feel different before meals than afterward? Take a chance that week. Indulge yourself in the foods you crave, and trust your body to know what it wants and needs.

You may be so numbed by chronic dieting that you never feel hungry or that you feel hungry all the time. If so, try eating on a four-hour schedule, at the same time each day. Eventually you'll start to get hungry before each meal. Once you can tune in to these sensations instead of tuning them out, as you've done for so long, you're on your way to a healthier pattern of eating.

THE NO-DIET APPROACH TO
HEALTHIER EATING

By now I hope you're beginning to realize that you don't have to keep on dieting to achieve bodylove. But you may have to change how you think about weight, food, and body image. In summary, here are some basic guidelines for replacing the dieter's mentality with a no-diet approach to healthy eating.

1. *Recognize hunger and eat in response to it.* Food is nourishment, not punishment. Eating is good for you, so stop feeling guilty when you do it. Once you accept that it's okay to eat, you may find it easier to stop eating when you're satisfied. Pause several times during a meal and ask yourself whether you feel full and have had enough. Notice the difference between hunger at the start of a meal and fullness at the end of it.

2. *Improve the quality of the food you eat.* Healthy food is high in nutrition and low in salt, fat, refined sugars, and sugar substitutes. (See the resource section on food and weight.) Start keeping track of the unhealthy foods you commonly consume. Gradually cut back by substituting more high-quality nutritious food for low-quality junk food. There are no foods that are totally taboo. Therefore, when you indulge in a fudge sundae it doesn't break your diet or give you an excuse to binge further. After a splurge, just get right back on the healthy eating track. Since you're not dieting, you can eat as much healthy food as you want.

3. *Accept your weight limitations.* Individual weight limitations are dictated by your setpoint and by your body shape. You can work to adjust your weight within your natural range by making permanent changes in what you eat and how you exercise. Nutritious food and moderate exercise that fit into your life-style will allow your body to comfortably maintain its natural setpoint. Get comfortable—in your clothes, in your eating patterns, and in your body image.

4. *Reduce the significance of weight.* Weight is not an accurate measure of self-worth; the value and beauty of a human being can't be measured on one dimension. What you are is much greater than what you weigh. By defining personal worth from within, you can close the gap between who you are and who you long to be. Self-acceptance is the most essential step in self-improvement.

5. *Actively combat the worship of thinness.* Whether it comes from the media, from others, or from your own head, the obsession with being thinner is destructive. Recognize fatism when you hear it, and realize that this prejudice hurts all of us no matter what we weigh. Fat and thin alike, we all deserve respect, including you.

After many months of resistance, Ellen is making progress. Some of the weight she gained when she stopped smoking has gradually dropped off. She has given up the goal of "breaking 130 pounds" and is starting to realize that life at 129 is not really much happier than life at 135. In fact, she has been able to announce to family and friends that she's accepting her current weight as right for her body and is no longer dieting. That was a difficult step, but it's helped to free her from feelings of shame and failure. Now she's concentrating on healthier eating and regular exercise to achieve a stable and comfortable weight.

MOVING BEYOND FAT

I've tried to show that dieting is an exercise in futility for most people. But physical exercise can be a fulfilling approach to weight control. Active people tend to be thinner than inactive ones, and heavy people tend to be inactive. Movement steps up metabolism. This means that calories are burned more rapidly, which may be nature's way of pushing the setpoint down somewhat. Weight maintenance through exercise feels different from dieting. You're not irritable, depressed, or chronically hungry.

We all differ in our desire for exercise, just as we differ in our needs for sleep or for sex. In the next chapter, you'll see how the joy of movement can help you overcome your resistance to exercise and add a dynamic lift to your body image.

Beauty can take many forms. Some of us are destined to be full figured or fat, some to be slim or curvaceous, others to be mighty and muscular. Yet all of us can feel attractive and lovable whatever the form our bodies take. If we challenge fatism by changing how we view our size and shape, society will slowly be reshaped as well. We do have some choice in the personal ideals we pursue and in the stereotypes we perpetuate.

ON THE MOVE

How does physical activity affect your feelings about your body?
    STRONG POSITIVE EFFECT
    SLIGHT POSITIVE EFFECT
    NO EFFECT
    SLIGHT NEGATIVE EFFECT
    STRONG NEGATIVE EFFECT

How often do you engage in vigorous exercise for at least twenty minutes?
    NEVER
    ONCE A MONTH
    ONCE A WEEK
    2–3 TIMES A WEEK
    ALMOST EVERY DAY

Compared to other women your age, how physically active are you?
    VERY ACTIVE
    FAIRLY ACTIVE
    AVERAGE
    FAIRLY INACTIVE
    VERY INACTIVE

Are you ever so obsessed with exercise that it becomes a compulsion?
    OFTEN
    SOMETIMES
    RARELY
    NEVER

Whenever I feel like exercising, I sit down until the urge passes. Fortunately it always does.

I AM exhausted but elated as I leave Vicki Stern's creative-movement class, where we've just marched to Mozart. "In this class you don't have to strain or strive for perfection," says Nena, a tall and heavyset woman. "It's a way to find out what makes your body special and different. I'm just too rebellious for other fitness classes, which are so regimented," she says. "But Vicki's is different. I feel at one with my body here, and have learned what it can and can't do."

Vicki Stern calls her approach "Working Out from Within," and her goal is to infuse the body with energy that makes it come alive. She believes we should feel animated all the time—not just when exercising, but as we move throughout the day. "So many people come in here ready to battle against themselves," she explains. "They approach exercise with an attitude of fierce determination, as though they were going to war. But their tension really stems from insecurity that prevents them from growing stronger mentally and physically. They have to stop looking from an external view and feel the body from the internal core of the self."[1]

Helping you to experience your body from that "internal core" is one goal of this book. Exercise is a fundamental way of moving toward that goal. Not only does it make you feel better physically but it also makes you feel better about who you are and how you look. It's another way to transform body image from within.

If you're able to walk a mile or run a marathon, you feel different about your body because you appreciate its potential for power and pleasure. When the body is energized and dynamic, then body image takes on those qualities, also. It shifts from a static to an active mode, as if a still photo became a motion picture. You can get to know and like your body by moving it in new directions. The message of this chapter is simple: you'll feel more attractive if you become more active.

THE EXERCISE EFFECT

Movement has many benefits, both physical and psychological. Just as mental images can cause your heart to race, exercise can change your mood and mind-set. Physical arousal leads to emotional arousal, so that "adrenalin makes the heart grow fonder," even of itself. Exercise stimulates the release of substances called endorphins. These seem to produce a "natural high" that decreases anxiety and elevates mood. Let's look at some facts about the effects of physical activity on self-image.[2]

- People who exercise regularly rate their bodies more positively than those who are inactive. Just six weeks of physical conditioning can produce better feelings about the body.
- College students who consider themselves physically fit have higher self-esteem and are more adventurous.
- Female athletes judge their bodies more accurately and more positively than nonathletes.
- When people who exercise regularly are deprived of activity for a month, they experience poor sleep, greater anxiety, and sexual tension.
- People who care about fitness and health have more positive feelings about their appearance than those who are more concerned about looks.

Take a moment to consider how physical activity influences your own perception of your body. Does it make you feel stronger, younger, more confident? Over 85 percent of those who took the Bodylove Survey felt it had a positive effect.

How does physical activity affect your feelings about your body?

56%	STRONG POSITIVE EFFECT
31%	SLIGHT POSITIVE EFFECT
11%	NO EFFECT
2%	SLIGHT NEGATIVE EFFECT
1%	STRONG NEGATIVE EFFECT

I asked Nena to describe how the creative-movement class influenced her. "The most obvious change is hard to put into words," she said. "My body looks the same, but I think I'm much less preoccupied with it, less self-absorbed. Somehow my mind feels quieter and I can focus more attention on other people. I get more deeply involved with them because I'm less concerned with how I look or how I move." While some women naturally gravitate to physical activity to feel better about their bodies, others find that social factors can get in the way.

YOUR BODY AS INSTRUMENT AND ORNAMENT

You may have some obstacles to overcome in getting your body into motion. As women, we've grown up in a culture that encourages us to view ourselves more decoratively than actively. Susan Kano points out that a boy is socialized to see his body as an "instrument," whereas a girl learns to view her body as an "ornament."[3]

The instrumental masculine body is stereotyped as a motion machine that conquers and wins. In contrast, the ornamental feminine body is supposed to attract attention and delight the eye. When Kano asked college students to talk about body satisfaction, she found that women usually discussed their appearance, while men discussed their health and athletic activities. It seems that for men, body esteem comes from feeling active, competent, and strong. For women, it comes from feeling well adorned and attractive.

Right from infancy boys are seen as hardy and are handled more roughly, while girls are considered delicate and are held more gently. Daughters receive fashion dolls for Christmas, while sons get action dolls. Gym teachers toss softballs to girls and hardballs to boys. Thus, daily socialization teaches children that "real" boys should be competitive, active, and athletic, while "real" girls should be less active and more attractive.

Actually some girls do pursue an energetic "boyish" life-style, at least temporarily. Can you remember being one of those tomboys who roamed like a tomcat over the rough masculine turf? Over half of adult women recall being tomboys when they were young. However, by college age girls typically give up their tomboy life-style. As one explained, "It was hard to be a jock while on a date. I realized that I was losing my femininity while trying to prove my athletic ability. So I tried to become softer looking and changed the way I dressed."

At some point during adolescence, most girls exchange the role of tomboy for that of Tom's girl. Personally, I remember leaving the track team for the cheerleading squad. Cheerleading became my only high school sport. While it was physically demanding, it also kept me preoccupied with my appearance, for a cheerleader's job is as ornamental as it is instrumental. Many years went by before I got myself "back on track."

Our early experiences with physical activity affect how we later move through life. Kim, another student in the creative-dance class, tells about the time she took her first ballet lessons: "I was only five and, of course, I ran right home to show Daddy what I could do," she confides. "But he only teased me and said that the classes were a waste of money. I was devastated, and from that day on until now I never danced in public again."

Take a moment to consider how childhood experiences shaped your attitudes and feelings toward movement. Think about how your parents encouraged or discouraged physical activity when you were little. Did they stress mastery or competition? Caution or fun? Perhaps you were steered into activities that were highly ornamental, like ballet or gymnastics. Or maybe you were steered away from those that were rough and dangerous. Some old photos may help you remember yourself as an active and playful child. Were your father's feelings about exercise different from your mother's? Were you a tomboy and did your behavior change during adolescence? As you reflect on these questions, try to understand how your past feelings about movement relate to your present activity patterns.

POWER AND MOVEMENT

As girls play the role of the fair sex, many start to feel like the weaker sex as well. When college students were asked to name the most powerful person they knew, over half of them mentioned their fathers. In contrast, very few of the men or women named their mothers.[4] Beauty *is* a form of social power. However, if you're decorated and displayed like a delicate ornament, you're likely to see yourself as vulnerable, and feel internally helpless as well.

It's easy to get pulled into the ornamental tide of the feminine role. And fashions are part of that undertow. Even when clothes create a more powerful look, they can produce a less powerful person. Tight corsets are a good historical example of how clothes cause constriction and dependency. But even today we still find ourselves wearing the narrow skirts that hem us in, or the pretty pumps that trip us up. These are the ornamental fashions that produce a more vulnerable woman—one who needs help climbing out of cars or into chairs.

One therapist who uses dream work to help people explore their feelings of helplessness found a common theme emerging in the content of her patients' dreams. Women of all social and economic levels reported being hampered and restricted by the clothes they wear in their dreams.[5] We all experience the interplay between psychological and physical powerlessness, though we're not always aware of the connection. One of my own clients described an incident typical of the conflicts women face when they want to act strong but are undermined by their outfits:

> All week I'd been trying to talk with Jim about the trust fund. Finally, on Saturday night as we drove to the city I managed to say some of the things on my mind. At first he was very defensive, but then he just gave me the angry, silent treatment. After we parked he started walking rapidly ahead of me to the theatre. I was already very upset over Jim's reaction, but I found myself slipping along the icy sidewalk in a long skirt and heels. I was furious at him for walking so fast that I couldn't keep up. It was as if he had abandoned me. . . . But I also felt quite helpless and realized how much I need him to lean on.

Take a look at the illustration on page 115. It's an outline of my bare foot (reduced for reproduction here), with my running shoe and my dressiest pumps superimposed on it. (You can easily make your own version of this drawing.) The shaded part shows the difference between my natural foot and my "ornamental, feminized foot." The area of constriction and altered balance caused by the high heel is impressive. Equally impressive is the difference in how I move in the two shoes and how I feel about myself when wearing them.

When my shoe misfits, not only is my foot misshapen, but my body image is altered as well. While Imelda Marcos may be the only woman who ever owned 3,000 pairs of shoes, many of us have had to try on that many to find just one pair we can wear, observes Ellen Goodman. "No one yet has designed a shoe that looks like a spike and fits like a sneaker," she adds.

Now that women have assumed new roles as workers, the conflicts between being a healthy woman and a healthy person are taking new forms. A good example is the beautifully dressed execu-

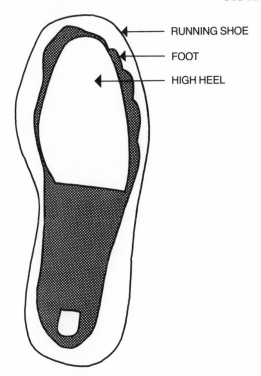

RUNNING SHOE

FOOT

HIGH HEEL

tive who leaves for work each day in her running shoes. Here is a woman who is as concerned with being a winner as with looking like a lady. She has reclaimed her right to move with speed and comfort. Merely by changing her shoes, she's exchanged the power to attract for the power to act.

Remember Vicki Stern's advice that our bodies should feel alive and active, not just during exercise time but throughout the day. Consider how your everyday outfits influence your capacity to move dynamically. Do they make you feel "at home" in your body and help you function as a strong, capable person? Do they allow you to express pride and strength? Or do they add to your feelings of fatigue and shame?

Feeling powerful and feeling good about your looks and yourself are closely connected. Confidence in your own potency builds ego strength. Susan B. Anthony once warned that women need strong bodies as well as quick minds in their struggle for equality. And exercise provides a power base for gaining a sense of control over your life. Movement puts muscle power into femininity. It can empower you with a "can do" mentality and an able body to go with it. As body strength grows, your body image will grow stronger, also.

By moving out of the powder room and into the locker room, you'll develop new forms of inner and outer strength—strength which can then be carried into the boardroom or into the bedroom. You don't need to try to become *as* powerful as possible or *more* powerful than others. Simply use movement to experience your body as a strong instrument, not merely as an ornamental object.

FIT OR MISFIT

We all differ in our need for physical exercise and in the pleasures and benefits we get from it. Fitness has many facets, such as strength, stamina, flexibility, and speed. One common measure of fitness is whether you exercise vigorously for twenty minutes at least three times a week. According to a government survey conducted by the Federal Center for Disease Control, only 41 percent of Americans fulfill this standard. About half of the Bodylove sample met this basic requirement.

How often do you engage in vigorous exercise for at least twenty minutes?

14%	NEVER
16%	ONCE A MONTH
16%	ONCE A WEEK
34%	2–3 TIMES A WEEK
20%	ALMOST EVERY DAY

Think about your own body. How fit or unfit are you right now? Do you exercise regularly or sporadically? Does your activity program develop strength and flexibility as well as stamina? Let's look more closely to see how movement can help or hinder your pursuit of bodylove.

Healthy Uses of Exercise

There are at least three good reasons for everyone to exercise regularly: to stay fit, to have fun, and to find fulfillment.

1. *To develop your body and stay fit.* The more you move, the freer you become to move even further. Fitness comes from working against gravity, from increasing your tolerance for fatigue, from learning new skills, and from testing limits and pushing against them. Greater fitness helps in all kinds of stressful situations, both physical and psychological.

2. *To enjoy yourself and have fun.* The joy of movement comes from social contact, from competing and playing with friends, and from touching other bodies. It comes from aesthetic experiences, like moving gracefully and feeling the sun on your face. It comes from fantasy and regression, as you daydream while splashing in the pool. If you're not having fun while you exercise, it's time to find some new games and rekindle the joy of childish play.

3. *To nurture yourself and find fulfillment.* Moving is a form of self-nurturance. Like eating and sleeping, it meets a basic human need. If you love your dog, you walk it. If you love your body, you move it. A sense of well-being comes from kinesthetic sensations such as lifting, gliding, and floating; from taking risks and discovering new capacities; from releasing anger, practicing self-discipline, or overcoming frustration. When mind and body are united through exercise, you can experience a unique feeling of fulfillment as a total person.

Unhealthy Use of Exercise

While movement should lead to fitness, fun, and fulfillment, like anything else it can be used improperly. If you're constantly getting injured or feeling oppressed by exercise, perhaps you're misusing it in ways such as:

1. *Focusing mainly on weight loss.* Shaping up primarily to shape down can be disappointing. Whether exercise will reduce weight depends on the kind and duration of activity, whether you're above or below setpoint at the start, and whether your setpoint is easily reset. In reality, building muscle doesn't guarantee a smaller or lighter body. Those who are preoccupied with the scale miss many of the other positive benefits that movement offers.

2. *Focusing mainly on competition.* If you find yourself constantly competing either with yourself or with others in your exercise regime, you're defeating the purpose. Activity that's merely an extension of a highly competitive life-style only adds another stress to your day. Of course, there is pleasure in winning or breaking personal records. But movement that's strictly goal oriented can be oppressive—and even dangerous when you push yourself beyond natural limitations.

Exercise should be done neither as a punishment for looking bad nor as a necessary evil for looking good. It's a gift you give yourself because you need and deserve it. So start playing to play, instead of to win, and you'll find yourself in a no-lose situation. Dinah Shore once said, "I've never thought of participating in sports just for the sake of exercise, or as a means to lose weight . . . or because it was a social fad. I really enjoy playing. It's a vital part of my life."

OVERCOMING RESISTANCE

Even if you appreciate the pleasures and benefits of physical activity, resistance may be holding you back. As we've seen all along, it takes thought and concentration to overcome resistance. About 10 percent of the women in our sample rated themselves as inactive, and another 30 percent felt their activity level was about average.

Compared to other women your age, how physically active are you?

27%	VERY ACTIVE
35%	FAIRLY ACTIVE
30%	AVERAGE
8%	FAIRLY INACTIVE
2%	VERY INACTIVE

Many of these women know that more activity would be good for them, yet they can't seem to get going or to stick with it. Lois tells me, "You can't imagine how many times I've tried to get involved in some kind of exercise program. I know I should, and I'd probably feel better. But for me it's harder than dieting." No doubt that some of the following resistance themes will sound familiar to you:

I'd really like to exercise more but just don't have the time.

I've tried, but could never find anything I liked.

I have weak ankles, bum knees, a bad back. . . .

I hate it, so don't bother me with the exercise bit.

I'm just too heavy, too old, too uncoordinated, too self-conscious. . . .

These resistance tactics are irrational, automatic responses that hold you back. Often they're based on faulty logic you've been using and believing for a long time. Once again, the triple-column technique can help correct cognitive errors that prevent you from making a commitment to regular exercise. First, write down your most common exercise excuses. Next, check them against the cognitive errors listed on pages 38–39 to see which types of faulty reasoning you're using. Then, work on some good, rational counterarguments to overcome resistance and help you get your body in motion. Nena explains: "For years I told myself I was too heavy to be seen exercising in public. And too rebellious to accept a rigid fitness program. By challenging these excuses I began to see that remaining inactive was itself a form of rebellion, and that it wasn't doing me much good."

Cindy realized that, "Exercise is the first thing I drop and the last thing I pick up during a work crunch." She challenged this tactic with the counterargument that exercise would help her get through a work crisis and keep her in balance during it.

MAKING TIME

In order for movement to become an integral part of your life, you'll have to solve the very real problem of finding time. How, you may ask, can I exercise regularly when I'm already overloaded with family responsibilities or a demanding job? It may not be easy but it is possible.

Besides the usual alternatives of waking up earlier or cutting out something else to make time for exercise, there are some less obvious ways to fit it into your day. For instance, try combining several things at once. Quality time with your family can be spent taking your children or spouse along for a walk or a swim. Maybe you can all work out together with video tapes. Even toddlers will love to dance with you or play tag outdoors.

Exercise can sometimes be built into your commute to work. Could you park farther away or get off a stop or two earlier and walk for a while? Could you exercise during lunch hour and eat a quick sandwich at your desk afterward? You might negotiate slightly different working hours that will give you time for an exercise class two days after work. Some companies have fitness facilities. Does yours, and have you used them?

Television time is ready-made movement time. While you're watching, start riding a stationary bike, running in place, jumping rope, doing floor exercises, or stretching. Be flexible in varying the amount of time you spend at movement each day. Five minutes of gentle yoga when you wake up or a short walk in the snow after dinner may not improve your stamina, but it can relax or stimulate you. These brief interludes of movement pleasure will keep your body image in top fitness form, even on the busiest days.

DO IT YOUR WAY

Another obstacle that got in Nena's way was perfectionism. In fact, you don't need to be a great athlete to get a great kick out of movement and a great benefit from it. The "I should do things right or not at all" syndrome is just another one of those automatic thoughts that inhibit growth.

In her movement class, Vicki Stern reminds us to "do what feels right for you and don't push yourself to keep up with the others. Exercise doesn't have to be done this way or that way, or even the right way. Just do the best you can." She encourages the class "to let go of the critical judgmental voice inside. Stop focusing on how well you're doing, and start focusing on how well you feel about what you're doing." Pushing causes tension, she warns, so concentrate on the process more than on the product.

This advice is especially important if you see yourself as too old, too fat, too awkward, or too self-conscious to attempt a new activity. As Nena explained, "Not having to do it the right way has freed me up. Now I can strive to do my best without feeling ashamed of being fatter or weaker than others. Instead of giving up in despair,

I'm more willing to explore my own limits, and I find that I'm getting stronger as a result."

Remember, too, that fatness does not preclude fitness. Thin people aren't always fit, nor are heavy people necessarily unfit. The great dancer Isadora Duncan was a "big woman," and 200-pound Virginia Zucci of the Russian Ballet was famous for her pirouettes.

Heavy women need to move as much as anyone else. A chain of health clubs called Women at Large has opened branches across the country. They cater to the 30 million American women who wear a size 16 or larger and who want to work out in an exercise class. This successful business was begun by "two heavy housewives" who were frustrated by conventional health clubs, "where the tyranny of the skinny and the tyranny of the fit made them feel unwanted." If you're resisting exercise because you're heavy, you might want to observe a class before you join, or bring along a friend for support.

Keep your special exercise needs in mind, such as advanced age, postmastectomy, postpartum, and other problems. These obstacles are real. It's important to face them and not let them keep you away from the physical activity you need and can enjoy. If you can't find an exercise group that meets your needs, start one yourself. Or try approaching your local Y about offering a safe and supportive program for people with your particular needs.

GETTING PHYSICAL

Once your resistance starts to break down, begin thinking about the kind of exercise that would nurture your self-esteem. Simple movement is rewarding in and of itself; so getting started is the most important step in proving to yourself just how true this is. The biggest mistake you can make is to push too hard, too soon. *Start slowly, start gently.* In fact, at the beginning it's best not to concentrate on goals or fitness at all. That will come on its own with time.

If you've been inactive, your first step is to make a one-month commitment to know and enjoy your body better through movement. Try to remember the pleasure you felt as a child at play, free of the rigid or competitive qualities you may associate with adult sports. Forget about weight loss. Forget about doing twenty situps or twenty minutes of jogging. Most classes and exercise tapes are too long and too demanding for beginners. You need time to move at your own pace before trying to keep pace with others.

EXERCISE • Expanding Activities

Take a few minutes to list some activities you've enjoyed in the past and some that you've always wanted to try. Keep the list short and include at least one activity you can do anytime at your own pace; one that involves other people; and perhaps one that can be done to music. Here are just some of the possibilities:

Walking—strolling, fast walking, race walking, hiking

Running—sprinting, jogging, long distance

Aerobic dancing—low and high impact

Swimming—laps, water ballet, water exercises

Dancing—folk, ballroom, disco, ballet, creative, tap

Racquet sports—tennis, squash, racquetball, badminton

Biking—stationary, cross-country

Skating—roller, ice

Martial arts—judo, karate, tai chi

Exercise machines—weights, treadmills, rowing machines

Team sports—softball, basketball, soccer, volleyball

Gymnastics

Yoga

Floor exercises—audio and video tapes, exercise classes

Skiing—downhill, cross-country, water

Horseback riding

Each activity has certain advantages and disadvantages, rewards and dangers, depending on the individual. You can always change your pattern, building up to more challenging activities as you grow stronger.

If nothing seems particularly appealing, or if you want to begin with the simplest and safest one, *just start walking.* You can walk alone or with others, indoors or out, slow or fast, in the rain, in a shopping mall. By simply walking in a variety of ways you can achieve the three basic goals of movement: fun, fitness, and fulfillment.

Once you begin to enjoy the basic sensations of simple movement, try stretching it into something more. Do it a little longer, a little faster. Walk a new route or try a pretty place at sunset. Perhaps some music or the company of a friend will add to your pleasure. Warm up before and cool down afterward with slow stretching. You should begin to view movement as a regular "time out from stress"—a gift that you look forward to each day.

Whatever exercise routine you choose, you're not a machine, so don't expect improvement overnight. Don't expect anything. Just see what happens by comparing your mind and body state before and after you exercise. Slowly warm your body up to the kinesthetic sensations it can feel. Hot, sweaty, breathless—these are all natural results of physical arousal. With time you'll learn to tolerate and even enjoy these feelings.

I often walk or run on our local school track. While the scenery is less interesting than the street, for me the track offers other rich experiences. Not having to watch the ground for hazards means I can turn my eyes to the open sky. I enjoy the sun hitting my face or the wind nudging me along from behind. Sometimes I pace myself with a stranger who then becomes a temporary friend. Other times I close my eyes and focus inward.

"I'm most closely in touch with my body when I'm outdoors doing physical things," explained Eileen. "Sometimes on a hike everything just clicks. The most strenuous parts fall into place with ease and my body seems to move effortlessly. It's wonderful when I feel my body responding in just the right way. I become at one with myself."

If you're exercising in the same way all the time, you're probably not getting the most from it. Perhaps you're stuck in a comfortable routine or are afraid to try something new for fear that you'll slack off or gain weight. Try to expand and shake up your exercise pattern. By breaking free of habits and limits, you'll fulfill more of your body's needs. For a few days, give up timing, counting, and the pressure to conform to a class or an instructor. Stop half-way or skip a day and really listen to what your body wants. Be sure that you're not abusing yourself by overexercising.

MOTION MADNESS—FITAHOLICS BEWARE

As we saw earlier, when exercise is misused it becomes unhealthy. Fitness is now being sold as basic insurance against becoming an ugly misfit. Actually, beauty has been paired with athleticism on and off since ancient Sparta. A hundred years ago, feminists like Elizabeth Cady Stanton were advocating exercise as the best form of makeup and the right road to beauty. Today, health-club ads warn us that "before you primp you've got to pump." More people report that they exercise in search of good looks than in search of good health (with weight loss as the primary motive among women). However, when fitness is peddled as a beauty imperative, it can become as oppressive as a tight girdle.

The multibillion-dollar fitness industry rakes in fat profits from our hunger to look like a lean machine. Whether you're flipping through a fitness or a fashion magazine, the contents are very much the same. Both are filled with beauty tips that include weight loss and exercise programs that demand self-control. The message of this new kind of enlightened narcissism seems to be based on health, yet it also carries with it a masochistic undertone that evokes guilt and shame.

Some women eagerly buy into the package and find themselves addicted to its contents. You may be one of them. Have you become a "fitaholic" in your search for good looks or good health? Fitaholics find that they just can't say no to the compulsive urge to run one more mile or take one more aerobics class. Fitness addiction is fairly common, and therefore must be recognized as an obstacle to body-love. In the Bodylove Survey about 20 percent of the women reported problems with overexercising.

Are you ever so obsessed with exercise that it becomes a compulsion?

4%	OFTEN
17%	SOMETIMES
25%	RARELY
56%	NEVER

Fitaholics endure physical risks including strained and torn muscles, stress, and disrupted menstrual cycles. They refuse to rest and recuperate after an injury. Moreover, the psychological risks are serious. Working out can serve as yet another handy excuse for not working on other problems. Controlling the body seems easier than controlling life. For some fitaholics there's also a self-destructive element, as they try to whip their bodies into shape. It's a kind of punishment for feeling ugly or inadequate.

Chronic dieting and compulsive exercising have been referred to as the "twin obsessions," since they frequently operate together in women who are trying to maintain a weight that's below their setpoint. Often these women are high achievers who are very demanding of themselves and others. Charlene described her problem this way:

> I denied it for months, then finally realized that I was preoccupied and obsessed with more and more exercise. It all started when I tried to get back in shape after pregnancy. I would get down to a certain weight, and then set another goal that was a few pounds lighter. If I wasn't taking classes at the club, I was working out at home. Somehow it proved to me that I was special. The thought of cutting back was so scary because it meant I'd become average, just like everyone else. Then I'd lose my whole identity.

Think about whether you may be a victim of the current fitness fad. Has movement become a form of punishment as well as pleasure? Here are some symptoms to consider.

- Do you compulsively pursue exercise while neglecting other basic needs for relaxation, laughter, love?
- Do you constantly measure your self-worth on a scale of fitness, like an anorexic measures hers on a scale of weight?
- Are you forever adding a new goal to your fitness program (another mile or another dance class)?
- Do you get upset when your fitness routine is changed? Does missing a few days feel frightening?

If these symptoms sound familiar, you're probably misusing exercise. It's important to identify your problems so you can start to work on them. Sometimes it's as hard for a fitaholic as for an alcoholic to recognize her difficulties. Admitting an addiction is frightening, especially when there's an underlying fear of weight gain. And withdrawal from any addictive behavior is a painful challenge. So begin slowly in small steps. Addicts may suffer withdrawal symptoms including anxiety, irritability, and depression if they cut back too fast.

EXERCISE • Gaining Control

Begin by gathering some baseline data to see just how much of your life is now committed to exercise. Record the number of hours a week you spend "getting fit" and how long you pursue each activity. When you miss a class or a session, how do you feel? Keep a record of the times you find yourself getting anxious about your exercise routine, and write down the specific thoughts that trigger your anxiety.

You only need three to four hours a week to achieve the fitness, fun, and fulfillment that movement provides. Try to reduce your exercise time gradually over the next few months, and give yourself at least one day of complete rest each week. Tone down your activity by doing it more leisurely. Stop timing yourself and stop counting. Try to focus more on having fun and less on staying fit. Perhaps you could turn your attention to the social side of movement or to other activities that are purely social or aesthetic.

As you slowly change your habits and attitudes about exercise, the compulsion will begin to fade. You'll be opening up your body's natural response to the joy of movement, and that's what bodylove is all about.

JOY IN MOTION

Humans are social creatures. Much of our time is spent trying to get connected with others, and physical activity can be a natural way of developing "your social body." Just watch children on a playground to see the rich potential for social movement—the cooperation on the seesaw and the competition to be first down the slide. Adults use movement in similar ways. Think of the nonverbal dialogue across a tennis net, or the camaraderie of hikers on a trail. A friend of mine recently built a lovely indoor pool for doing her daily laps. But then she found herself missing the banter in the locker room and the rhythmic flow of other swimmers in the water.

When exercise involves interpersonal contact, body image takes on a social dimension. Movement is a universal language that can bring people together in shared pleasure. If you can learn to use movement as a social instrument, you'll be less likely to focus exclusively on the ornamental image of yourself.

Music also brings people together while adding life to movement. A strong, steady beat sets off a primitive physical response that's hard to resist. Look around you at any concert from rock to Rachmaninoff; you'll see heads bobbing and feet tapping. Moving to music in pairs or in groups extends body boundaries beyond the self and adds yet another social aspect to body image.

You can have more fun and get more emotional satisfaction from exercise by simply adding music. Lightweight, portable music sources make it easy to add rhythm and melody anytime, anyplace. Working out to a beat keeps the pace steady and feels better.

Meredith recalled that, "Once someone brought a radio into the health-club pool. I never swam to music before, but I was immediately aware of how much nicer it was . . . less boring. There was a certain smooth flow to the sensations that was really a new experience." She went on to explain that, "The only exercise I really love to do is dancing. The rhythm and music keep you going. You do it without thinking that you're exercising, so it feels natural and painless."

Music plus movement is the basic equation for dance. You could meet most of your exercise needs simply by dancing at home. Dancing, like walking, builds strength and stamina. It can be done any time of day to any kind of music, for as long as you wish. If you've never turned on the radio and started moving as a form of exercise, try it once. You don't have to know a thing about formal dancing to do it, to like it, and to feel happier in your body. Start by slowly rocking and then expand with whatever comes naturally.

The popularity of aerobic dancing in recent years is evidence that music adds pleasure to movement. Here's a sport that's not traditional. There's no score, no winners or losers. But it challenges the body to a thorough workout, develops aesthetic grace, and provides the pleasure of social interaction—all at the same time. The aerobic dance class is a good place to explore the delights of your body as both instrument and ornament.

Dance studios offer another advantage. Lined with mirrors, the studio lets you study your own reflection as you move with others. Visual feedback enhances kinesthetic sensations by giving you a new perspective on your body in motion. Mirror-dancing also provides the perfect partner, one who always moves in harmony with you. Try it at home with your newest album.

My favorite form of dance takes place on ice. Tuesday evenings are always saved for the skating rink. No matter how tired I feel at the start, I know that an hour of ice dancing will melt down my stress and warm up my mood. It's my gift of movement to myself. I keep on skating year after year because ice dancing gives me such a rich mixture of fun, fitness, and fulfillment.

I find it an almost perfect blend of instrumental challenge and ornamental pleasure. There's the demand for high energy, balance, and technical skill. There's the sensuality of moving together with a partner as the music shifts our mood from tango to waltz. There's the fun of dressing up in skating costumes and socializing with friends on the ice. Sometimes there are even those rare magic moments when I feel weightless, gliding through space totally adrift in my fantasies. Make no mistake; I'm not especially good at this sport, but it's very good for me. I've given myself permission to skate like a star (and to see myself as one also). This is what movement can do for body image.

PLAYING WITH EMOTIONS

Another way that movement enhances self-image is by helping you feel and release emotions that are usually inhibited. If you think about it, emotional and physical arousal affect your body similarly, causing changes in temperature, pulse, respiration, and muscle tension. That's because mind and body are united; emotions are physical as well as mental. Our language is full of expressions that connect emotions to body parts:

He's hardheaded but kindhearted.

Don't keep such a stiff upper lip; get things off your chest.

I can't stomach her; she's such a pain in the neck.

I had a strong gut reaction, but my feelings got stuck in my throat.

Through movement you can feel emotions as part of your body and work toward "letting them go"—for instance, by jumping for joy or hitting hard. The following exercises will help you explore and express emotions in moving ways.

EXERCISE • Emotional Release

1. *Locating emotions.* Warm up your body by walking or jogging in place. While you're doing this, visualize a scene that evokes a particular emotion, like anger. Imagine someone stealing your parking space, for instance, and try to locate the places where your body feels the anger. Is it in your throat, your fists, your jaw? Tuning in to emotions is like tuning in to hunger. You have to search within for tension, pressure, subtle sensations. Now try to evoke some other emotions, such as grief, fear, or shame. Visualize a frightening scene and scan your body for feelings of fear.

2. *Expressing emotions.* After you've practiced arousing and locating your emotions, try to express them in movement. Get your anger going through visual imagery, and translate those feelings into action. Move around like the angriest woman on the block, or the saddest one. You can work with many positive and negative feelings (envy, fear, joy) by arousing them through imagery and releasing them through movement. This process should leave you less emotionally muscle bound and more relaxed.

3. *Incorporating emotions.* As a final step, try to incorporate emotional arousal and release into your everyday exercise routines. Take your feelings into the pool or onto the track. Run with anger or pleasure. Dance with elation or fear. As you move to release negative emotions or connect with positive ones, you'll also be nurturing your self-esteem.

EXERCISE • Meditation in Motion

Positive self-statements can be energized through movement. In her book *Transforming Body Image,* Marcia Hutchinson calls this "moving affirmations." During her workshops, she invites participants to move across the room, expressing affirmations such as:[6]

> I am a uniquely beautiful woman, inside and out, and I know it.
> I like myself and feel easy in my body.

Other affirmations that I've found useful include:

> My body is a powerful and beautiful instrument.
> I love the child within me and invite her to come out and play.

Recall some of the affirmations you rehearsed in front of the mirror (see page 72). Then try to express them through simple movement. Affirmations can also be carried into your everyday exercise routine, for instance, by repeating one while you're walking or biking. In this way, an ordinary workout is stretched to enhance its emotional value.

SOMETHING IN THE WAY SHE MOVES

With a little creativity, exercise time can help you achieve much more than mere fitness. Fantasy, music, social contact—these all serve to enhance body image through physical activity. As you move with strength and style, you develop both the instrumental and ornamental aspects of your self-image.

Exercise manuals often stress how long, how hard, or how fast you must work out to build muscles or raise heart rate. But don't forget about the feelings in your heart and the images in your head as you move your body. Kim, who once gave up dancing because of her father's ridicule, tells me that her husband gave her a course in creative movement as a birthday present.

> It's turned out to be a gift for both of us because it's really changed our marriage. I'm so much more open and accepting of my body. The judgmental part that made me feel inhibited is gone. Now I'm

freer to be myself, to give and take from the relationship. We move and touch with greater intimacy than we ever did before.

As Kim developed awareness of her physicality, she also became more sensitive to her sexuality. It's inevitable that the bodylove you gain through movement will carry over into other parts of your life, as well.

SENSUALLY SPEAKING

If you were more physically attractive, do you think your sexual life
would be (or would have been) more satisfying?
>DEFINITELY
>PROBABLY
>NOT SURE
>PROBABLY NOT
>DEFINITELY NOT

If you are married or in a coupled relationship, how does your
partner's physical appearance compare with your own?
>PARTNER IS MUCH BETTER LOOKING
>PARTNER IS SOMEWHAT BETTER LOOKING
>WE ARE ABOUT EQUAL
>I AM SOMEWHAT BETTER LOOKING
>I AM MUCH BETTER LOOKING
>I AM NOT COUPLED AT THIS TIME

How important to you is the sexual aspect of your life today?
>EXTREMELY IMPORTANT
>QUITE IMPORTANT
>OCCASIONALLY IMPORTANT
>NOT VERY IMPORTANT
>NOT AT ALL IMPORTANT

Do you think your body is sexually appealing?
>EXTREMELY APPEALING
>QUITE APPEALING
>SOMEWHAT APPEALING
>NOT VERY APPEALING
>NOT AT ALL APPEALING

Do your beauty routines involve other people touching your body
(i.e.: manicure, shampoo, massage)?
>SEVERAL TIMES A WEEK
>WEEKLY
>EVERY FEW WEEKS
>MONTHLY
>RARELY

Why not fall in love with the body you've been sleeping with all your life?

—STEWART EMERY

B Y now you know that this book isn't a sex manual, despite its title. It *is*, however, a guide to discovering and enjoying the pleasures your body can provide. How you see your body affects how you use it. Feeling ashamed about your appearance can inhibit your sexual expression. In turn, sexual shame may distort your body image.

This chapter explores the house of sensuality in which you live. By uncovering shame and discovering touch, you'll learn that your body isn't a den of iniquity, but really a pleasure palace. As you learn to fill up your senses with lovely feelings and become a more sensuous woman, you'll start to look lovelier in your own eyes.

In Vicki Stern's exercise classes, touch between members of the group is an important part of the dance routines. Participants also give each other a brief back massage to cool down at the end of the dance session. "Through these classes I've discovered that it's okay to touch—even to touch strangers," says Kim. "And I've also learned the joy of being touched in return. It's helped me to see my body differently."

Humans depend on vision more than many animals do. Today's world bombards us with constant imagery—from television, movies, computer screens—which only increases our visual dependency. Thus, we tend to experience our body more in terms of how it looks than how it feels. For women especially, the body becomes an ornament of visual display rather than an instrument of sensual pleasure. But other senses besides vision have an important effect on body image. Touch, in particular, has been called the mother of all senses and the language of love.

At the Vietnam War Memorial in Washington, D.C., where the names of the dead are carved in marble, visitors react in unexpected ways. Most reach out to touch the stone wall as if it were alive. "Perhaps by touching it, they renew their faith in love and in life," observes one writer. Touching creates intimacy. To be intimate is to be close in the literal sense of body contact. The opposite of intimate is distant. When you distance your body, you fall out of touch and out of love with it.

Love needs physical expression. We may whisper sweet nothings and gaze with adoring eyes, but above all, loving means physical contact. Touching turns strangers into friends and friends into lovers. We tell our friends to keep in touch, and are told to "reach out and touch someone." That someone can be yourself. Bodylove grows from body touch, for it's hard to hate a body that you love to touch.

GETTING IN TOUCH

From the moment we enter the world, the pleasure of touch is instinctive. "Welcome to motherhood," said the doctor, handing me a little bundle of life. As my newborn cuddled at my breast, her tiny fingers stroked my skin. This is how bodylove begins: with the touch of a hand. That moment felt as good to me as it did to her, for the mutual pleasure was part of nature's grand design to get us connected. Infants learn to "make love" with their bodies, thus forging the bonds that ensure survival.

My daughter caressed my skin and her fingers curled through my long hair in the same way that a baby monkey clings to its mother's furry belly or a toddler fondles a security blanket for comfort. In Harry Harlow's classic study, baby chimps were shown to bond more strongly to an artificial mother that's covered with terrycloth than to one that gives warm milk but feels hard and cold. It's not the food, but the soft touch of a sensuous mother that leads to love. The basic trust learned at a mother's breast lets us trust our own bodies enough to share them later on. In this way, a mother's hug paves the way for a lover's caress.

LOSING TOUCH

Because the road to intimacy was not well paved for her in childhood, Diane finds herself in a kind of sensual wasteland. "We haven't made love in months," she confides during therapy, quickly adding "though I'm not sure I care. Why do people make such a big deal about sex? I guess I'm just different." These comments come from a sexy-looking woman dressed in a hot-pink jumpsuit, with lips and nails to match. Artfully made up, she portrays the vision of a sensuous woman, yet under her sexy surface is a well of shame. In truth, Diane is often looked at but rarely touched. Though visually lovely, she's sensually lonely.

Diane's mother suffered on and off from depression when Diane was a child. "Mostly, Mom just wanted to be left alone, and I learned pretty early to stay out of her way. Now I'm worried because it's hard for me to get close to my own kids. Brian is two and constantly climbing all over me. I find myself pushing him away a lot. He messes up my clothes and makes me nervous." Deprived of good touching as a child, Diane feels threatened with intimacy and pulls back when others reach out to her. People who are comfortable with touching are found to be more satisfied with their body and their appearance. Conversely, those who have a poor body image have more trouble developing intimate contacts. They may sabotage relationships before they start or before they become really important.[1]

We're all born with sensitive, loving bodies, but unfortunately we get partly desensitized as we get civilized. Society trains us to keep our sensuality under cover. From an early age, children are socialized not only to play the masculine or feminine role but also to express intimacy in culturally acceptable ways. Think, for instance, how we put our babies to sleep in cribs, alone and "behind bars." Only in a "low-touch" culture like ours would we need bumper stickers that ask, "Have you hugged your child today?"

Society disrupts the natural expression of physical love and channels our instincts in the "proper" direction. Good girls should be seen but not heard, looked at but not touched. As Freud described it, the energy from the *id*, which is our basic drive for sensual gratification, is gradually redirected into activities that are more socially acceptable. After all, we can't just sit around all day sucking our thumbs and making love.

In analytic terms, the *superego* emerges to restrain the indulgent impulses of the id. Culture writes the rules and parents convey them. Then, as the child develops, the superego takes over as the internal voice of conscience. It demands self-control. So you learn to hold in, hold back, and behave properly. You learn which parts of the body are private and which bodily functions are naughty, ugly, dirty, and shameful. You learn that your body can't be trusted because it goes out of control and gets you in trouble. The role of the *ego* is to balance the tug-of-war between the pleasuring id and the punishing superego. Bodylove thrives when a strong ego can strike a healthy balance.

As we get properly connected to society, we get partly disconnected from our own bodies—and distanced from those with whom we are most intimate. My son, at the age of eight, is in the tub. Finding the door shut, I knock and start to open it but hear him say for the first time, "Don't come in." He's learned the rules and set a new boundary between us. Am I ready to give up the intimate pleasure of seeing that sweet little body I've nurtured for years? I recall how I cut off my braids and ended an intimacy with my father before he was ready to give it up.

Think back to your own childhood and try to remember the ways you were touched and permitted to touch. Was yours a low- or a high-touch household? Was touching mainly affectionate or also punitive? Who in your past has touched you most lovingly and helped you achieve basic trust in your body? Who has touched you aggressively or abusively, leaving behind a sense of mistrust or shame?

The boundaries of intimacy change throughout childhood and especially in adolescence. The baby cries to be held tight, the toddler says "put me down," and the teenager shouts "leave me alone." Diane was neither held tight nor left alone. As a heavy child, she became the object of ridicule from classmates who poked fun at her. "They called me Blimp, and I felt so ashamed. I just wished they would all get off my back and give me some peace." Diane had very few dates until college. Thus she missed out on the kissing and petting that help adolescents move into their sexuality. Her few teenage experiences with boys only left her feeling more rejected and self-conscious. Eventually Diane turned to cosmetics and self-adornment as a way to build self-esteem and to enjoy her body as a beauty object.

THE SENSUAL AND THE ORNAMENTAL WOMAN

One way that society causes us to lose touch with our sensuality is through media images that "objectify" women by splitting the mind from the body. We're all influenced by the provocative soft porn that surrounds us everywhere. As a result, we start to objectify ourselves through a kind of pornographic self-image. In Diane's case, for instance, looks dominate her awareness, even when she's making love. By acting out the ornamental feminine role she becomes a sex object to herself, and paradoxically this cuts her off from her own sensuality.

Kim found that the sensual movement she acquired in her dance class helped reduce her feelings of objectification and close the gap between mind and body. "I used to think 'I *am* what I look like.' Now I try to tune in to how my body feels as well as how it looks. My parents taught me that nice girls shouldn't like certain things, even if those things felt nice. I've learned to touch more freely and have become less embarrassed about sharing my body with David."

In effect, Kim has moved from an ornamental to a more sensual self-image. What exactly does this mean? Here are some characteristics of both the sensual and the ornamental woman that will help you understand the differences and evaluate yourself.

- A sensual woman sees herself as a whole person; an ornamental woman feels like a collection of parts.
- A sensual woman knows and meets her own needs for pleasure; an ornamental woman exists mainly for the visual pleasure of others.
- A sensual woman defines herself from within; an ornamental woman is defined by the outside viewer.
- A sensual woman is a subject to herself; an ornamental woman is an object on display.

Of course, beauty and body adornment are important to a sensual woman. However, she knows that the primary organ of sexual arousal is the mind. If you see yourself as attractive and desirable, then your body image can turn on your sexual appetite. Thoughts are a potent aphrodisiac, so body image plays a starring role in sexual fantasies. A beautiful body *is* a turn-on, whether you see it on the screen or project it into your own fantasies.

DO GOOD LOOKS MEAN GOOD SEX?

Appearance is certainly important to sexual attractiveness. The body signals we give off are part of the mating game. Like a peacock who spreads his gorgeous tail to seduce a passing hen, we show off our bodies to get noticed and loved. In cultures where people select their own mates, appearance is all the more important. Today, when women stay single for long periods—before marriage, after divorce, after widowhood—the rivalry to look fairest of all is heightened. Having lost twenty pounds, Sylvia declares, "I'm at the perfect hunting weight." And Rhoda, who's thirty-eight and still unmarried, admits, "I spend every extra cent, even go into debt, to look as good as I can for my vacation every summer. It's the only chance I have to meet men. Believe me, the competition is fierce on the singles scene."

Darwin explained that fancy feathers or flashy fins evolved through the process of natural selection and the competition for mates. But humans have become experts at creating unnatural lures. The bright red splashes on Diane's lips and nails grab attention. Her hot colors are seductive, creating the image of someone who's perpetually in heat. Cosmetic ads try to convince us that the one with the brighter lips gets the better lover . . . and therefore gets more love.

Unlike animals in heat, beautified women like Diane are often sending complicated mixed messages. They look like hot numbers, but actually they may be searching for attention, affection, or affluence even more than for sex. Turned on to the ornamental pleasures of body display, many women get turned off to the pleasures of sensual play.

Diane spends hours at the beauty salon and days in Bloomingdale's, but has little time for intimacy with herself or others. At thirty, she's more attractive than ever. People who see her assume that she's as sexually active as she is attractive. In fact, most pretty women are stereotyped as sexually warmer, more permissive, and more responsive than unattractive women. Looksism equates good looks with good sex.[2] But are these stereotypes true? Perhaps so, perhaps not.

In one study, good-looking college students were found to be more liberal in their sexual attitudes and to start having intercourse at an earlier age than their less attractive classmates. It may be true that "pretty girls do it sooner." A self-fulfilling prophecy could well be operating here. If pretty women are expected to be more sexually responsive, they may get more offers and thus engage in more sex. Or perhaps those with a stronger sexual drive work harder at looking good. In another study, young women who liked their bodies were found to be more sexually active than those who didn't like their bodies. Here, it's bodylove rather than beauty that correlates with increased sexuality.[3]

Over half the women who responded to the Bodylove Survey felt that being attractive was *not* directly related to sexual satisfaction in their personal lives. As one woman put it, "Being prettier would help me more at work than in bed."

If you were more physically attractive, do you think your sexual life would be (or would have been) more satisfying?

7%	DEFINITELY
13%	PROBABLY
26%	NOT SURE
39%	PROBABLY NOT
15%	DEFINITELY NOT

Take a moment to consider your response to this question and your own motives for pursuing physical attractiveness. Are you trying to attract a mate or arouse the one you have? Are you more concerned with how men react to your appearance or how women see you? Are you seeking affection, attention, or the pure power of looking provocative for its own sake?

It's true that good looks are important in the market of social exchange. Most people wind up with dates and mates who are equally matched to their own level of physical attractiveness, a fact confirmed by our sample. Half the women rated their partner's physical attractiveness as about equal to their own.

If you are married or in a coupled relationship, how does your partner's physical appearance compare with your own?

4%	PARTNER IS MUCH BETTER LOOKING
10%	PARTNER IS SOMEWHAT BETTER LOOKING
47%	WE ARE ABOUT EQUAL
13%	I AM SOMEWHAT BETTER LOOKING
4%	I AM MUCH BETTER LOOKING
22%	I AM NOT COUPLED AT THIS TIME

In terms of the mating game, like seeks like. Yet those who look seductive don't always act it. Sexually speaking, it's hard to judge a book by its cover. Most therapists quickly learn that an innocent face can mask a history of hard-core adventures, that some plain-Janes are Tarzans in bed. Sometimes, looking sexy can actually be a way of disguising and denying a strong fear of sexuality. Diane, for example, hides her anxiety under designer wraps and expresses her sensuality in the safe cosmetic arena. It's really her lack of sexual confidence that drives her to look as chic as possible.

According to the theories of Robert Brain, our preoccupation with female beauty grows from a fundamental fear and denial of female sexuality. "Beauty rituals are used primarily to make women socially acceptable," he writes. "A woman turns herself into a lovely lady in order to pursue social, not sexual satisfaction." Brain believes that cosmetic rituals are really a way of distracting the eye *away* from erogenous zones and of acting out sexual impulses in a socially acceptable way.[4]

SENSORY REINFORCEMENTS

In a culture that encourages the ornamental role so heavily, it's easy to become addicted to a diet of cosmetic adornment. Unless you open yourself up to the other essential nutrients, you may easily end up suffering, as Diane does, from a kind of sensual anorexia.

Remember that body image is more closely connected to self-esteem than to physical appearance. One way to feel better about your looks is to nurture your body through *sensory reinforcements.* These are rewards you give yourself simply because you need and deserve them. Sensory reinforcements are inexpensive, noncaloric, and readily available. So once you cultivate an appetite for these goodies, you can afford to feast on them whenever you like. "I try to have one terrific smell every day—I like to give my nose a snack," explains Lily Tomlin in a recent show. If you've been a compulsive dieter, or if you're frequently self-conscious about your looks, it's especially important to learn how to dish out nutritious sensory treats.

Start to overcome your sensual anorexia by tuning in to sensory hungers. This means paying close attention to the sensations your body enjoys. You'll recall that paying attention is a basic ingredient of bodylove. The next exercise shows you how to have fun attending to yourself as you would nurture a baby. You can increase

"Quick! Your gut reaction."

Drawing by Frascino; © 1980 The New Yorker Magazine, Inc.

awareness of sensual hungers by returning to the natural pleasures you felt in infancy, before your restricting superego took over.

EXERCISE • Exploring Primitive Pleasures

1. *Rocking.* Gentle rhythmic movement soothes the savage beast within. Start this exercise by rocking a bit as you might rock-a-bye your baby. You can use a swing, a rocking chair, a hammock. Try curling up on the floor, hug your knees to your chest, and slowly rock from side to side. Add some "rock" music with a steady beat and breathe in time to the rhythmic motion. Visualize your body gently swaying back and forth, and let the soothing rhythm seep into your body image.

2. *Mouthing.* Babies use their sensitive mouths to explore the world. (Some even suck their thumbs for comfort before birth!) Lips weren't designed only for lipstick, nor was your mouth meant only for eating. It's also sensitive to other kinds of sensory snacks. Try chewing on an orange peel or biting a pencil. Lick your own lips or the palm of your hand. Lick your skin to enjoy the salty taste after you exercise. Suck your thumb or a pacifier to indulge in the early joys of uninhibited sucking. Explore the different satisfactions of licking, sucking, and chewing, and learn how these "infantile" mouthings can give sensual satisfaction.

3. *Relaxing.* Reducing external stimulation is like returning to the womb. Relaxation can help you focus inward to feed your sensory needs. You might want to review the relaxation instructions on page 97. Basically, all you need do is get comfortable, close your eyes, relax your muscles, and breathe deeply. Tuck yourself in for a sensory nap each day and enjoy "the pause that refreshes" by turning off the TV, phone, radio, and people around you. Relaxation time can be as brief as two minutes or as long as you wish. While relaxing, try to focus your mind on a blank page or on a number. When thoughts intrude, just change the number or turn the page. With practice you'll achieve a "relaxation response" throughout your body, and this feeling of deep repose will gradually become part of your body image. Relaxation is a natural tranquilizer for reducing stress.

4. *Playing.* Through child's play you can rediscover how good your body can feel. Remember the fun you once had splashing in the tub? Put water-play back in your life. Try alternating hot and cold showers. Use a shower massage on different body parts and close your eyes to concentrate on the different sensations as you move it around. Take relaxation time into a warm tub and just let yourself luxuriate. (Or take a playmate into the tub with you.) Remember the fun of running naked? When you're home alone, strip down and feel what it's like to function in your baby skin as nature intended. Feel your bare feet on a soft rug or your bare bottom on a tile floor. Get a clear image of your nude body as you clean or dance to a favorite record. Let these visions sink into your head so they, too, become part of your body image.

You can also play with smells. Light a scented candle or incense while you eat. Rub an orange peel on your hands. Buy a new perfume to be used only when you feel like romancing yourself with pleasure. Explore the special smells of your body, also. Gather scent from your ears, your armpits, or your genitals and inhale these rich smells right into your body image so it comes alive. Any of these exercises in rocking, mouthing, playing can be as sensual or as sexual as you choose to make them. Trust your body to be your guide.

THE SENSUAL SIDE OF SEXUALITY

What's the difference between sensuality and sexuality? It's hard to say where the boundary lies. And it's probably futile to try to draw some arbitrary line between them since that point will vary depending on your background, your mood, your social situation.

In choosing *Bodylove* for the title of this book, I tried to convey the idea that self-image has sexual overtones. That's because body-love and sensuality are part of the broad foundation of healthy sexuality. Sensuality and sexuality both involve physical arousal and the pleasures of seeing, smelling, tasting, and touching. Both can be soothing or passionate. And we each vary in our needs for both, just as we vary in the sensitivity of body parts. Ginny, an athletic woman in her mid-forties, had this to say about sensuality and sexuality:

> I get a lot of pleasure from my body, but until recently I never thought I was very sexual. Although I always felt sensual. I love to feel the ground under my feet when I hike. I'll stop to explore the texture of a leaf or to smell the wet bark on a tree. When I'm playing good tennis, it's a tactile experience. I really feel the vibrations in my hand and I use my arm like a fine-tuned machine. Men have certainly picked up on the special way I have of exploring through touch. . . . Perhaps I'm actually more sexual than I thought.

An openness to sensuality leads naturally to sexuality. And without sensual awareness, sexuality is less likely to be fulfilling. Remember Diane's comments that, "Sex isn't something I think about very often." She suffers from "inhibited sexual desire," which is not uncommon among people with a poor body image. In the Bodylove Survey, the majority of women rated sexuality as quite an important part of their lives. Moreover, most of them saw themselves as sexually appealing to some extent; only 15 percent described their bodies as not very appealing.

How important is the sexual aspect of your life today?

14% EXTREMELY IMPORTANT
43% QUITE IMPORTANT
25% OCCASIONALLY IMPORTANT
15% NOT VERY IMPORTANT
4% NOT AT ALL IMPORTANT

Do you think your body is sexually appealing?

7% EXTREMELY APPEALING
30% QUITE APPEALING
48% SOMEWHAT APPEALING
11% NOT VERY APPEALING
4% NOT AT ALL APPEALING

Joyce observes that, "Although my dark skin has made me ashamed for most of my life, I still think I'm a sexually appealing woman. Maybe it's because I wound up marrying someone much lighter than I am and I know he finds me physically attractive."

Diane, on the other hand, doesn't see herself as sexually desirable despite her successful efforts to look pretty and feminine. Her preoccupation with the ornamental role and her denial of her sexuality leave her feeling emotionally distant. While making love, Diane sometimes experiences a form of "spectatoring." She sees herself from outside her body, almost like a voyeur. She's physically there but psychologically absent. This is true even in her erotic fantasies, where she feels as if she's watching the scene from afar. In Diane's case, the ornamental woman overpowers the sensuous woman, pushing her off to the sidelines.

SENSATE FOCUS

Earlier, we compared the differences between the sensuous and the ornamental woman. How can you become more sensuous? Actually, the answer lies right in the palm of your hand. Self-touch can be used as a vehicle to carry you away from the purely ornamental and toward the more sensual side of yourself.

Sensate focus is a technique developed by William Masters and Virginia Johnson to help people overcome their sexual problems. Starting with simple, nonthreatening touch, couples slowly move into more intimate erotic contact. Intercourse is forbidden at first, so they feel freer to touch without thinking about penetration, orgasm, or any other goals. Masters and Johnson suggest that for many couples, "The fundamental error is believing that touch is a means to an end. It is not. Touch is an end in itself."[5]

When you're sensate focused you concentrate only on experiencing the immediate physical contact—the pure pleasure of kissing, hugging, fondling. You tell each other what feels good, alternate between being a giver or receiver, overcome inhibitions in small steps. Sensate focus can be applied to self-touch as well as to another's touch, for touch serves as a bridge between mind and body as well as between people.

Following are a set of sensate-focus exercises that will get you in closer touch with your sensuality. They may be especially important if you recognize any of these issues in yourself:

You don't consider yourself sexually appealing.

You rarely experience sexual desire.

You don't think of your skin as an organ of pleasure.

You're reluctant to initiate sex and always depend on your partner to arouse you.

Prepare to take a sensual trip around your body. You'll need to set aside some private uninterrupted time and create a relaxed atmosphere with soft lighting and quiet music. Wear a loose robe so you can touch your body easily. And keep in mind that sensate focus has no goal except the experience of touch, pure and simple.

EXERCISE • Self-Touch

1. *Touch awareness.* Begin by gathering several interesting objects—an apple, a hairbrush, a silky fabric. Close your eyes to heighten tactile awareness and explore each object slowly. Start gently with your fingertips, then rub the object on your palm and enclose it in both hands. As you touch each object, try to clearly visualize it. Watch the image change in your mind as your hands move over the object, and notice the different feelings your hands can transmit: sharp, cold, soft, bumpy.

2. *Body awareness.* Lie comfortably and breathe deeply to relax and focus inward. Begin by placing your hands on the sides of your head and explore the qualities of your own head just as you did the other objects. Play with your hair, noticing its texture and softness. Now press your palms on each side of your temples and rotate them in a gentle massage. Keep your eyes closed to concentrate. Notice the pressure of your hands against your head and the size of your head in your hands. Next, let your fingers move over your face. Outline your features with your fingertips, and try to visualize each feature in your mind's eye. Spend as much time as you wish on each part of your face, experiencing its contours in a new way.

3. *Body exploration.* Choose another part of your body to explore through sensate focus. Start with a place that's safe: a part that you commonly touch and that feels attractive to you—for instance, your neck or arms. First, close your eyes and clearly visualize that part of the body *before* you touch it. Now, place your hands gently on it and let the inner image incorporate the feelings from your hands. Does it feel the way you thought it would? Outline the boundaries of that body part with your hands and with your mind, then gently stimulate that body part with your fingertips. How does the skin feel? Notice the differences among muscle, bone, and fat. Try various movements—scratch, tickle, rub, press. Try different speeds and notice the sensations you can arouse with your hands. Be creative in how you touch and focus on the sensations in a way that you've never done before. Don't rush, but take your time and try to stay completely here and now, in the sensation. See if you can integrate the physical feelings into your body image, so that the image itself feels stroked or rubbed.

4. *Becoming your body.* Try to express affection as you experience your body through your hand—skin to skin. Caress it with a loving, gentle touch and surrender yourself to the good feelings. Can you "become" that body part and identify with it as you focus on the sensations? Think about how that part likes to be stroked and held. Let that part speak to you in its own voice, and listen attentively to its message. Your hand is a delicate bow that can play magical melodies on the instrument of your body. Concentrate on letting go of the critical judgmental voice, and allow your body to give and receive affection as you become the object of your own attention. See if you can shift your awareness back and forth from the hand that is touching to the part being touched. Notice how touching adds intimacy to body image. Areas that aren't so lovely to look at can feel beautiful to touch.

5. *Going further.* After exploring some "safe" parts, journey on to a place that has more risk—perhaps your stomach or hips—and

repeat the process of touching, visualizing, and becoming that part. Relax with your eyes closed, and practice sensate focus as the feelings flow from your hand and back into it. Finally, visit a place that's more exotic and erotic to you—breasts, nipples, thighs.

6. *Sensual to sexual.* Sensate focus can be sensual, sexual, or both, depending on what you choose to make it. Can you tell where the sensual and erotic feelings blend? You may or may not wish to include genital touching in this exercise. But do realize that genitals are part of your body and therefore part of your body image. Masturbation is commonly practiced and enjoyed by most women as part of their sexual expression. Shyness and inhibition about touching your own body only restrict the full range of sexual pleasures available to you. No part of you need be "untouchable." No form of self-touch need be shameful. (See the resource section on sensuality for information on self-stimulation.)

Sensate focus can be practiced in the bath, in the dark, when lying in the sun. After repeating it several days in a row, you may notice the changes that come with practice. If you have an intimate partner, try exploring body-touch together. But remember that the purpose of this exercise is not to create intimacy with another, but to become more intimate with yourself. Touching your body as if it were a loving friend will help you see yourself as a lovelier woman—one who is more sensually responsive and more sexually appealing. It may also help you overcome feelings of body shame that often run deep.

FACING SHAME

Although Sylvia is thin and attractive now, she still feels ashamed of how she looked as a child. "My breasts started to develop when I was only nine, and I tried sleeping on my stomach to flatten them out. I did everything to hide them, but of course they showed anyway. For years my brother called me 'boobs.' Later he saw some tampons in my room and told me I looked ugly when I had my period. It was awful for me."

In earlier chapters, you saw the effects of shame on body image. Sexual shame may be one of your biggest obstacles as you strive toward bodylove. Remember that shame is "a feeling of inadequacy mixed with fear that some defect will be discovered by others." You can understand how sexual shame develops by looking at the taboos of menstruation. The Bible describes a menstruating woman as unclean, and prohibits her from eating with others or touching them. The menstrual shame of ancient times is still with us today. In a study conducted in 1980, one-third of those surveyed felt that women should hide the fact that they are menstruating from family members. And 12 percent of the men also thought that women "should stay away from other people" during their periods.

In the Bodylove Survey, almost half the women reported feeling worse about their bodies during menstruation. Of course, it's hard to know what part of these negative feelings is due to physical discomfort and what part comes from menstrual shame.

Do you feel different about your body just before or during your menstrual period?

0%	MUCH BETTER
3%	SOMEWHAT BETTER
32%	NO DIFFERENT
33%	SOMEWHAT WORSE
11%	MUCH WORSE
21%	I DO NOT HAVE MENSTRUAL PERIODS

To overcome negative feelings about yourself during menstruation, you may find it helpful to bolster your body image with positive affirmations, such as:

I welcome the cycles of my life that can create new life.

My womanly body is fertile and feminine.

Repeat these affirmations in front of the mirror as you dress or while you exercise. The joy of movement can also affirm that you're not "unwell" or unclean at that time of the month. Are you still keeping your periods hidden from certain family members? Consider why this remains a shameful secret that can't be shared with them.

There are many other aspects of sexual shame that distort body image. Touching becomes a shameful act when you've been touched by the wrong person, at the wrong time, or in the wrong way. Such experiences are usually shrouded in secrecy, and they're far more common than most people realize. It may come as a surprise to know that one out of every four American women is estimated to have suffered sexual abuse during childhood. All these victims, especially those who were subjected to incest, are left with painful and shameful memories. If you are one of them, you'll need to work hard to remove these shadows from your body image. Marjorie, who was abused by a stepfather, describes her feelings this way:

> I know now that what happened to me was terribly wrong and I'm trying not to blame myself. But you see, I let him touch me for so long and never told. My silence is what makes me most ashamed. Someday I hope I can be physically close to a man. Right now my body still feels too violated. I see it as used, a second-hand body. Even when I touch myself the old feelings of shame come flooding back.

If you've been a victim of sexual or physical abuse, please check the resource section on shame. However, these references are only a start and you'll probably need to explore other sources of professional help as well.

Above all, you should remember one thing: *there is no shame in being a victim.* Sexual abuse that occurred in childhood isn't your fault. Nor is violent abuse that occurs at any age. Sexual "choices" that you may have made under oppressive circumstances also aren't your fault. So stop blaming yourself and your body for things that were beyond your control, or for mistakes you may have made in the past. Instead, get angry at the abuser and at a shameful social system in which so many women wind up as sexual victims.

Teenage sexuality, adultery, abortion, and rape are all common events that are culturally taboo and therefore cause sexual shame. Rape shame persists when a victim feels that the rape was her own fault, or that her body was permanently defiled. When sexual shame is hidden deep in the unconscious, the body becomes a battleground for acting out these repressed feelings. Some women try to erase or conceal the evidence of their "shameful" past by binging, purging, or making over in order to cover up. What are the sexual traumas in your own life that have left you with shameful feelings that prevent bodylove?

No one is totally free of sexual shame. Donna, for example, was "caught" the very first time she had sex at seventeen: "My folks came home unexpectedly from a vacation. They switched on the lights and found me in bed with my boyfriend. I'll never forget the look on my father's face. I don't think he ever forgave me. It's been fifteen years, but I still get a rush of shame when I think of that terrible scene. And I still don't like to make love with the lights on."

REDUCING SHAME

In order to feel more at ease in our bodies, we all need to work on reducing shame. Your superego is the voice of conscience. Does it shout "shame on you" for touching or letting yourself be touched, now or in the past? When the id gets dominated by a punishing superego, it can't function properly as a source of sensual pleasure.

This is why Diane denies her desires, censors her sexual needs, and withdraws from intimacy into an ultrafeminine façade. "I do spend a lot on expensive jewelry and clothing," she admits. "Maybe it's an indulgence, but I feel I deserve to enjoy my looks now, after what I went through as a child." Diane also deserves to be touched with affection, but shame blocks her from "indulging" in such intimacy.

Visualization is a powerful tool for digging out the ghosts of guilt and shame that haunt your body image. You've practiced visualization in earlier chapters, so you should be able to create some spontaneous imagery on your own. Look over the following list to give you an idea of the kind of events that may still weigh heavily on your conscience:

Early sex play with friends during childhood

Masturbation

Attempted rape, actual rape, date or acquaintance rape

Having an abortion

Contracting a sexually transmitted disease

Catching your parents having sex

Getting caught by your parents

Group sex, kinky sex, or some form of "unacceptable" sex

Being a lesbian or having a homosexual experience

Cheating on a spouse or lover

None of these activities necessarily causes shame, but they often do. And there are many other sexual experiences that will apply to your personal case.

EXERCISE • Uncovering Shame

Choose an issue you want to explore further because you suspect there may be feelings of shame attached to it. Start by relaxing fully and trying out some pleasant images. Then create your own guided imagery to relive a shameful experience. Watch the details clearly and notice how you behaved and the expressions on your face. Try to remain as relaxed as possible as you repeat the visualization several times in a row to gather more detail and to experience the feelings more deeply.

Here are some follow-up questions:

- Where did you learn that this behavior was shameful?
- What precisely is wrong with it?
- Who is (was) hurt by it?
- Do you want to continue feeling ashamed of yourself or of your body?

EXERCISE • Overcoming Shame

1. *Challenging automatic thoughts.* Once you've uncovered, through visualization, some of the shameful issues in your life, you're ready to work on overcoming them. As you've seen, cognitive errors create negative feelings. This is especially true of shame. By challenging the automatic irrational thoughts that keep shame alive, you can gradually reduce its harmful effect on your body image.

Three types of cognitive errors in particular tend to arouse shame: (1) personalizing an event, (2) exaggerating its meaning, and (3) reasoning from your own emotions (see page 39). Use the triple-column technique to challenge the cognitive errors that lead to shame. For several weeks, make a list of the automatic thoughts you may have about your body that make you feel ashamed. Then try to figure out which cognitive errors (personalizing, exaggerating) trap you in these recurrent feelings of shame. Work to challenge your irrational thoughts with good counterarguments. Here are some examples from a woman who has had a venereal disease and felt guilty and ashamed because of it.

AUTOMATIC THOUGHT	COGNITIVE ERROR	RATIONAL COUNTERARGUMENT
"Getting chlamydia was my own fault. I should never have been that stupid and careless."	Personalizing	"Sexually transmitted diseases are so common in the culture that it's hard to escape them. I didn't do anything that I thought was wrong."
"I'll probably never enjoy sex again. No one will want me if they know."	Exaggerating the meaning	"The disease is over. I'm the same person I was before. In time I'll get over these feelings."
"I feel ugly and contaminated. Even my face shows that I've had VD."	Emotional reasoning	"Just because I feel bad doesn't mean I look any different. What I feel isn't the same as what others feel about me."

2. *Sharing secrets.* An important antidote to shame is self-disclosure. By speaking the unspeakable, you can conquer its hold on you and reduce your fear of being discovered. Psychotherapy is often effective simply because it provides a safe place to share shameful secrets. But you don't always need a therapist. This principle works in other safe situations as well. Most women experience a surprising sense of relief once they tell about the parts of the body or the events in their life that cause shame. When sexual secrets get aired and shared, the consequences are rarely as awful as imagined. Take some time to think about the body secrets in your life and use the following questions as a guide.

- What shameful things are you hiding from everyone, or from certain someones?
- Why are these things so shameful? Be specific. Define exactly what you think is wrong with your body or your behavior.
- What do you think would happen if you exposed that reality? Would the consequences really be worse than the shame you're now carrying around?
- Who can you trust to share these shameful secrets? Who do you *need* to tell in order to relieve the pressure?

Kathleen confided the following:

> I'd been married for nearly two years before I was able to tell my husband that I had an abortion as a teenager. From the time I first met him, I dreaded that he might find out because he has strong feelings about abortion. I was also worried that I might never be able to get pregnant again. Whenever we made love, the guilt and shame of that abortion welled up. I kept punishing myself for it. Finally I confided in a cousin who I really trusted. She urged me to see a particular priest who was tremendously helpful. He gave me the courage to tell my husband. It wasn't easy—for me or for him. But it's been a great relief. My body feels clean again, and I think my marriage may even be stronger than it was.

In most large communities, there are numerous support groups for incest survivors, herpes sufferers, rape victims, postabortion trauma, and many other common problems. A clergyman or physician can direct you to such groups. Or call your local mental health association for information about your special problem. These support groups provide a safe haven for sharing secrets and finding answers. By reaching out verbally you'll discover that friends and loved ones can accept you, despite your hidden secret. Sharing your "shameful" past with them creates a new, intimate bond. And strong social bonds are essential for building self-esteem.

CLOSE ENCOUNTERS

Chimps are social animals like us. They, too, reach toward each other to show affection and to make up after fights. Chimps spend hours at "mutual grooming," poking and picking over each others' fur as they create social bonds within the group. Being social means touching physically as well as verbally. As we've seen, however, society often inhibits us from touching spontaneously.

It seems as if we humans have "dehumanized" our grooming rituals and lost the social aspects that are so important to other primates. For us, being well-groomed means being neat and tidy, not well-touched by others who are personally connected to us. Few of us use grooming to show affection or to satisfy their need for personal contact. The majority of women in the Bodylove Survey said that their beauty routines rarely involved other people touching their bodies.

Do your beauty routines involve other people touching your body
(i.e.: manicure, shampoo, massage)?

1%	SEVERAL TIMES A WEEK
5%	WEEKLY
21%	EVERY FEW WEEKS
14%	MONTHLY
59%	RARELY

Perhaps we should follow the chimps' example and use grooming rituals to reach out and draw closer: by washing or coloring each
other's hair, by giving manicures and perms, by playfully making
each other over as adolescent girls do. These cosmetic "excuses" for
touching would feel especially good to the ill, the elderly, and the
handicapped who are so often deprived of human touch and who
may view their bodies negatively.

I gave my mother a pedicure machine for her last birthday. We
use it to play "beauty shop" together, mutually grooming each
other's feet by rubbing off the wear and tear and rubbing in some
soothing lotion. It's a way for us to keep intimately in touch.
Grooming others exposes you to the great variety of human bodies
and to the realities of aging. It builds tolerance for how bodies really
look as well as acceptance of your own unique features.

Are massages and facials part of your beauty routine? Why not
treat yourself to one as a special sensory reinforcement. An hour of
touch from a professional masseuse is as nourishing as dining out
once a month. It's a rich sensual dessert that you can buy, or can
get free from a friend, lover, spouse, child, or parent. If you find
yourself reluctant to ask, try using the excuse of a bad back or a
crimp in your neck to "justify" a request for some personal touch.
Or offer to give a massage to a loved one. It's an offer that few
people can refuse. Giving touch can feel just as satisfying as getting it.

STEPPING THROUGH RESISTANCE

You may find it difficult to get back in touch with your natural
sensuality, despite the pleasure it can bring. It's hard to break free
of a controlling superego that won't allow sensual pleasure; it's hard

to push out the boundaries of body image beyond the ornamental and to move from beauty bound to pleasure bound. The anxiety and sexual shame that prevents bodylove also causes strong resistance to change.

If you chip away at resistance long enough, however, it does break down, bit by bit. Little bits of change are less frightening because they still allow you to feel in control. Eventually small steps *can* yield big gains. Leo Buscaglia recommends what he calls a one-inch exercise: learning to love yourself one inch at a time. Think about how your resistance tactics prevent you from enjoying your sensuality. How could you slowly inch around them?

Diane used procrastination and avoidance to keep herself safely stuck. "No time" was her habitual excuse for not getting around to behavioral assignments. Working together, we developed a series of small steps that helped her tap into her sensuality. Beginning with a goal of just five minutes a day, Diane tried to connect sensual time with beauty time, since she already had committed many hours to beautifying. For example, she took a moment to massage her head while washing her hair and she practiced visualization while taking a shower. Diane decided to eliminate one hair appointment per month and substitute a body massage instead. Gradually, her "no time" excuse disappeared as she began to really enjoy her time out for sensuality.

Joyce, on the other hand, found that her resistance dissolved quite unexpectedly one day when she experienced a sudden shift in body image:

> The belief that my skin was too dark had really ground its way into my head when I was a child. Then last summer I started walking every day before work. I concentrated on tuning in to my body sensations. I was swinging my arms, enjoying the morning sun, when I got this rush of pleasure, thinking "my God, this arm is a beautiful color." I reached over to touch my skin in the sunlight and to really accept it as mine. Then I thought, how strange, at forty-one to feel good about something I'd been ashamed of for so long.

This kind of revelation at mid-life is not uncommon. Age is often kind to self-image, as we'll see in the next chapter. Many women seem to outgrow their shame and find self-acceptance with maturity.

CHECKLIST FOR SENSUAL GROWTH

While you work to become a more sensuous woman by adding sensuality to your body image, here are some key points to remember:

1. *Get more touch in your everyday life.* Find time to touch children, pets, and friends. Shake hands longer, hug relatives tighter, try mutual grooming and massage. Most of all, use the power of self-touch to touch up your body image.

2. *Pay attention to sensual needs.* Cultivate a healthy appetite for smelling, tasting, rocking, sucking, and relaxing. Use these sensory rewards to raise your body image out of a visual rut.

3. *Lift the barrier between sensuality and sexuality.* You need both of them to feel intimate with your own flesh. The more intimately you know your body, the more you can trust it enough to share it with others.

4. *Work to reduce body shame and sexual shame.* Use visualization to relive the traumas of the past and uncover the origins of shame. Share your "shameful" secrets with others and challenge the automatic thoughts that keep shame alive.

5. *Pursue sensual satisfaction as passionately as you pursue beauty.* The sensual woman within you can help keep the ornamental woman from dominating your self-image.

In order to receive love from another, you have to respect that person's choice of you as a worthy and attractive lover. Your body is the vehicle that can carry you down the road to self-love. Don't be afraid to allow yourself the sensual pleasures that nature intended to nurture body image. You're entitled to enjoy your body, not merely to display it as a beauty object. So try to worry a bit less about how good your body looks, and concentrate a bit more on how good it can feel.

TIMELY MATTERS

At what age do most women reach their peak of physical attractiveness?

At what age do most women feel best about their bodies?

How do your current feelings about your body compare with your feelings five years ago?

MUCH BETTER
SOMEWHAT BETTER
THE SAME
SOMEWHAT WORSE
MUCH WORSE

What do you think your feelings about your body will be five years from now?

MUCH BETTER
SOMEWHAT BETTER
THE SAME
SOMEWHAT WORSE
MUCH WORSE

I have everything I had 20 years ago, only it's all a little bit lower.
—GYPSY ROSE LEE

I HAVE good and bad news for you on the topic of aging. First, be reassured that there *is* life after youth. Not only life, but beauty, sensuality, and self-esteem, for time is on your side when it comes to bodylove. Growing older can mean feeling better about your body image.

The bad news is that life after youth isn't easy. As Bette Davis put it, "old age is no place for sissies." Looksism and ageism combine with a cult of youth that causes trouble. You'll find this mixed bag of news in the pages ahead, along with myths and facts about "older women."

This chapter isn't just for those of you who are past your prime, whenever that may be. It's for anyone who is facing a "big" birthday with trepidation. It's for those who are busy enjoying youth and who never give a thought to age. It's for women of every age, for we all must learn to live in a changing body. And we can learn to love it, even when it wrinkles.

I know that loving an aging body isn't always easy. It's hard to watch youth slip away in the mirror and realize that you're no longer growing up but growing old. Eventually the aging process forces you to give up an idealized forever-young image of yourself. How you feel about your aging image certainly influences your behavior and your self-esteem. "Dying is one thing, but looking awful for the next thirty years is even worse," declared one anxious candidate for middle age. Her anxiety may disrupt her relationships, inhibit her sexual expression, and limit the goals she sets for herself.

Self-acceptance must include the future self as well as the present one. If you can't imagine yourself growing gray, or if the thought of middle-age spread fills you with body loathing, then you're hiding from reality. By exploring the causes of age anxiety and learning some coping strategies, you can gain enough confidence to age more beautifully.

As Judith Viorst describes so insightfully in her book *Necessary Losses,* we grow by leaving parts of our life behind and letting go of them. Our losses feel threatening as we face an uncertain future. But

160

the losses of life are generally balanced by some gains. For instance, by giving up the tomboy role, you can then move on to the pleasures of adolescence. Or by letting go of your parents, you can explore the freedom of adulthood. A youthful body image is one of the prized possessions we have to give up in life, explains Viorst. Yet despite the loss of youthful beauty, bodylove can not only endure but help us move on to the next stage of growth.[1]

A WRINKLE IN TIME

After forty, wrote Camus, we become responsible for our own faces. What does this mean? How responsible are you for the necessary losses that age inflicts on beauty?

> *Peggy:* "I always thought that forty was over the hill. Now that I *am* forty, the landscape seems to have shifted."

> *Miriam:* "If I ever get to forty, I'll be so old I can get away with everything. Get fat, wear purple socks and feathered hats. I can look outrageous and no one will care."

> *Katha Pollitt:* "The funny thing about getting older is that I like it just fine. I'm happier now than I've ever been in my life; and all my younger-older-middle-age-elderly-mature friends feel exactly the same way."[2]

> *Ruth at 70:* "To me, forty is like springtime. A woman has years of good life ahead of her. To me a woman of forty is still a baby."

> *Gretchen:* "I'm almost forty and it's scary. I still look okay, but I'm afraid of being rejected or ignored. I'd hate to wake up one day and feel that I don't count anymore."

"My husband gave me a full-length mirror for my fortieth birthday to remind me I'd better keep an eye on my looks," says Elizabeth. How should you (do you) eye your looks after youth? With a watchful eye . . . a critical eye? When will you (did you) start to feel anxious about looking older?

Sometimes age anxiety begins quite early. Teen magazines warn girls that, "You're never too young to start worrying about preserving your looks." And they do worry. When I asked some fifteen-year-olds why they felt they absolutely had to wear makeup to class each day, one explained, "Because of these awful bags under my eyes . . . and to cover up all the little lines." These girls were already eyeing their faces for signs of wrinkles.

You've probably noticed that wrinkles are more than just skin deep. They bring us face to face with reality—the reality that some men do leave older wives for unwrinkled replacements, and the reality that some bosses do want pretty young secretaries. Therefore, like responsible housekeepers, we try to iron away the creases or cover them with makeup that gives the illusion of permanent press. "I always expected to grow old gracefully," says Lillian, "but now I'm busy fighting it as hard as I can."

Chronologically, we all age at the same rate of one birthday per year. But aging is also social, psychological, and biological. It's a state of mind as well as a state of matter. Two forty-year-olds may differ in physical age: Lois is vigorous and healthy while Sue is tired and out of shape. They may differ in appearance age: Lois easily passes for thirty while Sue is mistaken for fifty. They may differ in life stage: Lois is recently married and expecting her first child while Sue is already a grandmother. They may differ in psychological age: Lois feels like a young woman while Sue feels like she's getting old. Appearance is only one of many factors that influence body image as you age. But it is an important one.

While time is abstract, its effect on your body is all too concrete. Hair gradually loses its color. Skin becomes less elastic and weight increases as metabolism slows down. These changes force you to revise your body image, whether or not you're ready.

Often, body image lags behind the physical changes that occur. One day I saw a middle-aged woman reflected in a store window. She seemed to be walking alongside me when I suddenly realized, "Hey, that must be me." And another time I awoke from a dream, startled by the dream image of myself with reading glasses. After three years of wearing them, my glasses had finally become part of my unconscious state, signaling a shift in body image.

Ingrid Bergman once remarked, "You know, one looks at herself in the mirror every morning, and she doesn't see the difference. She doesn't realize that she is aging. But then she finds a friend who was young with her, and the friend isn't young anymore, and all of a sudden, like a slap on her eyes, she remembers that she, too, isn't young anymore."

As is true of any loving relationship, bodylove has to evolve to survive the aging process. This means readjusting your relationship with your own changing body. As time passes you're forced to revise your ideal about proper weight, about the kind of fashions you choose, about the way you decorate and display yourself. Betty explains, "I used to wear short skirts and high heels to show off my great legs. But now there's less to show off. So I'm wearing longer styles and darker stockings. I don't expect my legs to be noticed anymore, and that's starting to feel okay." Unless you revise, body-love can turn into body loathing.

Remaking your body image over and over is a life-long challenge. Viorst describes it as accepting the necessary loss of one's own younger self, "the self that thought it would be unwrinkled and invulnerable and immortal." If you cultivate the skill of readjusting while you're "younger," it comes more easily when you're "older."

AGE LABELS

What exactly do terms like "older" and "younger," really mean? Where are the boundaries between youth and middle age? That depends on whom you ask. One popular definition of an older woman is someone who's at least ten years older than you are right now. While beginning work on this chapter I accidentally typed "muddle" age and then laughed at the irony of the error. Indeed, age labels are muddled and messy.

There's no denying, however, that age labels do exist and are also quite important. What you call yourself does affect how you see yourself. Here's an exercise to help you become more aware of how you use age labels to identify yourself and others. First review these age-related terms:

Girl, young woman, adult, woman in the prime of life

Lady, middle-aged woman, woman of a certain age

Older woman, mature woman, aging woman

Senior citizen, old lady, Miss, Mrs., Ms.

Now consider what each of these words or titles means to you. What are the age boundaries that define each one, in your opinion?

Which of these labels fits you comfortably right now and which ones don't seem to fit at all? To see how you feel about these terms, try using each one in a phrase such as:

I am a . . .

I look like a . . .

You can further examine your attitudes and anxieties by completing the following sentences spontaneously and rapidly:

In terms of appearance, younger women . . .

In terms of appearance, older women . . .

In general, women are most attractive around the age of _____ because . . .

After "a certain age," most women become . . .

Jeanne found this exercise to be an eye-opener. "Without thinking, I wrote, 'In terms of appearance, young women look cute and girlish.' But you know, I always object when grown women are called girls. Especially when mature men talk about the girls they date. At thirty-six, I don't want to be one of the girls. Yet my response showed me I'm not finished with that term. I've always been called cute. Now I wonder what will happen when I'm too old to look cute anymore."

Vivian wrote: "After a certain age women become a little frantic about their looks." When I asked her why, she replied, "My best friend had her eyelids fixed last summer. She's not even forty, and I thought she was crazy when she told me she was going to do it. But when I saw how great she looked afterward it made me nervous. I felt like calling the surgeon myself. I guess I'm just not ready for middle age, so I try not to think about it. But when I do, I get a little frantic."

Our ideas about age labels come in part from our experiences with family members and from the attitudes of our friends. Check with your mother or other relatives of her generation to see how they feel about being "older women." Ask your children when they think middle age begins or ask your husband when the prime of life ends. As you compare your own feelings with theirs, think about how looksism and ageism combine to create the stereotypes that underlie these age labels.

"Some women to see you, Anne."

Drawing by Handelsman; © 1978 The New Yorker Magazine, Inc.

THE CULT OF YOUTH, THE CURSE OF AGE

Our ideas about the look of age are also shaped by media images. It's clear who counts most in commercial messages: those who look thin, pretty, sexy, and young. The first Miss America was only sixteen. And most beauty contestants today are in their early twenties, which reinforces the belief that female beauty peaks at that age.

Our culture equates looking good with looking young. When judges rated photographs of various kinds of people, they consistently picked white, teenage, female faces as the most attractive.[3] Whether we like it or not, we're all judged against that ideal. Susan Sontag observes that, "Only one standard of female beauty is sanctioned: the girl . . . thus, women are trained to want to continue looking like girls forever."

And so we apply cosmetic magic to impersonate the full, red lips of an infant, the pink cheeks of a toddler, and the wide eyes of a schoolgirl. Advertisers ask, "Can you compete with your little girl's looks?" and "Which are the mother's hands, which are the daughter's?" The message is clear: *don't grow up*. But of course we do. Geneen Roth observes that:[4]

> Once upon a time, I was beautiful. My hair was thick and dark and glossy. My skin was smooth and soft as a ripe peach . . . my mouth was dark pink and my teeth white and even. My eyes were large and clear, a deep blue-green. Beautiful. Unfortunately, I was four years old at the time. It's been downhill ever since.

Actually, the pleasure of being admired as a youthful beauty only sets us up for the pain of being rejected as an aging ugly.

The cult of youth artificially divides life into younger and older stages. These oversimplified categories feed the stereotypes of lookism and ageism. Young equals pretty equals good, while old equals ugly equals bad. Recall that thinking in extremes was one of the cognitive errors we discussed earlier. Splitting life into just two opposite extremes puts great pressure on you to remain in the younger half (or at least to pretend you're still there).

In addition to the child-woman, a second image has recently been added to the youth cult. This is the mature model who's frozen in time—the Jane Fonda, Joan Collins, Elizabeth Taylor, Raquel Welch version of middle-aged beauty that lasts indefinitely. Journalist Ellen Goodman labels this the cult of mid-life beauty. "The central notion of the middle-aged show and sell routine is that if she can look that good at fifty, so can you," writes Goodman.

But do these mid-life wonder women really make you feel better about yourself? Or do they only pressure you to preserve a girlish image? Miriam confides, "I'm exactly as old as Elizabeth Taylor. I have to admit I was secretly delighted a few years ago when she gained all that weight. But now she's thin and gorgeous again and I feel ashamed that I've given up so soon."

There's an insidious mixed message beneath this new middle-aged model. You're given permission to get older but not to look it, to live but not to change. When Gloria Steinem announced, "This is what fifty looks like," Ellen Goodman responded, "not necessarily."

The commercial implications of the youth cult are obvious. The greater your anxiety about looking older, the greater your desire for products to keep you looking younger. But the social and political implications of the youth cult are more subtle. When you're packaged in an adolescent image, you're less likely to be taken seriously, and you're also denied the vision of your own maturity. Remember that aging is determined by social as well as physical factors. The cult of youth further concentrates women's social power in the ornamental role. Yet it's only during and after middle age that most women are free to move beyond the constraints of child rearing, and to explore the full power of their potential. Because of the youth cult, women are less likely to embrace the possibility of feeling powerful in the second half of their life.*

When our sample was asked to pick the age when women reach their peak of attractiveness, the average age given by the group was thirty-three. This number reflects the cult of youth, but it also shows that prime time today lasts at least into the early thirties. Moreover, there was a distinct age trend in the responses to this question that is quite important. Whereas younger women picked twenty-six as the age of peak attractiveness, older women chose thirty-nine—a highly significant thirteen-year difference. Only 3 percent of the younger group felt that women reached their peak of attractiveness after the age of forty, whereas 44 percent of the older group felt this was true. These findings suggest that the cult of youth may diminish as the general population grows older.

How do your own feelings about the prime age of physical attractiveness for women compare with the sample? And where do you fit into this equation in terms of your present age?

At what age do most women reach their peak of physical attractiveness?

YOUNGER GROUP (UNDER 30)	AGE 26
MIDDLE GROUP (30–45)	AGE 34
OLDER GROUP (OVER 45)	AGE 39
TOTAL SAMPLE AVERAGE	AGE 33

---

*In order to analyze the survey questions by age, I divided the subjects into three parts: (1) younger women under 30, (2) middle group ages 30–45, and (3) older women over 45. I use the terms *younger, middle,* and *older* to refer to these three groups when presenting the research. However, I don't consider them definitive labels. Many women of 35 see themselves as young women. And 50-year-olds don't really belong in the same older category as their mothers of 70.

Another interesting age trend emerged from the Bodylove Survey. Although our sample believed that beauty peaks in the thirties, they thought that women feel best about their bodies at a somewhat younger age—during the late twenties. Here again the older the age of the sample, the older the age of their responses.

At what age do most women feel best about their bodies?

YOUNGER GROUP	AGE 23
MIDDLE GROUP	AGE 27
OLDER GROUP	AGE 31
TOTAL SAMPLE	AGE 27

If you, too, believe that women feel best about their bodies before age thirty, please remind yourself that this is part of the cult of youth, which assumes that being young equals being pretty equals feeling good about your looks. In fact, older women report feeling just as satisfied with their appearance as do younger women.

THE BRIGHT SIDE OF AGING

The surprising good news is that body image can withstand the test of time. Studies show that you'll probably be as satisfied with your looks in five years as you are right now. And that's a new wrinkle on the beauty horizon. Here are some myths and facts about age and appearance that show the bright side of aging.[5]

MYTH: As time passes we become increasingly unhappy with our physical appearance.

FACT: *Ratings of the body as a whole and of specific parts remain fairly consistent over time. When people in their twenties, thirties, and forties were asked how they felt about their bodies, no differences were found. All age groups seemed equally critical of their body image.*

MYTH: With age, we're more likely to want to make over our features.

FACT: *The desire to remodel one's looks declines with age. When asked which features they would like to remodel, young women chose a greater number of features than did older women.*

MYTH: With age we become more self-conscious about our looks.

FACT: *Self-consciousness tends to decline progressively with age. The older the woman, the less self-conscious she feels about her appearance.*

MYTH: One's level of attractiveness goes up and down periodically over the life span.

FACT: *Physical attractiveness does decline with age, as measured by outside observers. But compared to others of the same age, one's relative attractiveness tends to remain fairly stable. Once pretty, always pretty is the general rule that holds (especially for facial features, less so for body characteristics).*

All in all, we seem to become less critical and more accepting of our appearance as we mature into middle age. A sixty-year-old bookkeeper explained, "At my age I don't worry very much about whether I like my looks. . . . It's just one of those things that's part of me, so I simply don't dwell on it." Yvonne, at fifty-one, remarked, "I've come to realize that some things can't be changed . . . and really shouldn't be. Because they make me who I am. My face is no longer my fortune . . . it's my signature."

It's not that appearance stops being important for older women, but they typically gain self-assurance as they mature beyond mid-life. And this, as we've seen, is one of the most crucial factors in determining body image. Despite the physical changes older women must face, they usually feel quite good about themselves. Recall that body image and self-esteem are strongly related. Body image is generally positive when self-esteem is high, regardless of a person's actual appearance. A positive body image seems to be an important component of aging successfully.

The Bodylove Survey confirms the good news about aging and body image. When asked how their feelings about their body today compared with their feelings five years ago, three out of four women said they felt the same or better. A higher percentage of older women reported feeling the same about their body as five years ago, suggesting that body image tends to stabilize as time passes.

How do your current feelings about your body compare with your feelings five years ago?

	YOUNGER	MIDDLE	OLDER	WHOLE GROUP
MUCH BETTER	17%	16%	15%	16%
SOMEWHAT BETTER	27%	19%	11%	19%
THE SAME	31%	37%	57%	42%
SOMEWHAT WORSE	25%	27%	15%	23%
MUCH WORSE	0	1%	2%	1%

On the other hand, young women were much more optimistic about their future looks. Nearly half of the younger women in our sample expected to feel somewhat or much better about their bodies five years from now, compared to only 20 percent of the older women. Still, an impressive 84 percent of the older women expected to feel the same or better about their bodies five years from now. And relatively few of them expected to feel much worse.

What do you think your feelings about your body will be five years from now?

	YOUNGER	MIDDLE	OLDER	WHOLE GROUP
MUCH BETTER	19%	11%	9%	13%
SOMEWHAT BETTER	30%	27%	12%	23%
THE SAME	48%	54%	62%	55%
SOMEWHAT WORSE	3%	7%	14%	8%
MUCH WORSE	0	0	2%	1%

Since weight is such an important component of body image, it's interesting that the younger and older groups were about equally satisfied (or dissatisfied) with their weight. This was true, despite the natural tendency for most women to gradually gain weight with age.

Are you satisfied with your current weight?

	YOUNGER	MIDDLE	OLDER
VERY SATISFIED	19%	17%	17%
SOMEWHAT SATISFIED	27%	36%	32%
SOMEWHAT DISSATISFIED	27%	30%	40%
HIGHLY DISSATISFIED	28%	17%	11%

Overall, the Bodylove Survey supports the conclusion of other researchers that body image is surprisingly resilient over time. For most people, anxiety over loss of looks turns out to be worse than the reality. We can therefore gain an important new perspective on the beauty of aging simply by talking to family and friends who are ahead of us in the life cycle. How do they come to terms with the look of age? How have their ideas about "prime time" evolved over the years? Here are some comments that are typical of those who have adjusted well to their changing looks.

At sixty-five, Theresa had this to say: "When I was younger I was considered more attractive than I am now. I no longer feel as though people look at me and say 'Oh, wow, what a beautiful woman' the way they used to. And I feel sorry for them because really I'm a much more interesting person now than I was then. But that's their problem."[6]

Elissa Melamed reflects on her own self-image in her book *Mirror, Mirror:* "I realize that I like what my face has become. I could no longer conceive of it without its wrinkles. Anyone who is going to take me on is going to have to take on all of me, I'm afraid—with a full complement of years and the signs of their passage."[7] Trudy declares at forty-five: "My life is for me. If anyone says my dress is too short or my jewelry is too flashy I couldn't care less. It's time to look and act the way I want. I've reached a point that I don't give a damn about what other people think."

The sense of assurance that comes with age generally seems to add to a woman's strength and self-image. "One of the advantages of aging," says Marvine at seventy, "is that you can take or leave excitement of any kind. Which means that for the first time in your life you're truly independent, and that adds to your aura."

THE DARK SIDE OF AGING

But not all women are able to age so gracefully. The bad news is that growing older isn't always easy. Looksism plus ageism create a set of biased attitudes and sober statistics that creep into our lives no matter how good we feel about ourselves. With the loss of youth and beauty, some of us lose our positions in the world as well. The ultimate in a throwaway society is the disposable older woman who has been displaced as a wife, a homemaker, or a worker.

Loss of looks can threaten relationships. "One of your husband's basic needs is for you to be physically attractive to him," Mirabel Morgan warns the would-be Total Woman. "The outer shell of you is what the real estate people call 'curb appeal'—how the house looks from the outside. Is your curb appeal this week what it was five years ago?" asks Morgan. She also implies that you may wind up on the curb unless you quickly spruce up.[8]

Ironically, it's pretty women who have the most to worry about and the most to lose. When the happiness of middle-aged women was compared with their attractiveness many years earlier, an interesting finding emerged. Those women who had been the prettiest in college suffered more adjustment problems during middle age than those who were plainer looking when young. If you were one of the pretty young things, you may be especially vulnerable to the loss of beauty as you age.[9]

Some pretty women suffer a so-called narcissistic injury as they lose their youthful looks. They grieve over their fading beauty, as they would over the loss of any love object. Take Vivian, for example. "All my life I've felt so special wherever I went," she explains. "It came as a shock one day when I realized that I was no longer the belle of the ball. And that I never would be again." Vivian discovered that loss of beauty is one of the hazards of having it. Thus, pretty women can get tripped up by the transiency of their own attractiveness.

A young woman who relies heavily on her good looks may fail to cultivate her other talents to the fullest and then find that there's less to fall back on when beauty fades. Recall how Joyce concluded early in childhood that her dark skin meant she would never be pretty. "I knew I had to be better at everything else," she explains. "Now I feel I have a lot more going for me because I never expected to use my looks to get ahead."

Although she had not yet decided what she wanted to do with **heR** Life, Peggy's body had already Made up **its** Mind

DOUBLE STANDARDS—DOUBLE TROUBLE

Additional bad news is that men and women don't age at the same rates. Time hangs more heavily on female faces. Despite a life expectancy that is about eight years longer, middle-aged women are viewed as relatively older than their male contemporaries.

Looksism combines with sexism to create a so-called double standard of aging. This is evident in research comparing the attractiveness of older men and older women. When photos of the same person across the life span are rated, attractiveness is judged to decline more rapidly for women than for men. Moreover, ratings of a man's masculinity remain fairly constant over the years, whereas ratings of a woman's femininity are perceived to diminish rapidly between youth and middle age.[10] On her fortieth birthday, Grace Kelly complained that although forty was a terrific age for a man, it was torture for a woman, since it meant "the beginning of the end." It's not surprising that a woman may feel tortured at the same age that a man feels terrific. His star is still rising at forty, while hers may feel as if it's beginning to set.

"My husband is ten years older than I," observes Diane. "In the past year I've seen his tummy pouch and hairline go, but I see, too, that he looks more attractive and, that damn word, 'distinguished' as he ages. I keep seeing these lines and puffs on my face, and on me it doesn't look distinguished. I'm only thirty-two and already buying the propaganda that I'm losing my face."

The double standard of aging rests partly on social concepts of gender: the masculine role as instrumental and the feminine role as ornamental. Many women say they don't mind getting older; it's looking older and being treated older that gets them down.

Ann explains, "It makes me angry and frustrated to see my looks slipping away from me just when I'm beginning to feel like a whole person." And Cindy complains, "I work free-lance in a business that's very age conscious. I'm now thirty-nine, but mostly I deal with people younger than myself. Whenever I have to see a new client I worry whether I look young enough. At some point I know I'll start to lose jobs just because they don't hire middle-aged women to do this kind of stuff. It doesn't seem fair because my work really gets better each year."

These women feel as if they're being pushed over the hill into no-man's-land, considered old simply because they no longer look young. Elissa Melamed describes the phenomenon that faces women beyond a certain age: "We are put into another category by the eyes of others. What these eyes tell us is that they will no longer mirror us. The eyes make no contact: they glance and slide off as if they had seen an inanimate object."[11]

AGING YOUR BODY IMAGE

Being overlooked instead of looked over only adds to age anxiety. The silence of feeling unseen can be painful after a lifetime of listening for the compliment that confirms your power to please. You may not realize how much that power means to you until it starts to wane. "A whole week in Rome and I wasn't pinched once," complains a friend.

Vivian recalls a recent family wedding where she felt unseen and let down:

> I found the perfect dress and thought I looked terrific when we left for the affair. But my fifteen-year-old daughter had also found the perfect dress. All night relatives kept coming over to tell me how gorgeous she'd become. Of course I was pleased and proud for her, but also a bit let down because I didn't get the attention I'm so used to getting.

Vivian must learn to accept the loss of that kind of attention, and watch her daughter move into the limelight. She can ease herself into a new stage of growth by rehearsing it.

The following exercise helps you achieve a clearer view of your own body growing older. By rehearsing tomorrow's image today, you can reduce anxiety about it. There's a fundamental sense of self that transcends the necessary losses of aging. Your body image today is part of that continuity, and it includes your memories of the past as well as your expectations of the future. The power of visualization lets you create a filmstrip in your mind of what you may look like someday. Through imagery you adapt in advance, so to speak. This makes the losses that are inherent to the aging process easier to accept.

EXERCISE • Trying on Older Images

1. Begin by getting comfortable, clearing your mind, and taking a few deep breaths for relaxation. Imagine that you're facing a blank wall with a big picture frame on it. Project your current self-portrait onto this empty frame. See yourself just as you are today.

2. Change the time frame and visualize yourself at age twenty, perhaps as a student sitting in class. Notice your features, your weight, the texture of your skin. Try to imagine how that young woman feels about her body. Does she look grown up or still like an adolescent?

3. Add a decade of living. At thirty, notice how your appearance has changed. Are you blooming with life or weighted down by it?

Have you reached your prime of attractiveness at thirty, and are you content with how you look?

4. Move ahead to forty, the midpoint of life. Clearly visualize your features getting older. The lines of maturity are starting to show on your face. Are you past your prime or still moving toward it? Are you as attractive as you were a decade ago?

5. Picture your fiftieth birthday portrait. At the half-century mark you've reached middle age. Do you look it? Notice the wrinkles that define you, and the ones that disturb you. Which parts have shifted under the weight of time and which parts are the same as ever?

6. Roll the film ahead another decade and scan your sixty-year-old body from top to toe. How has it changed? Your hair may be thinner and your hips may be broader. Does your skin tell a rich tale and do your eyes still sparkle?

7. Try one final image at seventy. You're growing old, but may still live another twenty years. Which parts of you look strong, and which look frail? Are the expressions on your face the same ones you've worn all your life?

8. Now assemble all these images and project them onto the picture frame, one at a time. Watch as they pass before you in sequence, starting with your youthful face at twenty. After you've run them forward through the decades, rewind them going backward in time. Notice the continuity of body image even as it changes. Finally, review the whole montage by lining up the images in a row, like a portrait gallery.

These guided imagery instructions were all too brief. They're only meant to give you an idea of the exercise. When you practice it, be sure to go slowly enough to let your imagination fill in the details. Study each portrait of yourself until you are really comfortable with it and are able to clearly see the changes in your appearance that time dictates.

Angela, at thirty-five, described her reaction to this exercise: "I was enjoying the different views of myself until I got to age sixty. Then the picture frame just went blank for a while and I couldn't see myself at all. My mother's face suddenly flashed into view. She's now sixty-eight—an old-fashioned Italian mother who's rather plain. People always tell me I look a lot like her. And I guess I have trouble with the idea that I'll wind up like that. Though I have to admit, she doesn't seem to worry about looking older. I'm sure I'll have more trouble with it than she does."

Nancy had a different reaction: "I'm pushing fifty and feeling pretty confident about it. What surprised me was how much better I look today than I did at twenty or thirty. When I visualized those early images I was disappointed with what I saw. My face seemed kind of bland—like part of me wasn't really there. But I loved the older portraits . . . and I went on to imagine myself at eighty and ninety, to see how much living I could paint on my face. This exercise made me feel that I was really still a young woman compared to what I'll become someday."

Review your own responses to the visualization exercise:

- Were certain ages harder to see than others? If so, do you understand why?
- How did you feel as you saw yourself growing older? Do you think these feelings are based on truth or on myths about aging?
- Did you discover any "ancestral ghosts"—images of your mother or other relatives—that are part of your expectations for the future?

Take this exercise one final step and think about the elderly people who inhabit your inner scrapbook of memories. Most of us had no trouble loving the wrinkled faces of our grandparents when we were little. Recalling those warm feelings for our aging relatives can help us see our own future images as equally lovable.

PROTECTION THROUGH DECEPTION

As you face the loss of your youthful body, a new form of shame may develop: not sexual shame, not fat shame, but age shame. Few of us escape it unscathed, and some of us start lying to cover it up.

Age deception is part of the feminine mystique that's learned early in life. We make up our ages as we make up our faces, hoping to be seen as something we're not. Five-year-olds practice it when they use their makeup sets to pretend they're twelve.

Good girls are taught to please others. One way to please is simply to look pleasing. A pretty face is a pleasure to have around. Conversely, there's shame in looking "unpleasantly" old, shame in watching your role as an ornament slip away. The desire to be the "right age" has a special urgency for a woman it never has for a man, explains Susan Sontag. "Most men experience getting older with regret or apprehension. But most women experience it even more painfully with shame."

Not asking a woman's age, and not telling after a certain point, has become a universal joke. Be honest. Have you ever lied about your age? By mid-life those who do fib only hope they look young enough to pass. "Why should I tell my age when I don't look it?" says Margie. "If I have the choice I don't let on. But I don't exactly lie, either. I say 'I'm older than you think.' I find it intrusive when someone asks my age. It's none of their business." When Molly Yard (who is over sixty) was elected president of the National Organization for Women, she refused to answer questions about her age.

Sometimes, those who do answer honestly are made to feel as if they shouldn't. One actress reported the following after meeting with an agent: "She asked me my age. When I told her forty-nine—I never lie about my age, why should I?—she said in perfect seriousness, 'At forty-nine a comeback is still possible.' I said, 'Comeback! What do you mean comeback? I never left!' "[12]

If you're busy trying to look younger and not be treated older, you can get out of step with yourself. One day I overheard a friend say, "I never thought I'd do it, but I've started to lie about my age. And now I feel as ashamed of lying as I do about looking so old." Another day I overheard myself say, "What a shame. It takes me twice as long to look half as good as I used to." Shame is a powerful motive. And so we find ourselves buying into the cult of youth to protect ourselves from the shame of being seen as "too old." Gradually the distortion becomes part of our self-deception and we start to forget who we really are.

MODELS OF MATURITY

It's no wonder that age deception comes so naturally when we hear constant messages that encourage it:

"Are premature signs of age making you look older than you really are?"

"Nature is forcing you to make a decision—gray hair or Loving Care?"

"How is your face in general? Wrinkled? Put your hands to your temples and push up and back. Don't you look better?"

The media message is simple: pretty women don't look old. While actors may age into distinguished leading men, actresses often find themselves unemployable once they look sexually implausible. Joanne Woodward complains that husband Paul Newman gets handsomer every year while she only gets older.

An analysis of magazine ads between 1950 and 1980 showed that three-fourths of the women appeared to be under thirty years of age, while only 4 percent looked over forty. And a study of news anchorpersons found that nearly half the men but only 3 percent of the women were over age forty.[13] Media images are seductive. Unless we actively counteract them, they take control of our concepts of how people are supposed to look. We need more realistic exposure to wonderful older faces—models of successful, happy women who can show us what aging beautifully really looks like. These models are needed while we're still young, to give us a positive view of becoming older.

EXERCISE • Finding Classic Models

1. Browse through the Sunday paper, or through any magazine you generally read, to check the kinds of images that have long influenced your concepts of feminine attractiveness. Simply count the images of women who look over age fifty and those who look under thirty (include the photos in the ads as well as those in the text). What portion of these fall into the younger or older categories? When I tried this with the magazine section of the *New York Times,* I found a 4-to-1 ratio of younger to older women. The rarity of mature female faces conveys a subtle social message that certainly leaves its mark on body image. It's as if you're expected to vanish from polite company on your fiftieth birthday.

2. Now try to balance the media's influence by coming up with some classic role models who look and are at least middle-aged. They should be women of maturity whom you admire because

they've achieved distinction instrumentally, not ornamentally. Do not include any entertainers, singers, actresses, models, dancers, or TV personalities because their talents are always mixed up in the marketing of their looks. Think of scientists, athletes, writers, public servants, and heroines living or dead who achieved success in the second half of life: women like Margaret Thatcher, Margaret Mead, Lillian Hellman. Give yourself two minutes and see how many come to mind. Is your list impressively long or embarrassingly short? Ask a friend for some fresh ideas.

3. Each month, choose a new model of maturity as your "rolemate" of the month. She might be famous or simply a neighbor, but to you she's special in some way. Find out more about her. Clip her photo and put it on your refrigerator.

Study her body to see what an admirable older woman looks like in the bloom of success. Let her image counterbalance the cult of youth, and make room for a body like hers within your concept of beauty. How do you think she feels about her looks and how much of her energy do you think is poured into personal adornment?

The goal of this exercise is to expand the role models of maturity that are available to you. These centerfolds may not be young or glamourous, but they do have beautiful qualities: wit, warmth, strength, passion, commitment. Fill up your mental file cards with these oldies but goodies. They'll remind you that aging isn't the beginning of the end. It's a process that can propel you to new heights, long after your peak of physical attractiveness has past. My personal choice for rolemate this month is Ruth Rothfarb, who completed the Boston marathon at the age of eighty-five (in just over eight hours).

REMAINING AN ACTIVE WOMAN

Movement can enhance body image at every age, but especially during middle-age and beyond. Physical activity promotes good health, and a healthy woman not only feels better but looks better, too. On the other hand, lack of exercise breeds lethargy, stiffness, muscle weakness, and other symptoms associated with aging, which are also products of inactivity. Research shows that people in their sixties and seventies who gradually build up to a strenuous fitness program can achieve an aerobic capacity that is equal to the average thirty-year-old.

Whether or not you've been active in the past, it's never too late to make a commitment to the fun, fitness, and fulfillment of physical activity. Start slowly, start safely, by simply extending what you're already able to do: walking, climbing stairs, reaching, bending. As Gloria explains:

> I was forty-five and weighed over 200 pounds when I finally decided to get moving. I never liked exercise and it isn't easy to push this big body around. I found that even though I don't look terrific in a bathing suit, I'm a pretty good swimmer. Now I'm swimming farther and better all the time. Although my weight hasn't changed much, swimming gave me a new lease on life. I only hope I can do it for many years.

With age, you'll need to slow down and pay greater attention to safety. Athletic injury not only puts you out of commission but it in turn leads to body alienation and lowered self-esteem. Even the best athlete must eventually cut back, change her goals, and become less competitive with others or with herself. Old sports can be transferred to new arenas. Try fast walking instead of jogging, cross-country skiing instead of downhill, doubles in tennis instead of singles.

I no longer try to jump on the ice because the risks seem too great. Instead, I've turned to ballroom dancing as a replacement. My personal bias is for dance because it has the advantage of adding a social and sensual dimension to body image. Of course, I miss my younger self who could move more freely, yet I'm enjoying the novelty of a new activity. By cultivating a variety of physical activities when you're younger, you'll have more flexibility in finding some that can age well with you. Taking on a difficult physical challenge can do wonders for a middle-aged self-image, as Gladys discovered:

> I've been moderately active all my life, but on my sixtieth birthday I put myself to the test and joined a group for a week-long hike along the Appalachian Trail. Keeping up wasn't easy while carrying a backpack, but I managed to finish the trip successfully. I can't describe how terrific I felt about myself for doing it. My husband

was so proud he kept showing the pictures to everyone. I think he saw me differently after that. I know I had a new respect for what my body could do.

REMAINING A SENSUOUS WOMAN

Georgia O'Keeffe is one of my favorite role models for aging beautifully. She inspires me not only as a creative artist who continued to work throughout a very long life but also as a woman who continued to grow in terms of her sensuality. At ninety she was described as more feminine than at any time before. After a long marriage and decades of widowhood, she formed an intimate alliance with a man almost sixty years younger. According to one biographer, "Their relationship consisted of many elements: manwoman, parent-child, artist-artist . . . roles all inspired by sincere respect and genuine affection." Even when frail and elderly, Georgia O'Keeffe still looked sensually alive.

Remaining a sensuous woman after a certain age is a real challenge. The double standard of sexuality joins with the double standard of aging, and together they create a double bind that inhibits the sex lives of older women. Consequently, we often get caught up in a set of well-entrenched myths. Most of us have been taught to believe, for instance, that:[14]

Sex is mainly for the young.

Men are more sexually interested and active than women, all through life.

Having sex means having intercourse.

Sexual desire fades after menopause.

Myths like these are real obstacles to bodylove. They have a strong influence on the way you're seen and the way you see yourself as a sexually attractive older woman. Take a moment to reconsider your beliefs in light of these facts.

First, sex keeps rearing its lovely head all through life. There's a lot of postmenopausal passion floating around. Although older women may inspire less lust in others, their desire for a lusty life remains high. Someone once remarked that it was sex, not youth, that's wasted on the young. Not all of it is wasted, however.

"Now that I've decided that the rest of my life is for me, I'm shocked at how easy it is to get what I want," says forty-four-year-old Sharon. "There's hardly a thing I can think of sexually that I want to experience that I can't. I'm amazed and wonder why it took me so long not to stop being afraid to ask." An elderly woman says, "Age puzzles me. I thought it was a quiet time. My seventies were interesting and fairly serene. But my eighties are passionate. I grow more intense as I age."

Most males experience partial or situational impotence with age. This can cause performance anxiety, which in turn inhibits their sexual desire. Females, in contrast, suffer fewer sexual problems related to the aging process. Some even become orgasmic for the first time after menopause is over.

Aging women generally don't lose their sexual capacity or interest. What they do lose—all too often—is an available male partner. Beyond mid-life there just aren't enough men to go around. The ratio of single women to men after age sixty is about 4 to 1.[15] There are fewer men to dress up for and flirt with, fewer men to pursue and make love with. Even those lucky women who still have mates may not be sexually satisfied, for aging husbands sometimes withdraw sexually because of illness, lack of interest, or lack of potency.

Maureen confides, "My body still looks pretty good and I'm just as eager for sex as ever. But my husband died three years ago. There hasn't been any sex in my life since then. Here I am, single at sixty and still feeling so sexy—well it wasn't exactly what I expected."

Women like Maureen may need to broaden their sexual perspective as their circumstances change. Having sex doesn't necessarily translate into having a husband or into having intercourse. Alternatives include erotic contact with a man that doesn't focus on penetration, erotic contact with oneself that is sensual and satisfying, or erotic contact with another woman. This, too, is a viable sexual alternative that may feel threatening to many women, but that has proven personally satisfying to some.

Menopause can cause difficulties. Hot flashes are uncomfortable for a time, but they usually pass. Vaginal dryness is annoying, but treatable. For the most part, women are happy to be rid of a whole host of periodic problems. Best of all, they're finally free of the fear of pregnancy, which means a real gain in sexual freedom.

Menopause isn't a deficiency disease or a disaster but a natural process. Most women menstruate for about forty years, then live another thirty years after their periods end. That's a lot of postmenopausal life to enjoy. Whether it's ahead or behind you, stop for a moment to consider your attitudes toward menopause and how these influence your body image. If you're in the process of transition, you might want to consider joining or forming a support group to share experiences and coping strategies. Some groups have created rituals to celebrate this change of life as a rite of passage into new freedom.

Menopause does produce changes in appearances. Hair thins out, breasts become less firm, skin gets dryer. Yet despite all this, there's more good news about body image. Older women consider their bodies just as sexually appealing as do younger ones! In fact, women in the Bodylove Survey reported no decline at all with age when it comes to feeling sexually appealing. While 33 percent of the young women rated themselves as extremely or quite appealing, 36 percent of the older women rated themselves in those categories. These results were the most surprising of the whole survey. They again confirm the basic theme we've seen all along—that body image is more closely tied to self-esteem than to external signs of beauty.

Do you think your body is sexually appealing?

	YOUNGER	MIDDLE	OLDER
EXTREMELY APPEALING	5%	11%	5%
QUITE APPEALING	28%	30%	31%
SOMEWHAT APPEALING	48%	47%	49%
NOT VERY APPEALING	14%	10%	9%
NOT AT ALL	5%	1%	6%

When Georgia O'Keeffe was asked what stage of life was happiest, she replied, "There is no happiest stage, there are only happy moments." As a role model, she showed me that those special moments don't just belong to the young or the beautiful. In order to keep every stage of your life full of potential for happy and sensuous moments, remember the following:

1. *Get the facts about aging and sexuality.* Misinformation only perpetuates myths. (See the resource section on aging and sexuality.)

2. *Get enough touch in your life.* Use sensate-focus exercises like the ones described in Chapter 6 for reassurance that you're still sexually responsive. Women are lucky because we have greater freedom to touch our friends, to walk hand in hand, to hug and hold.

3. *Keep sensually stimulated.* You can do this through fantasy, candlelight dinners, exotic lingerie, erotic films and books. You don't have to be young to walk on the beach at sunset or to listen to music under the stars.

4. *Loosen up your view of proper sexual behavior.* What was right at thirty may not serve you well at sixty, so why not explore the endless variations on a sexual theme. An impotent husband can still be a potent lover if you find new forms of mutual pleasure. And friendships with women can also satisfy your needs for intimacy.

TIME OUT FOR INSTRUMENTAL AGING

The cult of youth stems partly from our fear of death. An aging body can feel like an "intimate enemy" as we try to deny our mortality by waging war against wrinkles. Cosmetic science now offers powerful weapons to stop the clock that ticks in your mirror. Some doctors even describe aging as a correctable deformity and a cureable disease. Should you or shouldn't you buy into their cures? There are no simple answers to this question. Decisions about self-preservation become harder as technology makes it easier to look younger. We'll see in the next chapter how cosmetic makeovers influence self- and body image. One woman observes that:

> Sometimes I think of the alternatives to looking older. And I wonder what it would be like to have my face frozen the way it was in my thirties. Then I think—that would be ridiculous! That's not me. It doesn't reflect the years I've lived and all the things I've experienced. I feel that if I dislike my aging looks, I'm denying all the wonderful parts of my life.[16]

I know there is real pressure on you to try to freeze your image at some preferred pretty stage. It takes courage to be seen as a full human being, not just as a girl forever; courage to look like a woman with a past. After a certain age film directors avoid closeups. They keep their cameras at a distance, filtering the effect with the softening lens of space. Stepping back from your mirror is a good defensive strategy. As your eyes grow dimmer, learn to use them differently. Back off a bit. Stop searching so closely with a critical eye, and instead, turn a more kindly eye on your reflection. This will help you look beyond the mirror's surface *into* yourself, not merely *at* yourself. Remember, at every age there is much more to you than meets the eye.

Each of us must develop our own personal approach to "aging beautifully." As you work toward bodylove, keep the major points of this chapter in mind:

1. *Develop a flexible beauty ideal.* Your ideal should be one that can grow older, heavier, wrinkled along with you. Remember that a negative body image is *not* a necessary side effect of getting older. Age can give you the confidence to create your own unique style.

2. *Identify with realistic role models.* Find older, unglamourous role models who are truly magnificent and hold them up as images with whom to identify. Also work hard to counteract your own ageism and looksism by trying to see older women as total women.

3. *Own up to your age.* Age acceptance doesn't mean resigning yourself to the stereotypes of ageism, but redefining those myths as time redesigns your body. If you learn to see yourself in terms of your total assets, not merely in terms of appearance, the loss of youthful beauty can be balanced by the accomplishments of age.

4. *Hang on to your sensuality.* Be daring and indulge your body in all the physical pleasures that you've earned by virtue of having lived this long. Keep enjoying the sensual side of movement and keep challenging your body with physical activity.

5. *Use the wisdom you've acquired over the years.* With maturity comes an understanding of what works well for you cosmetically, sexually, athletically, dietetically. This knowledge can help you nurture your aging body with attention and respect.

One sign of maturity is the ability to forgive oneself and others. Can you forgive your body for the flaws and failures of age? Forgiveness allows you to let go of anger toward your body, to forget what you can't change and to make peace with what you have. Those who age successfully—at every age—learn to compromise and to give up unrealistic demands for perfection. They stop evaluating their body in absolute terms of good or bad, young or old, and accept it with all its relatively imperfect parts. The goal is to work within the aging process and renegotiate a new relationship with your changing body all the time.

Coming of age successfully means integrating an ideal body image with a real body that shows the wear and tear of time. Whether you're younger or older, today's body image eventually becomes one of tomorrow's necessary losses. You can face it with courage or with cowardice, but in the end, time wears us all away. Bodylove can help you wear it well.

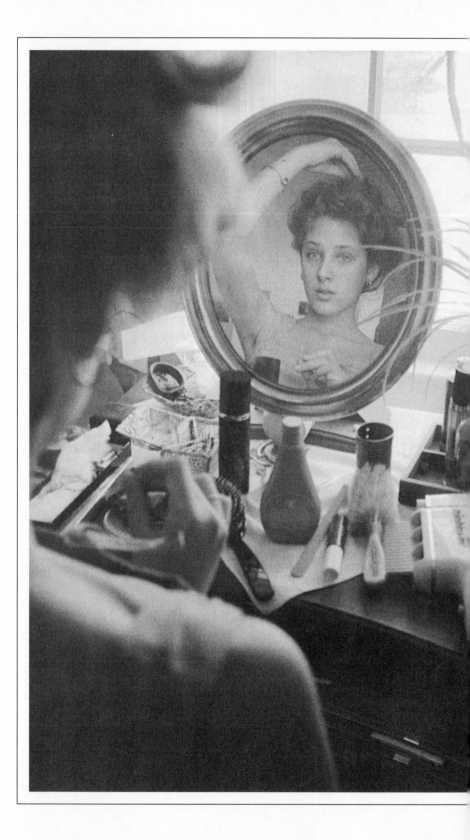

MAKING UP AND MAKING OVER

Compared to other women, how much do you use cosmetics and other beauty products?

    MUCH MORE
    SOMEWHAT MORE
    ABOUT THE SAME
    SOMEWHAT LESS
    MUCH LESS

How much time and effort do you usually spend getting ready before going out to a social event?

    A GREAT DEAL
    QUITE A LOT
    ABOUT AVERAGE
    NOT VERY MUCH

How much money do you spend on beauty products and grooming treatments?

    A GREAT DEAL
    QUITE A LOT
    ABOUT AVERAGE
    NOT VERY MUCH
    ALMOST NONE

> So I pumiced and brushed and sprayed and bleached and trimmed
> and squirted and rubbed . . . and I discovered a terrifying fact. If I
> did all the things the magazines told me to do, I'd spend my entire
> life in the bathroom.
>
> —CARYL RIVERS

CAN you remember the first time you wore makeup to a party, or the last time you partied without it? Most of us pass from girlhood into womanhood by detouring through the cosmetic department. There we buy the props and paint that help us become our own fairy godmothers.

Makeup is a basic part of the socialization of females. "When I was little I watched my mother cover her face every day and swore I'd never wear any of that stuff," recalls Pat. "Mom just looked at me and said, 'Wait till you're twelve, you'll change your mind.' And of course she was right." Watching my own daughter struggle through adolescence, I once wrote that a young girl's body will betray her unless she learns to tame it through cosmetic magic.

Our bodies continue to betray us throughout life. Mine has been turning gray for several years, which creates a cosmetic dilemma for me. Two out of five American women dye their hair, and I'm still among the three who don't. But I often wish I did, and maybe someday I will. There are times I long to be the dark-haired woman I was once, while at other times I'm content with the silver-streaked woman I am now. Decisions about my hair always feel tentative. They put me in conflict with who I am, who I was, and who I want to be. I'm sure you feel these conflicts, too. None of us escapes them.

Cosmetic problems surface in different ways for each of us. Joyce, for example, uses makeup freely. She loves feeling "beautified" and looking "exotic." However, she also gets anxious when caught without her face on. Eileen, on the other hand, ignores most cosmetic rituals. While she usually feels okay about her unadorned appearance, she also envies the more glamourized women around her.

> Sometimes I see women who are perfectly made up and fashiona-
> bly dressed with hair that's just been "done." Then I think that my
> looks aren't right. I feel inferior and socially noncompetitive.

They'll be noticed more and admired more. Part of me secretly wishes I could be like that and be more like everyone else. Somehow I won't or can't do it. When I do, I feel it's not me. Like a doll or something.

In Helen's case, it's her breasts that cause the greatest conflict. While her friends envy Helen's deep blue eyes and smooth skin, she's totally focused on her flat chest. "This boyish body doesn't seem normal," she tells me. "I just want to be like other women and feel more feminine." She's considering implants, yet hesitates about going ahead with the surgery.

Whether you like it or not, looks are important. It's true that if others see you as prettier, they may treat you better. Therefore, cosmetic transformations can have effects far beyond face value. Moreover, changing the outside can help you feel better inside. For these reasons, bodylove sometimes means making over to conform to social norms.

Most of us have some feature that causes embarrassment or shame: freckles, a birthmark, a body part that's too large or too small. When does it pay to transform your outer self in order to improve your inner image? When is making over a positive act of self-enhancement, and when is it a negative act of self-rejection? These are the questions we'll be facing in this chapter. The answers are neither simple nor clear, which is what makes cosmetic conflicts so confusing.

We'll explore the motives and fears behind such conflicts and weigh them against the costs and gains of makeovers. With new understanding, your beauty rituals *can* help you transform your body image and make you lovelier in your own eyes. The surface you project will then reflect the bodylove you feel.

THINKING OVER MAKING OVER

To understand your own cosmetic conflicts it's important to examine the underlying motives. As you read this list of common motives for cosmetic transformations, see if you can find an example of each one that relates to your own beauty routines.

Social conformity. To be like others and to be liked by them: "If I didn't wear makeup I'd feel odd. I want to fit in."

Fear. Of rejection, loneliness, looking ugly:
"You wouldn't ask why I wear it if you ever saw me without it."

Status. To convey social class and power:
"I move in sophisticated circles and have a certain image to uphold."

Lust and longing. To attract attention, affection, sexual pleasure:
"How do you like my new hairdo? I want to knock him dead tonight."

Pride. To display assets and show confidence:
"I'm doing great and I've never looked better, so why shouldn't I flaunt it?"

Shame and insecurity. To hide "flaws" or conceal age:
"Having the hair removed from my lip made me feel normal looking."

Aesthetic pleasure. To enjoy looking elegant, unique, or outrageous:
"I love color and feel like an artist when I make up."

Femininity. To confirm and display gender role:
"Cosmetics help me feel glamourous and feminine. It's as simple as that."

Comfort. To relieve pain or annoyance:
"After my breast reduction I could play tennis without dragging all that weight around."

Pleasing others. To conform to the expressed wishes of a loved one:
"My husband loves me as a blond and I like to make him happy."

That's a long list of motives, which is why cosmetic rituals remain so popular. None of these reasons is necessarily good or bad. All have the potential to promote bodylove or to cause body loathing, depending on the circumstances. However, there is a common theme that ties these many motives together—and that's the need for social approval. For a woman, gaining social approval usually means packaging oneself in whatever feminine image is currently fashionable.

SOCIAL PACKAGING

Cosmetic adornment varies the world over. In one place a woman stretches her lips with bone, in another she implants her breasts with silicone. Do these changes really make her look more attractive? Perspectives differ, yet her goal is the same in each case: to transform into the popular standard of feminine beauty, and therefore to feel more socially acceptable.

Our personal cosmetic motives and conflicts reflect the way society has taught us to look at beauty, and at our own bodies. With a quick rinse I can wash away my gray and package myself as a younger woman. Then, perhaps, I'll fit better into the cult of youth that I've learned to admire. For Helen, fitting in means filling out her bust size. "With bigger breasts, I'd be more appealing to men," she says, "and I'm sure my love life would improve." Thus, by making over our anatomy we hope to remake our social destiny as well.

Cosmetic packaging can change us from being merely female to being marvelously female. Fabricating a super-feminine façade isn't easy. How do we do it? Faces are peeled and painted with powder and blush. Ears are pierced. Brows are shaped. Lashes are darkened. Lids are lined. Lips are glossed. Noses are bobbed. Nails are polished. Hair is curled, rinsed, straightened, teased, sprayed. Breasts are reduced, lifted, padded. Rumps are plumped. Tummies are tucked, etc., etc.

Of course, none of us does all these things, yet few of us do none of them. We pick and choose what we think is needed to change from a "misfit" into someone who fits nicely into the social scene. "I won't even go to the mailbox without my lipstick on," says Irma. "Who knows what might happen?"

A little tube of color can become a pocket hand grenade of feminine power. It shows how much we depend on cosmetic packaging. Bella Abzug once quipped that women are trained to speak softly . . . and carry a lip-stick.

In a scene from a novel, a young woman is standing with her parents in a concentration camp lineup. Finding a lipstick in her pocket, she turns to quickly paint her mother's mouth, hoping to help her look young enough to be chosen to live. Recounting the planned suicide of her own mother after a long fight with cancer, Betty Rollin writes that her mother's final act before swallowing the fatal pills was to put on makeup. "My mother always liked to look her best," Rollin tells us. How else would a proud woman prepare for an important event?[1]

By taking charge of our lips or lashes, we try to take charge of our lives. It's a kind of fairy-tale mentality in which body transformations are used to solve problems and grant wishes. So the ladies room becomes the powder room, as well as the *power* room, where the magic rites of femininity are performed.

The power of cosmetic packaging can be a double-edged sword, however. We saw earlier the inherent tension in trying to be both a healthy woman and a healthy person. There may be a gain in power if you package yourself in the feminine image, but there can be a corresponding loss of power if you no longer resemble a healthy person.

Thus, beauty rituals can elevate a woman to a pedestal, even while they prove that she's "merely a woman after all." For example, in the nineteenth century, tight corsets were fashionable. The smaller her waist, the more attractive a woman was thought to be. But those same women who were so admired for their tiny waists were also considered stupid for wearing such ridiculous undergarments, and therefore not worthy of higher education. Even today, flashy blonds are stereotyped as beautiful but dumb, while large-breasted women are also viewed as less intelligent. This kind of cosmetic tension creates conflicts in the two major arenas of life—work and love.

PACKAGING FOR SUCCESS—IN WORK AND IN LOVE

Society is still uncertain about a woman's legitimate place in the work force and unsure about what she should look like once she gets there. Proper social packaging is confusing when the ornamental feminine image tries to merge with the instrumental corporate image. One career counselor finds that whenever she talks to women's groups, the question session always includes, "How should I dress?" Think for a moment about the image you present at work. How much making over must you do to "look your best" for bosses, clients, customers? What does "best" really mean in terms of career growth? It may vary from day to day depending on whom you're trying to impress.

We're told that, "a man should keep his nose to the grindstone, but a woman had better stop now and then to powder hers." It's not always clear, however, how much powder you need as on-the-job ammunition. Studies show that looking too pretty can be a problem for a woman who seeks a top managerial position. If she's seen as too attractive or too feminine, she's likely to be stereotyped as lacking the leadership and competitive qualities managers need.

The controversy between beauty and brains continues, and cosmetics can trigger it. For example, in one study, different photos were attached to job applications, with the candidates wearing either no makeup, moderate amounts, or heavy makeup applied by a cosmetician. For an accounting position, the applications were rated similarly regardless of the amount of makeup. However, for a secretarial job, the *less* makeup worn, the *higher* the rating of a potential candidate. Why? Because a "very attractive" (highly made up) secretary may be quickly stereotyped as more decorative than competent, while a "less attractive" (unmade up) one is assumed to have something on the ball.[2]

When you look "made up," you may threaten your credibility as a competent worker. Yet if you ignore the ornamental role and concentrate strictly on business, your achievements may go unnoticed. Take Lucy's case. At thirty-two, she's a successful marketing executive who describes herself as rather plain looking. She believes her success is due in part to a change in looks.

> When I was growing up, my sister was the pretty one, while I was the musician. In high school I lost the lead in a musical to a prettier girl who had much less talent. I've never forgotten that rejection. When I'd been working at the agency for a few years, and a friend told me that my image was keeping me from getting ahead, I took her advice seriously. I remembered the school show and didn't want to miss out again.

Impulsively, Lucy rinsed her hair to a strawberry blond. Contact lenses and more stylish clothes changed her appearance quite dramatically. Before long she got a promotion she well deserved, however her feelings about this are mixed. "I enjoy the extra attention, but feel a bit resentful. Inside I'm still the same person. I know that a man with my ability and an average face wouldn't need to remodel himself each day in order for his talents to be recognized." While Lucy's makeover paid off, her cosmetic conflicts persist, in spite of success. This, too, is part of looksism.

Even those women who reach the highest levels of achievement are still judged heavily by how they look. When Sandra Day

O'Connor was sworn to the Supreme Court, Chief Justice Warren Berger remarked to photographers, "You've never seen me with a better looking Justice, have you?" The *Washington Post* described her as, "an achieving woman who is good looking without being alienatingly beautiful." So we see that packaging for success in the workplace is complicated and fraught with cosmetic conflicts. Packaging for success in love is not any easier.

Cosmetics are a potent signal of sexuality as well as sociability. At one time or another, we've all used feminine packaging as a sexual lure. "Does she or doesn't she" was a powerful cosmetic ad because of its suggestive double meaning. With makeup you can create a look of childish innocence coupled with seductive allure. A pretty Cinderella is both sweet and provocative. She sends mixed messages: she looks ready to be turned on, then bolts before midnight (before it's too late).

Women walk a fine line between looking attractive and looking seductive, between wearing too little makeup and wearing too much. Though we may gain power on one side of the line, we may lose it on the other. A painted face can arouse the ambivalent feelings we all have about our own sexuality. Remember that, at one time, paint was the sign of a harlot or a loose woman.

Although men certainly enjoy cosmetic signals of sensuality, they also fear the power of the madeup woman to seduce or corrupt them. This ambivalence explains why most men say they prefer a woman who looks natural and wears very little makeup. (That's also why it takes us twice as long to touch up a face and make it look untouched.) Even the Bible warns, "Though you clothe yourself in crimson . . . and though you enlarge your eyes with paint, in vain shall you make yourself fair: your lovers will despise you."[3]

For her seventy-fifth birthday, my mother was given a "day of beautification" at a local spa. While there, she had her nails brightly polished for the first time ever. My father looked amazed when he saw her return, and insisted that she "take off the paint immediately." (She managed to hold out for three full days.) Thus, the use of cosmetics to attract or assure relationships can be tricky. Whether you're seen as tastefully well done or tastelessly overdone depends on who's watching. Given all these mixed feelings, it's not surprising that women wind up with a variety of cosmetic motives and conflicts that are hard to resolve. As one writer observed, there are three kinds of women in the world: those who wear makeup, those who don't, and those who try to look like they don't but do.

FOR APPEARANCE SAKE

Does making up and making over really work and what does it accomplish? Close your eyes for a moment and imagine yourself at a party, first with makeup on, then without it. How would you feel in each case? Most women report feeling more confident when visualizing themselves made up. Research shows that makeup has several consistent effects. First, women are seen as better looking with it on. Independent observers rate them as more attractive and more feminine when wearing cosmetics. Second, most women also feel better about their appearance with it on. Makeup can heighten a sense of confidence and sociability. For many women it seems to give a quick lift to the spirits (although its long-term effect on body image is less certain).[4]

Do those women who use more makeup differ from those who use less? Psychologist Thomas Cash, a pioneer in research on physical attractiveness, found that heavier users tend to be more self-conscious about their appearance and less satisfied with body parts. They also score higher in tests of feminine identity, which may be one of their motives for cosmetic use. However, wearing makeup apparently does not reduce self-consciousness on a long-term basis. This isn't surprising, since making up requires more mirror time, and mirrors tend to heighten self-awareness.[5]

Cash also suggests that heavier users may be trying to "correct or balance a flawed self-image." Do you consider yourself a light or heavy user of beauty products? Most of the women in the Bodylove Survey rated their cosmetic use as quite low. Perhaps they're reluctant to recognize or to admit their reliance on it. Barely 8 percent said they use more beauty products than average, while nearly 60 percent report using less than average. Either we are underestimating our own use or overestimating what other women are doing. In either case, the defensive denial seems quite common. Few of us are willing to acknowledge the extent of our "cosmetic habit."

Compared to other women, how much do you use cosmetics and other beauty products?

3%	MUCH MORE
5%	SOMEWHAT MORE
35%	ABOUT THE SAME
36%	SOMEWHAT LESS
23%	MUCH LESS

Although few women label themselves as heavy users, their comments reveal strong feelings about wearing makeup. "It's part of being dressed right, and putting on the finishing touches," says Elizabeth. "I wouldn't be noticed if I didn't wear it." On the other hand, Eileen experiences conflict. "Somehow I feel undressed without lipstick. Philosophically I say this is crazy. Why do I need it? But I do." Colleen believes that makeup is closely linked to her own inner strength. "I diet and use makeup for myself, not for men. It's my buffer against the world. It helps me gear up for the day and project an image of power." In contrast, Penny feels that not wearing any makeup says a lot about her strength of character. "I've never had any interest whatever in makeup. And always felt kind of smug about not wearing it. My husband doesn't care for it at all, which is great." Beth recalls that, "My ex-husband hated me to wear any makeup. He worried what his parents would think if I wore too much. It would look as if he didn't have much control over me."

The feelings we had as children when we watched our mothers make up their faces, and the feelings we had as adolescents when

Cathy. Copyright © 1977 Universal Press Syndicate. Reprinted with permission. All rights reserved.

we first used makeup to announce our passage into womanhood, linger on as part of our cosmetic mentality. Penny explains, "When I was little I used to call the beauty parlor the ugly parlor, because the process of becoming pretty had a stage of being ugly first." Jamie, age thirteen, received a cosmetic makeover at a salon for a birthday gift. "I think it's a great present," she says. "I can learn to put on shadow and eyeliner the right way. It's not pretty when you just gop it all on. When girls put on too much shadow, they look plastic."

We're constantly faced with the challenge of updating our attitudes as cosmetic fashions change and as our faces change with age. Just as hemlines and necklines rise and fall, cosmetic standards also shift. Brows go from pencil thin to shaggy thick. Lips go from glossy bright to ghostly white. Our strong need to fit in socially requires a constant update in self-presentation and a corresponding change in body image. Think about your own cosmetic evolution. How does your makeup use today compare with the makeup you used as a teenager? Or a decade ago? If there are big differences, do these reflect the changes in you, or changes that have occurred in cosmetic fashion? If you're still doing the same old things cosmetically, are you stuck in a rut that puts you behind the times? Of course, there is tremendous commercial pressure on you to constantly revise your cosmetic routines and experiment with new products.

NICE GIRLS SHOULD

Beauty products are big business and they get a big sell. Advertisers know a good market when they see one, and they carefully tune in to our motives to transform into the feminine ideal. "With makeup, a plain woman can be pretty, a pretty woman can be beautiful, and a beautiful woman can become a legend," we're told.

Actually our love affair with paint goes back a long way. In ancient Mycenae, women freely exposed their nipples and colored them red, much as we color our lips today. The Roman poet Ovid recommended crocodile dung for a glowing complexion. (No, I don't know if it works.) At one time, women ate a pinch of arsenic with breakfast to get the pale complexion that was so fashionable (and some died from it). During the Victorian era, paint was a sign of promiscuity. Cosmetics gradually became more socially acceptable, however, and by 1900, fashionable ladies were seen powdering their noses in public.

It was then that advertisers began to "democratize" beauty by spreading it around. Our view of cosmetic use slowly shifted—from nice girls don't, to nice girls can, and then to nice girls should. While ads promise beauty to all, they set standards that only a few can reach. This commercial campaign in effect triggers envy, self-consciousness, and body loathing because the magic is really in the ad, not in the bottle.

"Don't hate me because I'm beautiful," says the model. But the silent afterthought can also be heard, "Just hate yourself because you're not." Before and after shots with accompanying testimonials prove that nature needs only a nudge. There's a subtle message that "You owe it to yourself to try," otherwise "you have only yourself to blame." In this way, guilt is added to the stigma of looking plain or fat or gray.

How do you honestly feel about your appearance when you see such ads? Do they build self-confidence, or do they arouse new conflicts? In fact, people rate their own physical attractiveness as lower after exposure to pictures of beautiful models. Their self-evaluations drop in comparison to others who look so much better. As much as 50 cents of your cosmetic dollar pays for the ads that plant the seeds of doubt that ultimately grows into a desire to buy a lash enhancer. Not only must you want lovelier lashes, you must feel less lovable without them.

THE HIGH COST OF LOOKING GOOD

The term "cosmetics" comes from a Greek word meaning "the art of adorning." Cosmetics are supposed to adorn your body, not alter it. Since cosmetics aren't drugs, their effectiveness and safety don't have to be proven before they're sold. The Food and Drug Administration (FDA) can only protect you after a product is a proven health hazard. Worthless products are constantly being peddled, such as creams guaranteed to increase bust size "up to three inches in just eight days," or rubberized stockings "to trim thighs by making them sweat." Most cosmetic products are safe. Yet adverse reactions do occur more often than you would suppose. The most frequent problems are caused by deodorants, depilatories, moisturizers, hair spray, mascara, bubble bath, hair dyes, face creams, and nail polish.[6]

Sometimes the side effects are not so pretty. Mascara and eye shadow can cause serious eye infections, even blindness, if they contain bacteria. Tanning creams and sunlamp devices may damage the eyes or skin and lead to cancer. Face makeup often causes acne, and then it's used to cover the very problem it creates. Perfumes and makeup produce a wide range of allergic reactions such as headaches and rashes. Dyes in lipstick and hair rinses may be carcinogenic. (See the resource section on cosmetics and surgery.)

I've included this brief discussion to alert you to some potential dangers, even though I know that very few women pay much attention to health warnings about cosmetic products. Our motives for making over are so strong that we're generally willing to take the risk and pay the price in the name of beauty. We tend to agree with the woman who declared, "I'd rather die young than not dye at all." It's easy to rationalize that nothing can happen to us. Paying the price seems like part of the beauty game—part of the discomfort and inconvenience of looking and feeling more attractive.

All too often, beauty rituals do involve physical pain. Curling, bleaching, piercing, dieting, waxing, plucking, girdling all hurt, so that feeling bad becomes a prerequisite to looking good. When Cinderella's stepsisters each try to squeeze their foot into the glass slipper, their mother urges them to slice off a heel or toe. "Once you're queen you won't need to walk anymore," she shouts. The fairy-tale message is simple: beauty is worth it at any price, even a pound of flesh.

Here's where masochism enters the picture. It's strange but true that pain can feel pleasant when it proves your commitment to looking good. Self-sacrifice shows that you really do care about your image and about what others think of it. It's a signal that you're willing to make the effort and pay the price. Helen rationalizes:

I know there's risk involved in breast surgery. But I'm so miserable when I look at my body. If I don't do something to improve it means that I don't care. My grandmother used to say, "if you really want to feel pretty you have to suffer." It's true. Let's face it. Some things may be uncomfortable, but they really look so much better. Why not sacrifice an hour or two, or sacrifice your comfort, to really look good. Sometimes I wear jeans that are so tight I can't breathe in them. But I do wear them, just as an exception. I don't mind how they feel.

Masochism has been called an "inherent feminine trait." However, I would agree with those who argue that the masochistic need to suffer for beauty is a by-product of women's dependent role.[7] Like Helen, we choose to pay the price quite simply because we feel we can't afford not to. After all, having beauty is like having an American Express card. It can be cashed in for goodies anytime, and that's why we're afraid to leave home without it. That's why we're so willing to suffer in its pursuit.

Pain is only part of the high cost of looking good. Cosmetic rituals also require expenditures of time, effort, and money. These costs are probably greater than most of us realize. In the Bodylove Survey, the majority of women rated their investments as rather small.

How much time and effort do you usually spend getting ready before going out to a social event?

2%	A GREAT DEAL
10%	QUITE A LOT
66%	ABOUT AVERAGE
23%	NOT VERY MUCH

How much money do you spend on beauty products and grooming treatments?

3%	A GREAT DEAL
8%	QUITE A LOT
41%	ABOUT AVERAGE
42%	NOT VERY MUCH
8%	ALMOST NONE

Only 11 percent of the sample felt they spent more than an average amount on cosmetic products, while half the group felt they spent less than average. These, of course, are subjective reports. What does average really mean? Americans reportedly spent about $10 billion on cosmetic products in one recent year. Where are all the women who are buying and using these beauty products? Is it that we just don't realize how much we invest in personal adornment? The amount of floor space devoted to cosmetic display in any large department store is impressive proof that business is brisk and profits are high. Yet the strong defensive denial found in the responses to these questions suggests that there may be some embarrassment or even shame attached to making up and making over. Apparently we do it, but don't like to admit it, even to ourselves. Therefore it's important to take a closer look at our everyday cosmetic behavior.

EXERCISE • Cosmetic Assessments

1. *Taking inventory.* Gather some baseline data to find out how much you're really investing in the beauty game. What does "average" or "almost none" mean in your life? Take inventory of the beauty products you own. Gather together all the lipsticks, sprays, perfumes, conditioners, moisturizers, styling combs, pencils, brushes, mirrors, dryers, curlers, and polishes that fill your purse and bathroom shelves. Try to guess the cost of the whole pile, then roughly figure out the total. Sylvia admits, "It was a real eye-opener to see it all piled up on the table. 'Average' turned out to be more than I expected. . . . I guess fifteen lipsticks might be a bit much." Don't forget to add in the cost of professional beauty services that you are currently buying.

Now take inventory of your cosmetic activities. Start keeping track of the time you spend washing, combing, drying, dressing, shaving, putting on your face and taking it off. Add in the weekly or monthly manicures, facials, hair appointments, and shopping sprees for cosmetics. Then figure out the minutes per day and hours per week it takes you to create the ornamental feminine image.

Ask yourself some questions. Does this collection of cosmetics— and the time, money, and effort you spend—seem like a healthy "average" to you? Do you think your use of cosmetics makes you more or less self-conscious about your looks? Most important, does it pay off in terms of bodylove? Think about whether you might want to reinvest some of these resources in other self-nurturing ways—ways that are less ornamental but more nourishing for your body image, such as playing, touching, moving. On the other hand, would a greater investment in beauty routines give a valuable boost to your self-esteem?

2. *Exploring conflicts.* After you've taken stock of some of your cosmetic habits, choose one particular routine that's causing you some conflict. It may be something you're doing reluctantly or compulsively. Perhaps it's something you're considering but can't quite decide on. For me it's whether to stay gray. For Helen it's whether to stay flat-chested.

Now think about your motives for that particular makeover. Why do you do it, or want to do it? Use the list of motives on pages 191–192 to help assess your feelings. Are you driven by fear, shame, or longing? A desire for comfort? For conformity? Helen is ashamed of her breasts and afraid that men won't find her attractive. She wants to feel more feminine, and also to find a husband.

After you've decided on the most obvious motivation behind your desire for this makeover, think about it further to see if you can discover additional motives that are more subtle and perhaps harder to admit. Why is this cosmetic change causing conflict? Is it more painful or less socially acceptable than your other beauty rituals?

Perhaps there are factors in your life history that are troubling you. When I think about my hair, for example, I recall that my mother turned gray at thirty-five and has lived happily with it ever since. But do I need to follow her example? I know I don't feel as content with my gray as she did with hers. And maybe I'm not quite ready to look like her yet. For Helen, breast surgery is connected with the memory of her aunt's mastectomy. She's afraid that implants might make it harder to detect breast cancer some day. Consider the role that masochism may play in your conflicts. Inflicting pain, or some other discomfort, is sometimes a way of punishing your body for betraying you. How much do you really want to suffer in order to look good?

3. *Catching cognitive errors.* As we've seen in other chapters, the way you think about your body has a greater influence on body image than how you actually look. Cognitive errors can add to your cosmetic conflicts. Examine your motives once more to see if they may be based on automatic irrational thoughts. The list of cognitive errors on pages 38–39 will remind you of some of your entrenched tendencies to exaggerate or personalize.

For example, when Helen says, "I'll always be ashamed of my flat chest. . . . I need bigger breasts to feel like a real woman," she's jumping to conclusions. Her shame comes from taking things personally. After all, breast size is genetically determined. We may not like a particular trait and we may want to alter it, but we aren't responsible for it. You can use the triple-column technique to challenge irrational thoughts about cosmetic change and to correct the faulty thinking that may be causing cosmetic conflicts.

WINNING THE BEAUTY GAME

We saw earlier that cosmetic use can sometimes create a more attractive image as well as boost self-esteem. There is, therefore, a cosmetic route to bodylove. Makeup can help you achieve a better body image, while having fun in the process.

EXERCISE • The Creative Use of Makeup

This exercise taps into your motives for novelty and aesthetic change. It will help you step back from your critical mirror and step up to a friendlier one. For a moment try to forget the compulsive use of makeup for correcting or perfecting. Instead, experiment with using cosmetics less fearfully and more joyfully.

1. Begin by putting aside half an hour at home alone. This is a time for fun, fantasy, and regression—a time to indulge your imagination in healthy narcissism as you turn your body into an "ambulatory art form." You'll be using props and paint to create someone special. First set the mood with music. Then start to think up a new image for yourself. At first you may find it hard to give yourself permission to let go, to allow your looks to express parts of your personality that rarely show. If you practice a few times, this exercise will get easier and more spontaneous.

2. Now dress up and make yourself over to look girlish, clownish, vampish—as silly or sultry as the mood inspires. Cheap makeup in strong colors and other props such as hats, body paints, and costume jewelry will help you create the image you want (so start to gather them in advance). Be creative and above all have fun. Paint a flower on your cheek, a heart on your breast. Wear one long earring and make up differently on each side of your face. Put on war paint or a silly clown's smile. Take enough time to really become this new character and to live in the role for a little while.

3. Finish the exercise by standing quietly in front of the mirror. Study your reflection and let the made-up vision sink into your

body image as you take a mental photo of it. Now look into your eyes and repeat a mirror affirmation such as, "I can create and enjoy all the different images waiting within me." By playfully making over your image, you may find new uses of props and paint that can carry over into "real" life. For example, one woman found that she could be more flexible in using cosmetics—wearing almost none to work on some days and a great deal on other days, depending on her mood. As you try to creatively expand this exercise, just remember that the overall goal is to play with cosmetic transformations so they enhance body image.

EXERCISE • The Sensual Side of Makeup

Your daily beauty routines can become rituals of nurturance and sensuality. It's easy to add a bit of self-indulgence as you groom, by paying attention not only to the mirror image but to the body image within. For example, I end each day over a bowl of hot water. I find it relaxing to press warm washcloths onto my face, to feel the contours of my features and visualize them while smoothing away the wrinkles. When my skin is flushed from the heat, I enjoy seeing a glowing face in my mirror. Here are a few suggestions for ways to expand the meaning of your cosmetic routines.

1. Before putting on lipstick, close your eyes and run your tongue over your lips to feel their texture and shape. When grooming your nails, study your hands not just as ornaments but as instruments of touch and creativity. When you make up your face, visualize the tiny muscles beneath the skin and the many emotions they communicate. Occasionally take an extra moment in the shower or bath to imagine yourself floating in a pond or standing under a waterfall. Afterward, put on body lotion and fantasize that a loving partner is caressing your skin.

2. Try using makeup for self-seduction. Play out a sensuous fantasy by putting on the trappings of a seductive woman. What would it mean to be visually provocative to yourself?

By taking the time to let your body come alive during your cosmetic routines, you can enhance your body image on a daily basis. And don't forget the power of self-praise through mirror affirmations. While you work on your appearance, also work on giving yourself compliments from your praise list.

EXERCISE • The Social Side of Makeup

As mentioned in Chapter 6, grooming rituals can be used for social contact and to get more touch into your life. By manicuring, shampooing, or making up with a friend or loved one, you can experience your body through another person's hands (or experience someone's body through yours). Mutual grooming reshapes body image by the touch of real flesh. It changes the process of making up from a lonely competitive routine to a ritual of social connection. Eva tells me, "My neighbor Georgette comes over every few weeks and we play 'toilette' together. She tweezes my eyebrows because I can't see well enough to do it on my own. Sometimes we paint toenails or color our hair. She's not my closest friend, but she's my special cosmetic friend. It becomes a kind of game—we giggle a lot, like teenagers."

THE CHISELED PROFILE

As new cosmetic technologies are perfected, the surgical route to beauty becomes more and more tempting. Surgery does offer many advantages that previously were unavailable. However, it's an option that also creates greater conflicts because of its permanence and because of its dangers.

If you're hungry for a cosmetic fix, doctors offer a full menu that includes breast remodeling, tummy tucks, face-lifts, chin implants, dermabrasion, collagen injections, eyelid tucks, permanent eyelid lining (tatoo), nose jobs, chemical peels, hair transplants, surgical body contouring, and, last but not least, fat suction—the newest and most popular form of cosmetic surgery performed today.

Surgeons seem as adept at publicizing their operations as at performing them. "Nature makes mistakes," says one. "We can do better." They make it look so simple. However, these operations aren't always as safe or predictable as the promotions claim. Of course, there are risks.

Complications and even deaths occur in all forms of cosmetic surgery. The list of potential hazards includes infection, nerve damage, anesthesia reactions, unusual scarring, blood clots, asymmetry. For example, face-lifts can leave some patients with crooked smiles or difficulty closing their eyes. Ann Scheiner published the following diary entries after a face-lift at the age of fifty-four:[8]

Day 2—My face feels like broken glass, like frostbite. . . . eyes are blurry. Will I be able to see clearly again?

Day 15—My smile seems frozen . . . spontaneity is gone. And my eyes are still swollen . . . the lids feel glued.

Day 19—Before the operation I rationalized that I wanted my face-lift so my exterior would match my interior. Now I am more out of sync than ever before. I realize I was lying to myself. I just wanted to look younger and prettier.

Day 42—Finally I can work again . . . I tally the score. On the plus side, a smoother cheek and neck line . . . fewer lines. On the minus side, serious eye problems, hideous swelling . . . numb face and neck. Loss of identity. Loss of work. No exercise for weeks. The results will last only four to eight years. After that, it's sags and bags again.

The average age of face-lift patients has reportedly dropped from sixty to fifty, with many forty-year-olds now facing the knife.[9] In the Bodylove Survey, 22 percent of the women said they would consider having a face-lift and 1 percent already had; 2 percent had undergone breast implant surgery and 5 percent said they would consider it; 1 percent had undergone breast reduction surgery and 6 percent would consider it.

In fact, the bust-alteration business is booming. In one recent year 150,000 breasts were lifted, implanted, or reduced, for the sole purpose of "enhancing their aesthetic appeal" (at a cost of $2,000 to $4,000 each). Clearly, the cultured bosom is inflated with meaning that nature never intended. In the 1970s, a wave of feminism swept in the small-breasted look of an athlete. Now, with "family values" back in vogue, fuller breasts are spilling over strapless gowns.

"What are breasts for anyway," asks Geraldo Rivera on a talk show about men's view of bosoms. "Tits are mostly for tots," I explain. They're designed to feed babies and provide erotic sensation for women, neither of which is related to bust size. Sometimes the ornamental bosom loses its instrumental role, however. "I knew that if I had a breast reduction I might lose nipple sensitivity and not be able to breastfeed," says Michelle. "Those things didn't seem important compared to what I suffered every day."

The problems and self-consciousness surrounding breast size can be very real, as Michelle explains. "Life isn't easy if you're five feet tall with 34DD breasts. I suffered constant pain in my shoulders and back. I was humiliated by hoots and whistles everywhere I went. There were times at work when all eyes were glued on my bust and whatever I was saying was totally lost."

For Helen, the sense of humiliation was just the opposite. "My breasts just never developed. As a teenager I prayed every day for God to turn me into a real woman. I felt ashamed whenever I looked in the mirror. My boyfriend didn't push me into having the implants, but I knew he wasn't happy with my shape."

Helen finally decided to go ahead with the surgery and, a year later, is basically pleased with the results. "It was more painful than I expected," she says, "but my figure looks so nice now. I love to put on a bathing suit and parade on the beach. It didn't make much difference to my boyfriend, though. We broke up anyway. And my breasts don't feel as natural as they look. I'm inhibited about being touched, so I'm having some trouble sexually. Yes, I'm glad I did it. The best part is that I just don't think about my breasts so much anymore."

Today, there's much less stigma attached to cosmetic surgery than there was a decade ago. It's even considered a quick form of psychotherapy, a useful way to get rid of an annoying problem and to get on with other things. Research shows that a woman like Helen who seeks breast surgery is just as psychologically stable as other women. The only difference is her negative view of her body and her greater preoccupation with looking attractive.[10] In other words, she's a mentally healthy woman who suffers from heightened self-consciousness about her appearance.

According to Thomas Cash, many people who seek surgery have an "exaggerated sense of how bad they look." Their basic problem is often one of poor body image, he concludes, which may or not be tied to objective reality. Self-perception is the underlying problem and improvement hinges on a change of self-perception after surgery. When someone thinks she's unattractive, it affects her behavior. If surgery can correct the self-stigmatizing belief, the patient may feel better as well as look better.[11]

Does cosmetic surgery work? Yes, generally it does work in the same way that makeup works. First, most patients are pleased with the results—even more so than the surgeons! They do look better after surgery, as judged by themselves and by others. Follow-up studies consistently show a high rate of satisfaction for most forms of cosmetic surgery. Second, patients not only look better but they're seen as more socially desirable in other ways. Remember that looksism produces positive stereotypes. When before and after photographs are judged, patients are seen as more likable, happier, and potentially more successful in the "after" shots. Clearly, these benefits can reduce self-consciousness and improve body image.

Cosmetic surgery can accomplish some things but not everything. It isn't magic. It won't radically transform your personality or instantly deliver new love. If you expect miracles you're likely to be disappointed. It can enhance appearance and help you like yourself better—sometimes. However, the surgical route is not the only way to accomplish these goals, as I've tried to show throughout this book. The potential costs and risks of surgery are relatively high, compared to other methods for achieving bodylove.

SHOULD I OR SHOULDN'T I?

Having cosmetic surgery is "neither a salvation nor a sellout." If you're considering surgery, the following questions will serve as a helpful guide:

- What do you want to accomplish? Be specific. Identify precisely what's wrong with your body and what you hope to look like afterward.
- Is it possible to achieve the results you want? If so, will the changes last, or will the operation need to be repeated?
- What are your motives? Go over the list on pages 191–192 to see which ones are creating this conflict. Consider whether your motives are rational or are based on cognitive errors.
- Why are you seeking surgery right now? Did something trigger your current need, such as a change of job or loss of mate? Are you in a good emotional state to make this decision, or are your feelings likely to change over time? Perhaps you should wait and see.
- What are the overall costs in terms of time, money, stress? How much pain can you expect and how long must you give up work, exercise, driving, sex?
- What complications sometimes occur, and what are the risks for someone in your physical condition?

Above all, make sure you have enough information to be an informed consumer and avoid making an impulsive decision. Consider whether there are other ways to accomplish your goals that are less costly or less risky. If you decide to go ahead, you should give at least as much care to picking a surgeon as you do to picking a hairdresser. The mark of good surgeons may not be the cases they do, but the ones they turn away. One doctor describes the ideal candidate as someone in good health, highly motivated, with realistic expectations about recuperation and final results. Her goals should be based on the reality of her own body, not on some arbitrary ideal.

In fact, one of the best reasons for considering cosmetic surgery is to correct a major flaw or "abnormality." By eliminating an obvious cosmetic problem such as a birthmark, scar, or other disfigurement, you may indeed find a real improvement in how others see and treat you.

So give yourself a chance to reconsider your assets and liabilities. Are there obvious problems that dominate your appearance or your self-image, such as facial hair, dental defects, complexion problems? Is improvement possible, and at what cost? By doing nothing about them, you may be suffering a social handicap unnecessarily. It's a disadvantage to be so unattractive that your looks distract others from getting to know who you are. Looksism is real. Small changes can sometimes produce big gains if they fix a flaw that dominates your image. You don't have to be beautiful. But trying to look average (for your age) is a worthwhile goal.

When is a feature truly abnormal or unsightly? That's not always clear. Just because Helen was obsessed with her small breasts doesn't mean they needed fixing. The overall impression you make is often much more important than any single feature. If you're in doubt about how you really look to others, get an opinion from a therapist or from a few honest friends. Your outward appearance may be less of a problem than you suppose.

Beware that you don't destroy your individuality in search of normality. When Sylvia was asked which cosmetic decisions helped define her personal image, she said, "I decided not to get a nose job." Bette Midler's bust or Barbra Streisand's nose make them memorable because of the "flaws" that remain unfixed. Although beauty norms are narrow, they can be stretched when you confidently accept and display a distinctive feature. Like Helen, Rhoda is also small-breasted. Unlike Helen, she pokes fun at herself and wears sexy blouses to flaunt what she doesn't have. She proves that liking your looks matters as much as what you look like.

FINDING A BALANCE

Social pressures are strong. Few of us can confidently get away without any makeup at all and still feel attractive. That's why it's valuable both psychologically and socially for you to spend some effort at self-adornment—but not too much. Some transformations are worth it, up to a point. After all, there's no end to the makeovers that could make you prettier. As in the opening quote of this chapter, if you tried to do everything that "nice girls should," you might never get out of your bathroom. Struggling for perfection can be a tormenting waste of time. For you to be reasonably well groomed and attractive shouldn't require pain, preoccupation, or self-sacrifice on the altar of beauty.

In fact, facial expression is a key factor in whether you're seen as attractive. Try putting on your face by looking alive, interested, turned on by those around you. When you radiate these qualities, you'll immediately be seen as a lovelier woman, regardless of the size of your breasts or the color of your hair.[12]

How about Helen? Do you think she made a good decision? She's happier about her breasts and less obsessed with them. However, socially she's still lonely and sexually she's more inhibited. Was hers an act of self-enhancement or one of self-rejection? Probably both.

In one sense she was motivated by healthy narcissism. She wanted to feel more feminine and enjoy her body more fully. Yet she was also trapped by unhealthy masochism; by the mistaken belief that her breasts were unfeminine and needed correction at any cost. Her body loathing was due in part to a culture that neurotically worships busts out of all proportion to their importance. This led to her cognitive errors and to her feelings of shame. Helen's decision isn't clearly right or wrong. It does show, however, that a reasonably attractive woman may not gain as much as she expects from a cosmetic transformation.

Making over can sometimes create as many problems as it corrects. And the mere possibility of change adds stress to your life. "Does she or doesn't she" translates for each of us into "should I or shouldn't I?" Why or why not? When and how much? Before the days of implants, Helen might have felt unhappy with her breasts, but not conflicted over seeking a surgical solution. One important effect of makeovers is that they raise beauty standards. When more and more people wash away their gray, for example, it becomes harder and harder for me to feel content with mine.

As you can see, making healthy cosmetic decisions that promote bodylove is complicated. Sometimes beauty transformations are worth it, other times they're not. In facing your own conflicts about making over, remember these points:

1. *Assess your motives carefully.* Why does a change seem so important right now? Consider the underlying factors that may be influencing you. Perhaps you're seeking a cosmetic solution to problems that could best be handled in other ways.
2. *Take small steps in revising your beauty routines.* Make them more fun, more flexible, and more sensuous. Look for alternatives that are less painful or less costly. Try to use the process of adornment to nurture and enhance your body image as well as your mirror image.
3. *Consider the long-term effects of a cosmetic change.* Will it help you accept and appreciate yourself? Will it improve body image in the long run, or is it merely a short-term distraction?
4. *Recognize and resist the commercial messages.* There is constant pressure on you to buy beauty at any price. But you alone will profit when you make over body image from the inside out.

TAKING
CHARGE
OF
YOUR IMAGE

In the long run, we shape our lives and we shape ourselves. The process never ends until we die. And the choices we make are ultimately our own responsibility.

—ELEANOR ROOSEVELT

WHETHER your image is plain or fancy, you may have trouble facing up to it sometimes. Perhaps you cringe when trying on bathing suits, confronted with the naked truth in a three-way mirror. Cathy Guisewite, author of the *Cathy* comic strip, admits she once broke down and wept at that moment of truth. Body loathing troubles most of us in one way or another. Throughout this book you've had a chance to identify it in your own life, and you've seen many examples of it in the Bodylove Survey and in the case studies.

Body loathing caught Ellen in a dieter's mentality that kept her hungry and deprived. Lynn felt a painful self-consciousness at work, and Susan's dreams were haunted by her fear of rejection on her wedding day. Whatever form it takes, body loathing distorts body image. So that you wind up feeling less attractive than you want to be.

The consequences of body loathing are physical and emotional distress. It causes shame about eating compulsively and shame about touching intimately. Some women become addicted to exercising while others suffer the risk of costly surgery. A few simply stay at home to avoid being seen. Body loathing keeps us beauty bound. Caught up in the mirror's reflection, we forget to take care of the person within the image.

Just as your relationships influence body image, your body image also spills over into your relationships. Body loathing may prevent you from reaching out and connecting with people, or from interacting spontaneously with them. Unless you respect your body along with yourself, you can't respect someone else's choice of you as a friend or lover.

Body loathing isn't inherited, but it is contagious. You catch it from others when you inhale the social air that's loaded with stereotypes. Looksism equates how you look with who you are. It thereby traps you into believing that good looks guarantee success and happiness. Learned through socialization with family and friends,

216

looksism is constantly reinforced by media images. We all perpetuate these stereotypes by buying into them unconsciously.

Annette, for instance, is one of the 70 million viewers who faithfully turns on the Miss America Pageant each year. She watches as the camera slowly pans up and down each contestant's body. During one commercial, Annette's seven-year-old daughter puts on a bathing suit and starts parading in Mommy's heels, with a wiggle and a smile. She fully expects to grow up looking like Miss Texas—and most likely she'll wind up disappointed. This is how looksism and body loathing get passed on to our children.

BUILDING BODYLOVE THROUGH SELF-ESTEEM

If body loathing is a contagious "dis-ease," the healing antidote is bodylove—an elixir of positive emotions, attitudes, and actions. Loving your body means enjoying it—using it, touching it, and seeing it with pleasure. Despite the messages of looksism, bodylove has very little to do with how you actually look. It's not beauty, but self-esteem that builds bodylove. That's because body image is quite independent of physical appearance. Someone with high self-esteem tends to view her body favorably, regardless of how she actually looks.

The weak connection between body image and physical appearance means that changing your looks won't guarantee a lasting improvement in self-esteem. In fact, looksism works in both directions. It equates beauty with goodness, and it also equates goodness

Cathy. Copyright © 1987 Universal Press Syndicate. Reprinted with permission. All rights reserved.

with beauty. If you radiate good qualities—such as confidence, humor, sociability, charm—you'll probably be seen as more attractive. A woman who projects admirable traits finds admiration reflected back from those who look at her.

"Most people don't act, they react," observes Annette. "I know that if I feel good and give out positive vibrations, others get that message. It makes a difference in other people's eyes and in your own eyes, also. Of course it's nice to have the outer package, but that's not a substitute for inner confidence."

To achieve bodylove you need to get past your appearance and focus on your other personal strengths as well. It's true that making over your looks can sometimes boost self-esteem. However, in the end it's how you feel about those outer changes that really counts most of all.

This book has given you some techniques for taking the basic steps toward improving body image. First, you should pay close attention to your body's needs and respect them: your needs for nourishment and comfort, for movement and touch. Paying attention will then help you appreciate the many pleasures your body naturally provides, such as the great taste of food or the sensual joy of intimacy. You'll find that by appreciating your strengths, you can then accept your limitations more easily. Accepting the unique features that make you distinctive will free you from the frustrating pursuit of perfection.

WHEN AVERAGE IS MORE THAN GOOD ENOUGH

Bodylove can't flourish if you keep on judging yourself against impossible standards. There's no doubt that some of your features will always disappoint you. So it's important to realistically assess and acknowledge what is possible and what is not. Whether your anatomy becomes your destiny depends on how you view your weaknesses. Aiming for perfection is a self-defeating goal that only sets you up for failure.

Your perfectionistic "shoulds" were absorbed throughout life from parents and peers, from a critical mate, and from a culture that breeds looksism. Sometimes these unrealistic goals are based on myths or on cognitive errors. As long as you cling to them, you'll continue to pay a high price in terms of insecurity, shame, and body loathing.

The old saying that "moderation is best" applies when it comes to pursuing beauty. You really don't have to look gorgeous to get ahead in life. You don't have to be super-thin, super-fit, or marvelously made up to be successful. In fact, super-beautiful people have only a slight social advantage over those who are only average looking. Which means that it isn't crucial to correct every flaw or remodel every part. Looking okay is almost always good enough to achieve what you want in life, especially when you actively display your other valuable assets.[1]

Just set modest goals and realistic expectations. Then you won't be disappointed as you face your reflection (even when trying on a bathing suit). What do realistic expectations mean in everyday terms?

For Cynthia, it meant giving away all the clothes that were too tight and accepting the reality of her heavy body. She decided to shop in large-size stores and thus avoid the frustration she always felt among the regular sizes. She also took the "thin" pictures of what she looked like as a teenager out of her wallet and stopped showing them to people. For Maggie, it meant cutting her running routine from seven to four days a week, and joining an art class instead. For you it might mean spending less time in front of the mirror or less energy worrying about what to wear. Take a moment to review the goals that you set for yourself in Chapter 1. Are they moderate and how can you begin to translate them into everyday behavior?

Setting appropriate goals is an important part of the cognitive and behavioral exercises that were presented in each chapter. These exercises really *can* help you achieve bodylove. In one study, for example, a group of women who used similar exercises to work on self-image felt more confident about their appearance in just six weeks.[2] Their self-esteem rose and they were able to see themselves as more attractive. This research shows that you don't have to change your outer appearance to feel better about your looks and yourself. But you won't discover this unless you try.

Pursuing bodylove does require effort and practice. Have you read through this book without doing the exercises? If so, now is the time to go back to those sections that are most relevant to your needs. Start to overcome resistance by taking some action. Unless you risk a few small steps in a new direction, resistance will keep you stuck in your old patterns of self-rejection.

GUIDELINES FOR CHANGE

While working on the exercises, try to keep some basic guidelines in mind:

1. *You can gain greater self-control.* Monitor your behavior and take charge of it. For example, gather accurate data so you really know what you're doing and thinking. Then you'll be able to measure your progress. Jane became less obsessed with her complexion simply by getting rid of a magnifying mirror she'd been using each morning that exaggerated every flaw.

2. *You can increase positive feelings.* Focus on your strengths and reduce self-criticism. For example, develop a healthy praise list, rehearse positive affirmations in front of the mirror, and learn to receive compliments graciously. As Lynn walked to work, she repeated positive statements about her looks and found that she felt more confident when dealing with clients.

3. *You can understand social influences on body image.* Become more sensitive to looksism. For example, think about how you use age and weight labels, how your family has shaped your ideas about attractiveness, and how the media promote a particular feature. When Nancy discussed aging with her husband, she realized that her fears about looking older came from his desire to see her as young and beautiful forever.

4. *You can develop sensory awareness.* Tune in to your body. For example, listen carefully to feelings of hunger and to the effects of movement or touch. Diane worked on her sexual inhibitions by practicing relaxation in the bath and by exploring different body sensations.

5. *You can correct faulty beliefs.* Challenge irrational thoughts. For example, learn to refute your cognitive errors with good counterarguments. Get the facts about weight control or cosmetic surgery, and use these truths to replace the myths that cause body loathing. Ellen reviewed a list of diet myths each day during breakfast until she could easily challenge the dieter's mentality and rationally reject it.

HEALTHY AND UNHEALTHY NARCISSISM

In a way, the active pursuit of bodylove makes you more narcissistic. Narcissism means choosing and valuing yourself as a love object. It can be either healthy or unhealthy. Narcissism is healthy when it promotes a realistic body image that's created from within, not dictated from without. It's healthy when it helps you accept yourself as imperfect but still lovable. We all need to feel attractive to ourselves and to others. When self-love is shared, it unites people through visual and physical intimacy. In effect, healthy narcissism lets you shout, "Hey, look at me so we'll both be delighted."

Sometimes narcissism gets stuck at a childish level, however. Then, the need for attention dominates, as it did in infancy. Narcissism is unhealthy when it excludes concern for others or when it's totally invested in appearance alone. Those who suffer from unhealthy narcissism become self-absorbed or chronic show-offs. They must constantly shout, "Hey, look at me so I can feel secure."

Women find it especially hard to strike a balance between healthy and unhealthy narcissism. After all, beauty is so central to femininity, and packaging the feminine image often requires preoccupation with endless details of appearance.

Betty, for instance, exercises an hour a day at dawn, then devotes the next hour to showering, doing her hair, and making up. She works for eight hours in the high heels she needs for her corporate image. Lunch hours are often spent shopping for clothes or visiting the beauty salon. By mid-afternoon, her back aches and she wonders why she can't get through the day without wilting. Like Betty, you may wind up blaming your body or yourself because you can't comfortably function in a decorative mold that was really designed for a Barbie doll's life.

As you play out the feminine role, you may feel yourself being pulled between healthy and unhealthy narcissism—torn between the healthy woman within you who wants to look prettier, and the healthy person within you who doesn't want to suffer in the pursuit of beauty. There's an inherent tension between being an ornamental female who sees herself (and is seen) as a decorative object and being an instrumental female who sees herself as a competent person. This basic feminine conflict is a major cause of body loathing. It surfaces in many different ways, so trying to maintain a secure balance between healthy and unhealthy narcissism is precarious.

WOMEN'S STRENGTHS

Although women do have special problems with looksism and with body loathing, we also have special strengths that can help us. First, such physical challenges as menstruation, pregnancy, and menopause naturally force us to reconstruct a new image over and over as our bodies change periodically. Thus we're used to revising our body image. This can be a real asset as you work to cast off an ill-fitting beauty mold and recast yourself in a more comfortable one.

Women also have the so-called feminine traits of patience, gentleness, compassion, and concern: patience to let the body set its own proper weight; gentleness and tender concern for living flesh; compassion and forgiveness for "shameful" past experiences. When these traits are turned back toward the self, they become powerful tools to nurture bodylove.

Finally, women know how to be good friends. We can offer empathy and understanding, which help reduce the isolation of body loathing. Through the eyes of friends you can see your body with new admiration. From their mouths you'll hear the praise you need and deserve.

In the safety of formal or informal support groups, you can admit weaknesses, share secrets, seek help, and speak out about body-image problems. Campus networks for women with eating disorders illustrate the effectiveness of support groups. So do the dance and exercise classes discussed earlier. In such groups you'll find beautiful role models of all ages and sizes with whom to identify. These are not the ornamental females seen in advertisements, but real, flesh-and-blood women, whose imperfect bodies are more like your own. Gladys related this experience:

> After my breast was removed, I was in a state of mourning. I felt damaged and missed the part of me that was lost. My local Y had a postmastectomy group, which I joined reluctantly. But it turned out to be terrific. When I looked around that room I saw women

who I knew were beautiful and whole. They really understood my sense of loss, and with their help I began to think differently about my body.

Unfortunately, the competitive pursuit of beauty that's encouraged by our society often alienates us from other women. We start to envy or fear those who make us feel inadequate. Remember that this form of competition only adds to body loathing. By working on self-esteem through the support of other women, you'll be in a much stronger position to expand your concepts of personal attractiveness.

EXPANDING THE IMAGE OF BEAUTY

There's a lot of pressure on you to conform to a narrow beauty standard—one that's thin, young, and idealized. The pressure comes from the stereotypes of looksism. It comes from commercial messages selling makeover magic. It comes from your mirror and from your own deep needs to fit in and feel socially secure. But you do have the power to exert some counterpressure.

We can't directly control how others view us. But we do have some control over how we view ourselves. After all, we are the ones who make the appointments, buy the fashions, and apply the products. The choices we make also influence social standards of physical attractiveness.

Our personal and social definitions of beauty can stretch to make room for the stouter, the older, the plainer, and funny faced among us. They can stretch to embrace ethnic and racial differences. So try to resist the narrow media images that exclude so many, and instead, seek new role models that include the great diversity of human characteristics. Within a broader definition of beauty you'll be able to relabel your "flaws" as differences, and to count them as part of your personal assets. You are unique in body and spirit. Don't let the pressures to conform destroy your individuality.

While outer beauty is certainly an asset, bodylove has an even greater payoff. What will you gain by actively pursuing it?

- Freedom from tormenting self-consciousness, insecurity, and shame.
- Comfort and health as you nurture your body and care for its needs.

- Greater resources to invest in work and play.
- Better relationships as you strive to connect rather than compete with others.

You have a right—and a responsibility—to judge yourself according to realistic standards. A right to feel comfortable in your own skin.

Throughout these chapters, I've tried to show how to take charge of your body image. It's possible to reduce preoccupation with appearance, to break destructive habits, and to find more constructive alternatives. This book is a resource. But knowing what to do is not enough. Doing is essential. So start somewhere. Work to adore your body as well as adorn it.

Cinderella really can't live happily ever after on the brief advantage that a pretty face provides. Think about whether you spend more time making up than making love? Whether you work harder at making over your looks than making over your life? In order to achieve bodylove you must strike a balance between your ornamental needs for adornment, your instrumental needs for achievement, and your sensual needs for fulfillment. In the end, self-esteem comes through personal development—through becoming a competent and caring human being. By transforming your image from within, you can move beyond body loathing and toward bodylove.

APPENDIX: THE BODYLOVE SURVEY

Note: Figures are percentages of the responses of the group. The total does not equal 100% for some questions because of multiple choices or missing data.

1. Age _____

2. Sex M _____ F _____

3. In which state do you live? _____

4. Highest level of education completed:
   a. LESS THAN HIGH SCHOOL (1)
   b. HIGH SCHOOL GRADUATE (9)
   c. SOME COLLEGE (29)
   d. COLLEGE GRADUATE (25)
   e. SOME GRADUATE WORK (12)
   f. GRADUATE DEGREE (26)

5. Marital status:
   a. NEVER MARRIED (37)
   b. FIRST MARRIAGE (34)
   c. DIVORCED (12)
   d. SEPARATED (2)
   e. REMARRIED (11)
   f. COHABITING (2)
   g. WIDOWED (4)

6. How many children do you have? _____

7. How do you spend most of your time?
   a. AS A HOMEMAKER AND/OR MOTHER (15)
   b. AS A STUDENT (19)
   c. WORKING FULL TIME OR PART TIME (54)
   d. OTHER _____

8. Describe your economic level:
   a. QUITE POOR (0)
   b. GETTING BY (11)
   c. SOMEWHAT SECURE (43)
   d. FAIRLY PROSPEROUS (35)
   e. AFFLUENT (11)

9. Are you self-conscious about your appearance?
   a. CONSTANTLY (21)
   b. OFTEN (23)
   c. SOMETIMES (40)
   d. RARELY (14)
   e. NEVER (2)

10. During the course of the day, how often do you check yourself in a mirror?
    a. CONSTANTLY (2)
    b. OFTEN (20)
    c. SOMETIMES (53)
    d. RARELY (25)
    e. NEVER (2)

11. When you do check yourself, how does it make you feel?
    a. MUCH BETTER (9)
    b. SLIGHTLY BETTER (33)
    c. NO CHANGE (43)
    d. SLIGHTLY WORSE (12)
    e. MUCH WORSE (3)

12. Is physical attractiveness important in the daily lives of most people?
    a. VERY IMPORTANT (39)
    b. SOMEWHAT IMPORTANT (56)
    c. NOT SURE (3)
    d. UNIMPORTANT (1)
    e. VERY UNIMPORTANT (1)

13. Do you agree that "good-looking people are usually happier and more successful than less attractive people?"
    a. STRONGLY AGREE (11)
    b. AGREE (37)
    c. NOT SURE (16)
    d. DISAGREE (33)
    e. STRONGLY DISAGREE (4)

14. How do you feel when someone compliments you about your appearance?
    a. VERY DELIGHTED (46)
    b. SOMEWHAT PLEASED (44)
    c. MIXED FEELINGS (5)
    d. SELF-CONSCIOUS (5)
    e. VERY UNCOMFORTABLE (2)

15. What were your mother's attitudes toward your appearance when you were growing up?
    a. VERY POSITIVE AND ACCEPTING (33)
    b. GENERALLY POSITIVE (37)
    c. MIXED (13)
    d. GENERALLY NEGATIVE AND CRITICAL (8)
    e. VERY NEGATIVE (3)
    f. I DON'T KNOW (6)

16. What were your father's attitudes toward your appearance while you were growing up?
    a. VERY POSITIVE AND ACCEPTING (26)
    b. GENERALLY POSITIVE (38)
    c. MIXED (13)
    d. GENERALLY NEGATIVE AND CRITICAL (5)
    e. VERY NEGATIVE (3)
    f. I DON'T KNOW (15)

17. Are you physically disabled or disfigured?
    _____ No _____ Yes
    If yes, please describe _____

18. If you could change one thing about your body, what would it be? _____

19. When you take a long look at your nude body in a full-length mirror, how do you feel?
    a. PROUD (8)
    b. CONTENT (30)
    c. MIXED FEELINGS (47)
    d. ANXIOUS OR DEPRESSED (14)
    e. REPULSED (2)

20. Are you satisfied with your current weight?
    a. VERY SATISFIED (18)
    b. SOMEWHAT SATISFIED (32)
    c. SOMEWHAT DISSATISFIED (33)
    d. VERY DISSATISFIED (19)

21. How often do you weigh yourself?
    a. RARELY (28)
    b. ONCE A MONTH (21)
    c. ONCE A WEEK (20)
    d. EVERY FEW DAYS (15)
    e. ONCE A DAY (15)
    f. TWICE A DAY OR MORE (2). IF MORE, HOW OFTEN? _____

22. At the present time, are you dieting in order to lose weight?
    Yes (28)   No (72)

23. During the past ten years, have you used any of the following methods to control your weight?
    1=often   2=sometimes   3=rarely   4=never
    _____ MODERATE CALORIE RESTRICTION
    _____ CRASH DIETING
    _____ INTENSE EXERCISING
    _____ FASTING/STARVING
    _____ DIET PILLS
    _____ LAXATIVES
    _____ DIURETICS (WATER PILLS)
    _____ VOMITING
    _____ OTHER MEDICATIONS
    _____ LIQUID-FORMULA PROTEIN DIETS
    _____ WEIGHT-WATCHING CLUBS
    _____ DIET SPAS

24. Do you believe that your current weight is:
    a. MORE THAN 15 POUNDS *UNDERWEIGHT* (3)
    b. 3–10 POUNDS *UNDERWEIGHT* (3)
    c. JUST RIGHT (17)
    d. 1–5 POUNDS OVERWEIGHT (17)
    e. 5–10 POUNDS OVERWEIGHT (23)
    f. 10–20 POUNDS OVERWEIGHT (22)
    g. 20–50 POUNDS OVERWEIGHT (11)
    h. MORE THAN 50 POUNDS OVERWEIGHT (5)

25. What do you think your weight will be five years from now?
    a. MUCH LESS [20 OR MORE POUNDS] (11)
    b. SLIGHTLY LESS [5–10 POUNDS] (23)
    c. THE SAME (52)
    d. SLIGHTLY MORE [5–10 POUNDS] (13)
    e. SOMEWHAT MORE [10–20 POUNDS] (1)
    f. MUCH MORE [OVER 30 POUNDS] (1)

26. How do your current feelings about your body compare with your feelings five years ago?
    a. MUCH BETTER (16)
    b. SOMEWHAT BETTER (19)
    c. THE SAME (42)
    d. SOMEWHAT WORSE (23)
    e. MUCH WORSE (1)

27. What do you think your feelings about your body will be five years from now?
    a. MUCH BETTER (13)
    b. SOMEWHAT BETTER (23)
    c. THE SAME (55)
    d. SOMEWHAT WORSE (8)
    e. MUCH WORSE (1)

28. At what age do most women reach their peak of physical attractiveness? _____ (33 was average age selected)

29. At what age do most women feel best about their bodies?_____ (27 was average age selected)

30. When you were growing up, did classmates ever make fun of you because of your appearance?
    a. FREQUENTLY (9)
    b. SOMETIMES (30)
    c. RARELY (25)
    d. NEVER (36)

31. Compared to other women your age, how physically active are you?
    a. VERY ACTIVE (27)
    b. FAIRLY ACTIVE (35)
    c. AVERAGE (30)
    d. FAIRLY INACTIVE (8)
    e. VERY INACTIVE (2)

32. How often do you engage in vigorous exercise for at least twenty minutes?
    a. NEVER (14)
    b. ONCE A MONTH (16)
    c. ONCE A WEEK (16)
    d. 2–3 TIMES A WEEK (34)
    e. ALMOST EVERY DAY (20)

33. How does physical activity affect your feelings about your body?
    a. STRONG POSITIVE EFFECT (56)
    b. SLIGHT POSITIVE EFFECT (32)
    c. NO EFFECT (11)
    d. SLIGHT NEGATIVE EFFECT (2)
    e. STRONG NEGATIVE EFFECT (1)

34. Are you ever so obsessed with exercise that it becomes a compulsion?
    a. OFTEN (4)
    b. SOMETIMES (17)
    c. RARELY (25)
    d. NEVER (56)

35. How often do you dance or move to music (alone, with a partner, or in a group)?
    a. WEEKLY (48)
    b. MONTHLY (17)
    c. RARELY (27)
    d. NEVER (8)

36. If you are married or in a coupled relationship, how does your partner's physical appearance compare with your own?
    a. PARTNER IS MUCH BETTER LOOKING (4)
    b. PARTNER IS SOMEWHAT BETTER LOOKING (10)
    c. WE ARE ABOUT EQUAL (47)
    d. I AM SOMEWHAT BETTER LOOKING (13)
    e. I AM MUCH BETTER LOOKING (4)
    f. I AM NOT COUPLED AT THIS TIME (22)

37. Do you think your body is sexually appealing?
    a. EXTREMELY APPEALING (7)
    b. QUITE APPEALING (30)
    c. SOMEWHAT APPEALING (48)
    d. NOT VERY APPEALING (11)
    e. NOT AT ALL APPEALING (4)

38. How important to you is the sexual aspect of your life today?
    a. EXTREMELY IMPORTANT (14)
    b. QUITE IMPORTANT (43)
    c. OCCASIONALLY IMPORTANT (25)
    d. NOT VERY IMPORTANT (15)
    e. NOT AT ALL IMPORTANT (4)

39. If you were more physically attractive, do you think your sexual life would be [or would have been] more satisfying?
    a. DEFINITELY (7)
    b. PROBABLY (13)
    c. NOT SURE (26)
    d. PROBABLY NOT (39)
    e. DEFINITELY NOT (15)

40. Do you feel different about your body just before or during your menstrual period?
    a. MUCH BETTER (0)
    b. SOMEWHAT BETTER (3)
    c. NO DIFFERENCE (32)
    d. SOMEWHAT WORSE (33)
    e. MUCH WORSE (11)
    f. I DO NOT HAVE MENSTRUAL PERIODS (21)

41. Compared to other women, how much do you use cosmetics and other beauty products?
    a. MUCH MORE (3)
    b. SOMEWHAT MORE (5)
    c. ABOUT THE SAME (35)
    d. SOMEWHAT LESS (36)
    e. MUCH LESS (23)

42. Do your beauty routines involve other people touching your body (i.e.: manicure, shampoo, massage)?
    a. SEVERAL TIMES A WEEK (1)
    b. WEEKLY (5)
    c. EVERY FEW WEEKS (21)
    d. MONTHLY (14)
    e. RARELY (59)

43. How much time and effort do you usually spend getting ready before going out to a social event?
    a. A GREAT DEAL (2)
    b. QUITE A LOT (10)
    c. ABOUT AVERAGE (66)
    d. NOT VERY MUCH (23)

44. How much money do you spend on beauty products and grooming treatments?
    a. A GREAT DEAL (3)
    b. QUITE A LOT (8)
    c. ABOUT AVERAGE (41)
    d. NOT VERY MUCH (42)
    e. ALMOST NONE (8)

45. Check any of the following surgical procedures that you have had or would consider having *in order to look more attractive.*
    1 = have had   2 = would consider having
    _____ NOSE JOB
    _____ EYELID SURGERY
    _____ SKIN PEELING FOR WRINKLES
    _____ FACE-LIFT
    _____ CHIN SURGERY
    _____ BREAST IMPLANTS
    _____ BREAST REDUCTION
    _____ BREASTS LIFTED
    _____ LIPOSUCTION [FAT REMOVAL]
    _____ TUMMY TUCK
    _____ BUTTOCKS RESHAPED
    _____ TEETH CAPPED
    _____ TEETH STRAIGHTENED
    _____ ELECTROLYSIS
    _____ OTHER

46. What is your ethnic or racial background?
    a. ASIAN   (4)
    b. BLACK   (5)
    c. CAUCASIAN   (87)
    d. HISPANIC   (2)
    e. OTHER   (2)

47. What is your religious background?
    a. NONE   (10)
    b. PROTESTANT   (37)
    c. CATHOLIC   (26)
    d. JEWISH   (19)
    e. OTHER   (9)

RESOURCES

GENERAL REFERENCES ON BEAUTY AND BODY IMAGE

Baker, Nancy. *The Beauty Trap: Exploring Woman's Greatest Obsession.* New York: Franklin Watts, 1984.

Freedman, Rita. *Beauty Bound: Why We Pursue the Myth in the Mirror.* Lexington, Mass.: Lexington Books, 1986.

Hutchinson, Marcia. *Transforming Body Image: Learning to Love the Body You Have.* New York: Crossing Press, 1985.

Moffatt, Betty. *Looking Good: A Woman's Guide to Personal Unfoldment.* Gloucester, Mass.: Para Research, 1984.

Sanford, Linda and Mary Ellen Donovan. *Women and Self-Esteem.* Garden City, New York: Anchor Doubleday, 1984.

AGING

Butler, Robert and Myrna Lewis. *Love and Sex After 40: A Guide for Men and Women for Their Mid and Later Years.* New York: Harper & Row, 1986.

Doress, Paula, Diana Siegal and the Midlife and Older Women Book Project. *Ourselves, Growing Older.* New York: Simon and Schuster, 1987.

Hot Flash: A Newsletter for Midlife and Older Women. National Action Forum for Midlife and Older Women, Box 816, Stony Brook, New York 11790-0609

Lederach, Naomi, Nona Kauffman and Beth Lederach. *Exercise as You Grow Older.* Intercourse, Penn.: Good Books, 1986.

Walker, Barbara. *The Crone: Woman of Age, Wisdom and Power.* San Francisco, Calif.: Harper & Row, 1985.

COSMETICS AND SURGERY

Brumberg, Elaine. *Save Your Money, Save Your Face: What Every Cosmetic Buyer Needs to Know.* New York: Harper & Row. 1986.

Isaac, Katharine, ed. *Being Beautiful.* Center for the Study of Responsive Law, P.O. Box 19367, Washington, D.C. 20036

Moynahan, Paula. *Cosmetic Surgery for Women.* New York: Crown, 1988.

Stabile, T. *Everything You Want to Know About Cosmetics, or What Your Friendly Clerk Didn't Tell You.* New York: Dodd Mead & Co., 1984.

For recent publications on cosmetic contents and allergies, write to: Division of Cosmetic Technology, U.S. Department of Health and Human Services, Food and Drug Administration, 5600 Fishers Lane, Rockvile, Maryland 20857

MOVEMENT

Kuntzleman, Charles and the Consumer Guide Editors. *The Complete Book of Walking.* New York: Pocket Books, 1986.

Rush, Anne. *Getting Clear: Body Work for Women.* New York: Random House/ Bookworks, 1975.

RELAXATION

Benson, Herbert and William Proctor. *Beyond the Relaxation Response.* New York: Berkley Publishers, 1985.

Borysenko, Joan. *Minding the Body, Mending the Mind.* New York: Bantam Books, 1988.

Davis, Martha, Mathew McKay and Elizabeth Eshelman. *The Relaxation and Stress Reduction Workbook.* Oakland, Calif.: New Harbinger Publishers, 1982.

Kravette, Steve. *Complete Relaxation.* Rockport, Mass.: Para Research, 1979.

SENSUALITY

Barbach, Lonnie. *For Yourself: The Fulfillment of Female Sexuality.* Garden City, New York: Anchor Press, 1975.

The Boston Women's Health Book Collective. *The New Our Bodies, Ourselves.* New York: Simon and Schuster, 1984.

Dodson, Betty. *Sex for One: The Joy of Selfloving.* New York: Crown, 1987.

Olds, Sally. *The Eternal Garden: Seasons of Our Sexuality.* New York: Times Books, 1985.

SHAME AND SELF-HELP

Bass, Ellen and Laura Davis. *The Courage to Heal: A Guide for Women Survivors of Child Sexual Abuse.* New York: Harper & Row, 1988.

Ledray, Linda. *Revcovering from Rape.* New York: Henry Holt, 1986.

National Self-Help Clearinghouse, 33 W. 42 Street, New York, New York 10036. (212)840-1259.

Warshaw, Robin. *I Never Called it Rape.* New York: Harper & Row, 1988.

WEIGHT AND FOOD

Bennet, William and Joel Gurin. *The Dieters's Dilemma: Eating Less and Weighing More.* New York: Basic Books, 1982.

Brody, Jane. *Jane Brody's Nutrition Book.* New York: W. W. Norton, 1987.

Kano, S. *Making Peace with Food: A Step-by-Step Guide to Freedom from Diet/Weight Conflict.* New York: Harper & Row, 1989.

National Association to Aid Fat Americans (NAAFA), Box 188620, Sacramento, Calif. 95818.

Nutrition Action Newsletter. Center for Science in the Public Interest, 1501 16th Street, N.W., Washington, D.C. 20036.

Polivy, Janet and Peter Herman. *Breaking the Diet Habit: The Natural Weight Alternative.* New York: Basic Books, 1985.

Roberts, Nancy. *Breaking All the Rules: Feeling Good and Looking Great No matter What Your Size.* New York: Penguin Books, 1987.

Roth, Geneen. *Breaking Free From Compulsive Eating.* New York: New American Library, 1986.

Schoenfielder, Lisa and Barb Wieser, eds. *Shadows on a Tightrope: Writings by Women on Fat Oppression.* San Francisco, Calif.: Spinsters/Aunt Lute Press, 1983.

NOTES

CHAPTER 1

1. Rossner, J. (1983). *August.* Boston: Houghton Mifflin, p. 376.
2. For a general discussion of this point, see:
   Hatfield, E., and Sprecher, S. (1986). *Mirror, Mirror.* Albany, N.Y.: State Univ. of New York Press, pp. 31–33.
   Ruff, G. A., and Barrios, B. A. (1986). Realistic assessment of body image. *Behavioral Assessment,* 8, pp. 237–251.

CHAPTER 2

1. Gallup, G. G. (1977). Self-recognition in primates. *American Psychologist,* 32, pp. 329–338.
2. Thompson, K. J. (1986). Larger than life. *Psychology Today,* April, pp. 36–44.
3. For a general discussion, see:
   Hatfield, E. and Sprecher, S. (1986). *Mirror, Mirror.* Albany, N.Y.: State Univ. of New York Press, pp. 238–246.
   Fisher, S. (1986). *Development and Structure of Body Image,* vol. I. Hillsdale, N.J.: Lawrence Erlbaum, pp. 127–132.
   Lasky, E. (1979). Physical attractiveness and its relationship to self-esteem. In *Love and Attraction: An International Conference,* M. Cook and G. Wilson, eds. Oxford: Pergamon Press, 1979.
4. Feeling fat in a thin society. *Glamour,* February 1984, pp. 198–201.
5. Alta (1971). Pretty. In *Woman in Sexist Society,* V. Gornick and B. Moran, eds. New York: Basic Books, p. 3.
6. Berscheid, E., Dion, K., Walster, E., and Walster, G. (1971). Physical attractiveness and dating choice: A test of the matching hypothesis. *Journal of Experimental Social Psychology,* 7, pp. 173–189.
7. Cavoir, N. (1970). Physical attractiveness, perceived attitudes, similarity and interpersonal attraction among fifth and eleventh

grade boys and girls. Ph.D. dissertation. Houston: Univ. of Houston.

Dacey, J. (1979). *Adolescents Today.* Santa Monica, Calif.: Goodyear.

Cash, T. F., Winstead, B. A., and Janda, L. H. (1986). The great American shape-up. *Psychology Today,* (April), pp. 30–37.

Fallon, A. E., and Rozin, P. (1985). Sex differences in perceptions of desirable body shape. *Journal of Abnormal Psychology,* 94 (1), pp. 102–105.

Feeling fat in a thin society, *Glamour,* February 1984, pp. 198–201.

For a general review of women's special problems with physical attractiveness, see:

Freedman, R. (1986). *Beauty Bound.* Lexington, Mass.: Lexington Books.

8. Broverman, I., Broverman, D., Clarkson, F., Rosencrantz, P., and Vogel, S. (1970). Sex-role stereotypes and clinical judgments of mental health. *Journal of Consulting and Clinical Psychology,* 34, pp. 1–7.

9. Hildebrandt, K. A., and Fitzgerald, H. E. (1978). Adults' responses to infants' varying in perceived cuteness. *Behavioral Processes,* 3, pp. 159–172.

Adams, G. R., and Cohen, A. S. (1974). Children's physical and interpersonal characteristics that affect student-teacher interaction. *Journal of Experimental Education,* 43, pp. 1–5.

Krebs, D., and Adinolfi, A. (1975). Physical attractiveness, social relations, and personality style. *Journal of Personality and Social Psychology,* 31, pp. 245–253.

Heilman, M. E., and Stopeck, M. H. (1985). Attractiveness and corporate success: Different causal attributions for males and females. *Journal of Applied Psychology,* 70, pp. 379–388.

For a general overview, of facts about looksism, see:

Driskell, J. E. (1983). Beauty as status. *American Journal of Sociology,* 89 (1), pp. 140–165.

10. Dion, K., Berscheid, E., and Hatfield, E. (1972). What is beautiful is good. *Journal of Personality and Social Psychology,* 24, pp. 285–290.

11. Snyder, M., Tanke, E., and Berscheid, E. (1977). Social perception and interpersonal behavior: On the self-fulfilling nature of social stereotypes. *Journal of Personality and Social Psychology,* 35, pp. 656–666.

12. Cash, T. F., Cash, D. W., and Butters, J. W. (1983). Mirror, mirror, on the wall . . . ?: Contrast effects and self-evaluations of physical attractiveness. *Personality and Social Psychology Bulletin,* 9, pp. 351–358.

13. For an overview of the effects of mirrors, see:

Fisher, S. (1986). *Development and Structure of Body Image,* vol. I. Hillsdale, N.J.: Lawrence Erlbaum, p. 133.

14. For an understanding of cognitive theory and its application, see:

Burns, D. (1980). *Feeling Good.* N.Y.: Morrow.

15. Beck, A. T., Rush, A. J., Shaw, B. F., and Emery, G. (1979). *Cognitive Therapy of Depression.* N.Y.: Guilford Press.
    Beck, A. T. (1976). *Cognitive Therapy and the Emotional Disorders.* N.Y.: International University Press.

CHAPTER 3

1. Rubin, J., Provenzano, F., and Luria, Z. (1974). The eye of the beholder: Parents views on sex of newborns. *American Journal of Orthopsychiatry,* 44, pp. 512–519.
2. For an overview of children's perception of physical attractiveness, see:
    Langlois, J. H., and Stephan, C. W. (1981). Beauty and the beast: The role of physical attractiveness in the development of peer relations and social behavior. In *Developmental Social Psychology,* S. Brehm, S. Kassin, and F. Gibbons, eds. New York: Oxford University Press, pp. 152–168.
3. Offer, D., Ostrov, E., and Howard, K. (1981). *The Adolescent: A Psychological Self-Portrait.* New York: Basic Books.
    Musa, K., and Roach, M. (1973). Adolescent appearance and self-concept. *Adolescence,* 8, pp. 385–394.
4. This procedure was developed by Butters, J. W., and Cash, T. F. (1987). Cognitive-behavioral treatment of women's body-image dissatisfaction: A controlled outcome study. *Journal of Consulting and Clinical Psychology,* 55, pp. 889–897.

CHAPTER 4

1. Fallon, A. E., and Rozin, P. (1985). Sex differences in perceptions of desirable body shape. *Journal of Abnormal Psychology,* 94 (1), pp. 102–105.
2. Fat facts. See:
    Brody J. *New York Times,* March 18, 1987.
    Gray, J., and Ford, K. (1985). Incidence of bulimia in a college sample. *International Journal of Eating Disorders,* 4, pp. 201–210.
    Thompson, K. J. (1986). Larger than life. *Psychology Today,* April, pp. 36–44.
    Kolata, G. (1986). Weight regulation may start in our cells, not psyches. *Smithsonian,* May, pp. 91–97.
3. Fallon and Rozin, Sex differences. (See ch. 4, note 1.)
4. Playboy centerfolds, see:
    Garner, D. M., Garfinkel, P. E., Schwartz, D., and Thompson, M. (1980). Cultural expectations of thinness in women. *Psychological Reports,* 47, pp. 483–491.

Advertisements and plump models, see:
Ms., May 1987, p. 33.

5. Richardson, S., Hastorf, A., Goodman, N., and Dornbusch, S. (1961). Cultural uniformity in reaction to physical disabilities. *American Sociological Review,* 26, pp. 241–247.

6. For a review of weight bias, see:
Hatfield, E., and Sprecher, S. (1986). *Mirror, Mirror.* Albany, N.Y.: State Univ. of New York Press, pp. 204–223.

7. Bennett, W., and Gurin, J. (1982). *The Dieter's Dilemma: Eating Less and Weighing More.* New York: Basic Books.
Polivy, J., and Herman, P. (1983). *Breaking the Diet Habit—The Natural Weight Alternative.* New York: Basic Books.

8. Kano, S. (1989). *Making Peace with Food.* New York: Harper & Row.

9. Polivy, J., and Herman, P. (1985). Dieting and binging: A casual analysis. *American Psychologist,* 40 (2), pp. 193–201.
Wooley, S. C., and Kearney-Cooke, A. (1986). Intensive treatment of bulimia and body-image disturbance. In *Handbook of Eating Disorders,* K. D. Brownell and J. P. Foreyt, eds. New York: Basic Books, pp. 476–502.

CHAPTER 5

1. Vicki Stern. Body Music, 59 Carmine Street, 2E, New York, N.Y. 10014.

2. Facts about physical activity and self-image.
Joesting, J. (1981). Comparison of students who exercise with those who do not. *Perceptual and Motor Skills,* 53, p. 426.
Ryckman, R., Robbin, M., Thornton, B., and Cantrell, P. (1982). Development and validation of a physical self-efficacy scale. *Journal of Personality and Social Psychology,* 42, pp. 891–900.
Snyder, E. E., and Kivlin, J. E. (1975). Women athletes and aspects of psychological well-being and body image. *Research Quarterly,* 46, pp. 191–199.
Baekeland, F. (1970). Exercise deprivation. *Archives of General Psychiatry,* 22, pp. 365–369.
Cash, T. F., Winstead, B.A., and Janda, L. H. (1986). The great American shape-up. *Psychology Today,* April, pp. 30–37.
For a general discussion, see:
Fisher, S. F. (1986). *Development and Structure of Body Image,* vol. 1. Hillsdale, N.J.: Lawrence Erlbaum, pp. 139–143.

3. Kano, S. (1989). *Making Peace with Food.* New York: Harper & Row.

4. Lips, H. (1981). *Women, Men, and the Psychology of Power.* Englewood Cliffs, N.J.: Prentice-Hall, p. 9.

5. Ibid., p. 77.

6. Hutchinson, M. (1985). *Transforming Body Image.* Trumansburg, New York: Crossing Press.

CHAPTER 6

1. Thayer, S. (1988). Close encounters. *Psychology Today,* March, pp. 31–36.
2. Hatfield, E., and Sprecher, S. (1986). *Mirror, Mirror.* Albany, New York: State Univ. of New York Press, pp. 167–172.
3. Kelley, J. (1978). Sexual permissiveness: Evidence for a theory. *Journal of Marriage and the Family,* 40, pp. 455–468.
4. Brain, R. (1970). *The Decorated Body.* New York: Harper & Row.
5. Masters, W. H., and Johnson, V. E. (1975). *The Pleasure Bond.* Boston: Little, Brown.

CHAPTER 7

1. Viorst, J. (1986). *Necessary Losses.* New York: Ballantine Books.
2. Katha Pollitt, *New York Times,* Hers column, January 16, 1986, p. C2.
3. Cross, J., and Cross, J. (1971). Age, sex, race, and the perception of facial beauty. *Developmental Psychology,* 5, pp. 433–439.
4. Roth, G. (1982). *Feeding the Hungry Heart.* New York: New American Library, p. 40.
5. Myths and facts about aging, see:
   Berscheid, E. E., Hatfield (Walster), E., and Bohrnstedt, G. (1973). The happy American body: A survey report. *Psychology Today,* 7, pp. 119–131.
   Fisher, S. (1986). *Development and Structure of Body Image,* vol. I. Hillsdale, N.J.: Lawrence Erlbaum, pp. 246–251. (For myths 2 & 3)
   Adams, G. (1977). Physical attractiveness, personality, and social reactions to peer pressure. *Journal of Psychology,* 96, pp. 287–296.
6. Doress, P. B., Siegal, D. L., and the Midlife and Older Women Book Project (1987). *Ourselves, Growing Older.* New York: Simon and Schuster, p. 44.
7. Melamed, E. (1983). *Mirror, Mirror: The Terror of Not Being Young.* New York: Linden Press/Simon and Schuster, p. 156.
8. Morgan, M. (1973). *The Total Woman.* Old Tappan, N.J.: Fleming H. Revell, p. 92.
9. Berscheid, E., and Walster, E. (1974). Physical attractiveness. In *Advances in Experimental Social Psychology,* Vol 7, L. Berkowitz (ed.). New York: Academic Press, pp. 157–215.
10. Deutsch, F., Clark, M., and Zalenski, C. (1983). Is there a double standard of aging? Paper presented at the annual meeting of the Eastern Psychological Association, Philadelphia.

11. Melamed, p. 75.
12. Lichtendorf, S. (1982). *Eve's Journey.* New York: Putnam, p. 15.
13. England, P., Kuhn, A., and Gardener, T. (1981). The ages of men and women in magazine advertisements. *Journalism Quarterly,* 58, pp. 468–471.
14. See Doress et al., *Ourselves Growing Older,* note 6.
15. Witkin-Lanoil, G. (1984). *The Female Stress Syndrome.* New York: Newmarket Press, p. 164.
16. See Doress et al., *Ourselves, Growing Older,* note 6, p. 38.

CHAPTER 8

1. Rollin, B. (1985). *Last Wish.* New York: Linden Press/Simon and Schuster.
2. Heilman, M., and Stopeck, M. (1985). Attractiveness and corporate success: Different causal attributions for males and females. *Journal of Applied Psychology,* 70 (2), pp. 379–388.
   Cox, C., and Glick, W. (1986). Resume evaluations and cosmetics use: When more is not better. *Sex Roles,* 14, pp. 51–58.
3. Old Testament, Jeremiah 4:30.
4. For an overview of the meaning of cosmetics, see:
   Graham, J. A., and Kligman, A., eds. (1985). *The Psychology of Cosmetic Treatments.* New York: Praeger.
   Graham J. A., and Jouhar, A. J. (1980). Cosmetics considered in the context of physical attractiveness: A review. *International Journal of Cosmetic Science,* 2, pp. 77–101.
5. Cash, T., and Cash, D. (1982). Women's use of cosmetics: Psychosocial correlates and consequences. *International Journal of Cosmetic Science,* 4, pp. 1–14.
   Cash, T., Rissi, J., and Chapman, R. (1985). Not just another pretty face: Sex roles, locus of control, and cosmetics use. *Personality and Social Psychology Bulletin,* 11 (3), pp. 246–257.
6. Department of Health, Education and Welfare, Food and Drug Administration (1979). HEW publication no. 78-5007.
7. Caplan, P. (1984). The myth of women's masochism. *American Psychologist,* 39, pp. 130–139.
8. Scheiner, A. (1986). My face-lift: A cautionary tale. *Ms.,* November, p. 58.
9. Moynahan, P. (1988). *Cosmetic Surgery for Women.* New York: Crown.
10. For a general discussion of cosmetic surgery, see:
    Fisher, S. (1986). *Development and Structure of Body Image,* vol I. Hillsdale, N.J.: Lawrence Erlbaum. pp. 146–150. See also Hamburger, A. (1988). Beauty quest. *Psychology Today,* May, pp. 27–32.
11. Cash, T., and Horton, C. (1983). Aesthetic surgery: Effects of rhino-

plasty on the social perception of patients by others. *Plastic and Reconstructive Surgery*, 72, pp. 543–548.

12. Shulman, G., and Hoskins, M. (1986). Perceiving the male versus the female face. *Psychology of Women Quarterly*, 10, pp. 141–154.

CHAPTER 9

1. Freeman, H. R. (1985). Somatic attractiveness: As in other things, moderation is best. *Psychology of Women Quarterly*, 9 (3), pp. 311–322.
2. Butters, J. W., and Cash, T. F. (1987). Cognitive-behavioral treatment of women's body-image dissatisfaction: A controlled outcome study. *Journal of Consulting and Clinical Psychology*, 55, pp. 889–897.

INDEX